A WONDERFUL-TERRIBLE GOD

In The Light of Love, There Is No Darkness

THE REV. JUDITH W. LETHIN

A Journey of Spiritual Awakening in Native Alaska

Cirque Press
Copyright ©2024 Judith Lethin
All rights reserved. No part of this publication may be reproduced, distributed or transmitted in any form or by any means, including photocopying, recording, or other electronic or mechanical methods, without the prior written permission of the publisher and author, except in the case of brief quotations embodied in critical reviews and certain other noncommercial uses permitted by copyright law.

Published by
Cirque Press

Sandra Kleven — Michael Burwell
3157 Bettles Bay Loop
Anchorage, AK 99515

Print ISBN:
979-8-89660-352-8

cirquejournal@gmail.com
www.cirquejournal.com

Author photo by Linda Smoger
Book Design by Moontide Design

There are ways in, journeys to the center of a life, through time, through air, matter, dream and thought. The ways in are not always mapped or charted, but sometimes, being lost, if there is such a thing, is the sweetest place to be. And always in this search, a person might find that she is already there, at the center of the world. It may be a broken world, but it is glorious nonetheless.

Linda Hogan
The Woman Who Watches Over the World:
A Native Memoir

I acknowledge the land I am living on today is the traditional territory of the Sugpiaq Alutiiq people, who have cared for this land from the beginning of time. I am grateful for their stewardship and care of creation.
I pledge to respect the spiritual values and traditions of the Sugpiaq people, and all Indigenous Peoples.

Dancing Eagles sits on the boat harbor on Seldovia Bay and has been the home of the Lethin family since 1979.

For the Children and the Daffodils
You are Joy and Wonder Incarnate

Students from St. Paul's Episcopal Church in Grayling enjoying a "Noxzema" facial during a youth retreat.

Judith singing *If You're Happy Clap Your Hands* with children from St. Luke's Episcopal church in Shageluk.

Acolyte training with students from Christ Church, Anvik.

THE PARABLE OF
TWO BUCKETS OF WATER

In the old days people make everything they have from what they catch.
When the time comes, they have a celebration in thanksgiving for what they have.
Men talk to young boys.
Women talk to young girls.
The Elders teach about God and how to live good.
There are no accidents because everybody follows the rules.
The buckets are full. The people all come. Everybody drinks and is filled.

The first Christians come. They have teachers.
They teach about God and how to live good from books.
The Elders fell silent. Hard times come. Difficulties come.
People forget how to live good.
Accidents happen because people no longer follow the rules.
The buckets are empty. All the water goes out. The people are thirsty.

Now the Elders are speaking again. Now the people are singing again.
Now the Elders and Teachers are teaching about God and how to live good.
The buckets are filling. The people are coming.
Everyone who drinks is filled.

Spoken by the Rev. James Gump, Hooper Bay
Recorded by the Rev. Judith Lethin, Seldovia

THE PARABLE OF TWO BUCKETS OF WATER
INTRODUCTION
CHAPTERS

1.	Dance	*1*
2.	Porcupine	*11*
3.	A Tangle of Yellow	*19*
4.	Pyroclastic Flow	*23*
5.	Do You Love Me?	*35*
6.	Women's Work	*45*
7.	Is Anything Broken?	*59*
8.	Daffodils and Chrysanthemums	*69*
9.	Shattered Dreams	*89*
10.	No Time to Grieve	*99*
11.	Sam Houston	*105*
12.	A Place to Come to Life	*111*
13.	Potlatch	*123*
14.	There Is No Darkness	*149*
15.	First Beaver	*153*
16.	The Doll Maker	*161*
17.	Grandma's Medicine	*169*
18.	Dappled Light	*175*
19.	Robins And Rainbows	*183*
20.	The FBI	*203*
21.	I Adopt You	*209*
22.	Old Fox	*215*
23.	Wolverine Medicine	*219*
24.	Fire Bath	*227*
25.	Nativity	*233*
26.	Yer Hungry?	*243*
27.	Blessings	*247*
28.	Light Inaccessible	*255*
29.	Twice Blessed	*261*

KATHERINE'S POTLATCH
ADMONITION
THE LORD'S PRAYER (IN DEG XINAG)
EPILOGUE
ACKNOWLEDGMENTS
ABOUT THE AUTHOR

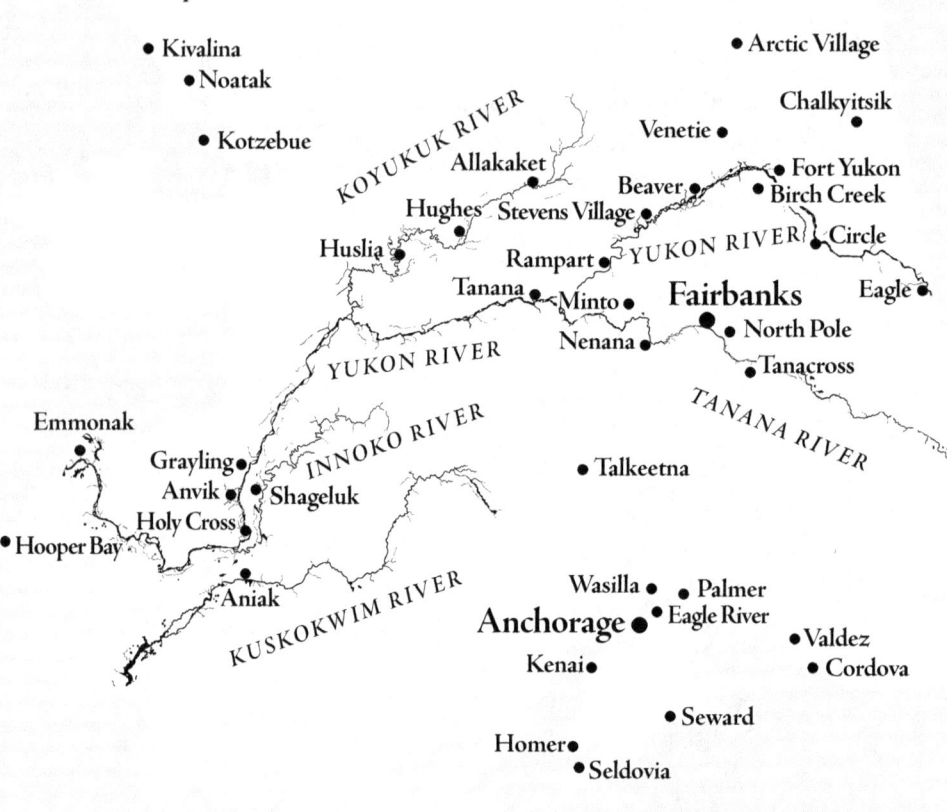

- Haines
- Juneau

Sitka • • Petersburg
 • Wrangell

 • Ketchikan

A COWBOY NEVER SITS
WITH HIS BACK TO THE DOOR.

—Attributed to "Wild Bill" Hickok

The Rosalind Theater was built by Rosalind and Bill Wegman in Homedale, Idaho in 1947.

INTRODUCTION

Homedale, Idaho, 1947

I watched the gathering crowd stream in from the lobby and down the two aisles on either side of me as I waited for Gramps to join me on the bench that he'd constructed out of a board across the two middle seats in the back row. Gramps was bowlegged and crippled from spending his life on a horse, and he couldn't get in and out of the soft, low theater seats. The bench also allowed me to see over the heads of those in front of me. As I sat alone in the dark, a tingling anticipation mixed with fear filled my small body. One of the ushers would bring my customary supper: popcorn, Coca-Cola, and either a soft ice cream cone or an Idaho Spud candy bar. I would let the crunchy, salty, sweetness blot out the rumblings as I pretended to be brave.

Suddenly the lights dimmed, a lion roared, and music began to play. Gramps slipped onto the bench beside me just as the velvet curtains glided open. Larger than life cowboys, shooting rifles and six-shooters over their shoulders, galloped through a red rock canyon pursued by whooping and hollering Indians who were chasing them off their land with bows and arrows. Sometimes beautiful women sang and danced in low cut, ruffled dresses in a saloon filled with rowdy cowboys drinking shots of whiskey. Sometimes a lost girl skipped down a yellow brick road with a tin man, a scarecrow, and a lion looking for the Wizard of Oz, or a cinder child, dressed by her Fairy God Mother for the Ball danced with the prince until midnight.

I'd stay at the theater until bedtime when my much-older half-sisters would walk me home and put me to bed in a dark house. As I fell asleep, fragments of movie scenes and dialogue mashed together with stories about my great-grandfather, Arthur Pence, Sr., who left Iowa in 1864 and followed the Oregon Trail into the Idaho Territory. He rode into the Bruneau Valley in 1869 and met a beautiful young woman with violet-colored eyes, Mary Sydney Wells. They married in 1877 and settled in the valley where they had four children and ran sheep, and later cattle, in the sagebrush hills above the Bruneau Canyon. My Gramps, Arthur Pence, Jr., lived his whole life there on the Hot Springs Ranch until I was born and he and my grandmother, Edith, moved to be near us in Homedale, Idaho. There he sold tickets at the theater my father built for my mother.

In my dreams, family legends were joined by film legends. In one, my great-grandparents were befriended by a Shoshone Indian called Bruneau John, who warned them about a party of young Bannock warriors riding into the valley to kill white settlers in retaliation for depredations they had suffered from the U.S. Army and the settlers in Oregon. My great-grandparents hid in the Roberson Caves and survived. Excitement and terror collided with images of Bannock Indians chasing cowboys.

Growing up watching movies and listening to my grandfather, I learned a story is never just a story. There are layers of meaning, characters with conflicting motivations, sacrifices that must be made, and longings that may never be met. I learned to join the fight on the side of the underdog even when the odds of success were long; to challenge authority; to shoot first and ask questions later. My heroes laughed out loud when they should have kept quiet, wore flamboyant hats when modesty was called for; and did what they thought was right, even if it put them in danger. I learned that bad people are never entirely bad. Good people have flaws, or secrets that drive them mad until they confess and make amends. I learned to pay attention to small things: tone of voice, a subtle glance, a raised eyebrow, a shoulder that turned away just before a kiss, the crescendo of violins, the wind in the trees. I knew from experience there wasn't always a happily-ever-after.

By 1950, people stopped going to the theater for entertainment. Black-and-white television sets were commonplace, bringing the movies into the home, even ours. My parents sold the theater in 1955 and moved the family to the Sheldon Wildlife Refuge in Northern Nevada. My father and his brothers operated a sandstone mining company, and my mother took the teaching position in a one-room school house in Denio. Without the movies and my grandfather's stories to feed my imagination, I devoured the stories of Alaska by Jack London and James Oliver Curwood. I dreamed of a life of friendship like my great-grandfather and Bruneau John had and surviving in the Alaskan wilderness with my loyal malamute husky dog.

Dreams and reality often collide. In Nevada our family faced poverty, alcohol abuse, parental fighting, threats of divorce, promiscuity, sexual abuse, and mental health issues. My mother suffered from unresolved grief from her first marriage and often cried behind a closed door. My father, carrying his own secrets into their marriage, would jump into his truck and drive off whenever they fought. Is it any wonder I felt safer facing the door with my back to the wall? The stress of always having to keep my eye on the action prevented me from practicing good self-care my entire life. As a young woman, I didn't know the meaning of *moderation, calm,* or *kind.*

I survived by playing two major roles: hero and rebel. In Winnemucca I was Worthy Advisor of the Rainbow Girls, DeMolay Sweetheart, first runner-up in the Miss Winnemucca pageant, and Sunday school teacher at St. Mary's Episcopal Church. At home, I cussed with the best of them, drank whiskey straight up, argued with authority, and ran away from home three times.

By the time I was eighteen years old, my mother was exhausted. She bought me a one-way ticket to Anchorage, Alaska to visit my sister and our aunt and uncle for the summer. Alaska! I met Kris Lethin four days after I arrived, certain my life of adventure had begun. Kris reminded me of Clarke Gable in "Gone with the Wind"—good-looking and kind, and he said he loved me. I had no idea what love was, but I accepted his proposal of marriage knowing he was my ticket out of Nevada.

Our early marriage was stormy. I was Cinderella looking for prince charming, and Kris was the tin man looking for a heart. Carmen Miranda had taught me to samba with a bouquet of flowers on my head, Debbie Reynolds inspired me to sing and dance in the rain, and Judy Canova allowed me to laugh at myself even as I blundered into trouble, but somehow those weren't the qualities needed for a successful marriage or when raising four sons.

Forty years into marriage and motherhood, a therapist helped me realize that while my parents were busy surviving their own drama, dozens of actors had been auditioning for their jobs. I came to realize just how damaging to a young developing psyche all those conflicting role models were. I had developed such a permeable inner self from sitting through adult movies night after night that I found myself feeling the feelings and experiences of others as though they were my own. I couldn't find the essential Judith because I was a chameleon. I could play any role, speak in any voice, discern plot twists and who-done-it long before the story ended. I also hid my true feelings and fears in a bag of popcorn or a bowl of ice cream, or a shot of whiskey.

In spite of this, my grandfather and our family hero stories instilled in me a desire to help people. I wanted to be generous and kind like my great grandparents, and courageous enough to stand up for people who are different like Bruneau John, but most of all I wanted my grandfather to be proud of me. I became active in the Episcopal Church and was eventually invited to the village of Minto by three new Alaska Native friends to fast and pray for the condition of the world. They initiated me into their world view and culture and quite probably saved my life. Bishop George Harris from the Episcopal Diocese of Alaska invited me to sing, pray, and lead values clarification exercises in many of the Native Episcopal churches along the Yukon River. I sensed a growing call to Holy Orders and was ordained to the priesthood on the Feast of St. Brigit of Kildare on February 1, 2004 by Bishop Mark MacDonald.

Working with people who suffered from intergenerational trauma caused by colonialism, the influenza epidemic of 1918, and boarding school helped me examine my own wounds and the need for healing. I grew up suspicious, afraid of the dark, hypervigilant, hiding behind a smile or a song, more at home in the garden and with the chickens and my dog, Pal, or actors on the silver screen than with kids my own age. I loved story but I had such a sensitive, permeable ego that it was often hard to separate what was happening "out there" from what was happening "in there." When I had children of my own, I overcompensated. One example: I never had any clean clothes as a child and when I confessed that to my prayer partner, she asked to see my children's underwear drawers. We went downstairs and opened their drawers. There were 36 pairs of shorts and t-shirts neatly folded *each*. Then we went upstairs and opened my underwear drawer. Rags. She marched me to Sears and Roebuck's and insisted I spend $100 on new undies—that's equivalent to $780 in today's dollars!

That's a long way of saying, my growing up in a movie theater has had lasting repercussions, and that the people I've encountered throughout my life have led me to deeper understanding, to integration, to love, and healing. The stories I'm telling are my way of finding and integrating the real Judith, the essential Judith with the woman hiding behind hats, and shawls, and a happy face. I want to show the struggles. I want to finish coming out of hiding, and I want to assure you that everyone can come out of hiding. That children need to be protected and nurtured and grow up safe, not thinking they have to or can protect their parents. That the journey of integration is never really over, and that when we do find our tribe somehow, journeying together makes life a whole lot more meaningful, purposeful, and even more joyful.

Judith, Billy, Johnny Wegman, 1947.

Johnny, Billy, Judith Wegman, 1949.

NO ROOTS. NO ROOTS.
I'M JUST LIKE THAT LITTLE TREE, THERE,
GROWING OUT OF THAT ROCK.
I HAVE NO ROOTS

—Marie Tyson, Emmonak

1.

DANCE

"In the old days," said the Rev. James Gump, "People make everything they have from what they catch."

"What was that like?" asked the Rev. Scott Fisher, matching the slow cadence and rhythm of this young Yup'ik Eskimo man from Hooper Bay.

"It was just good," said James thoughtfully, as he looked around the room. Others in the circle nodded and sighed audibly and then settled more comfortably into their folding chairs. James was a deacon in the Roman Catholic Church and was a natural storyteller and teacher.

"In fall time all the peoples would come together and have a celebration in thanksgiving for what they have. It was a time of feasting; a time of dancing. The elders would teach the children the rules and how to live good."

I couldn't take my eyes off of this small man who had traveled 600 miles for this meeting. In Hooper Bay, the wind-driven sea ice hugs the shore for most of the winter months, and people shelter in dwellings atop a hillock just 26 feet above the Bering Sea. I felt that that landscape had instilled in him a wisdom that compelled him to contextualize his life experience. In his worldview everything is connected. Nothing can be left out. His words, deceptively simple, seemed to have the power to gather up the spiritual values and traditions of the people and make them visible to the generations who may have forgotten how their people once lived. I was drawn into the story as I faithfully recorded his words.

A candle flickered on a table in the center of the room. Ghostlike shadows danced up the walls behind us, as though the ancestors had come to lend support to the work we were about to do. An undercurrent of energy seemed to circle around and under the gathering. A strange awareness began to surface, something hidden was about to be revealed.

I had come to the Ecumenical Consultation in Wasilla, Alaska by invitation of my Bishop, the Rt. Rev. George Harris. I'd been a member of the Gospel Mission Team for two years, along with the Rev. Scott Fisher from the Bishop's staff in Fairbanks, the Rev. David Salmon from Chalkyitsik, the first officially ordained Athabascan priest from Interior Alaska, the Rev. Titus Peter from Ft. Yukon, and a number of Native leaders from other Episcopal villages. We flew from village to village in a kind of mini revival, sharing the teachings of Jesus, and preparing families for baptism and confirmation. Coming to the Consultation, we hoped to deepen our relationship with Alaska Native people from the other main-line denominations—Roman Catholic, Lutheran, Moravian, and Methodist—as we all shared the difficulties we were facing in our respective villages. This was no easy task in Alaska.

The forty-ninth state is big, really big, fully one fifth the size of the continental United States. There are over 200 villages scattered across 665,400 square miles of tundra, boreal and spruce forests, and along the 34,000 miles of shoreline. There are eleven distinct Indigenous cultures, each with unique values and traditions, and 23 distinct Indigenous language groups. To bring this diverse gathering of nearly one hundred people together, organizers of the Consultation decided on the time-honored strategies of small groups and storytelling.

Scott and I were grouped with eight Native delegates in a small room in the basement of Meier Lake Conference Center north of Wasilla, Alaska. He would serve as moderator, and I would serve as scribe. This arrangement allowed the delegates the freedom to simply listen deeply to one another and share from their own experiences. There were eleven other groups just like this one in different rooms throughout the conference center. The stillness in the room deepened as James continued to speak.

"Old men would talk to young boys," James confided as he opened his hands in a gesture of welcome. The men leaned in close, lending strength to his words, their brown weathered faces crinkling as if remembering a distant time. "Old women would talk to young girls." The women nodded and rocked back and forth, then closed their eyes, also remembering. "They would talk about God and how to live good," said James. "There were no accidents because everybody followed the rules. It's like the buckets were just full of water. All the peoples come. Everybody drinks and is filled."

Scott's respectful way of listening allowed the conversation to move forward at a very slow pace. At last, he whispered, "What happened?"

"White people come. They start to talk about God and how to live good from books." An aching tension quickened the stillness that had fallen over the gathering as we watched and waited for James to tell us what happened. Nobody moved. "The elders don't say nothing." I scanned the stony faces, but no one looked up. "Hard times come. Difficulties come. People forget how to live good." Everyone leaned forward at once.

"Then what happened?"

"Accidents happened. People no longer followed the rules. The buckets are just empty now. All the water has gone out. The people are thirsty."

Once James finished sharing, a litany of accidents began to flow from the gathered leaders like spruce sap from scraped bark—slow, steady, sticking to everything, impossible to wash off: a popular basketball player walked out onto the tundra alone after breaking up with his girlfriend and shot himself, and then multiple copy-cat suicides followed. Young people ran out of gas in a spring snowstorm traveling by snowmachine to a nearby village to buy alcohol from the bootleggers and froze to death. An old woman, covered in vomit, died alone from alcohol poisoning. An entire family perished when the parents drinking late into the night failed to notice the red-hot chimney igniting the wood rafters of their log cabin. A daughter, drinking on Fourth Avenue in Anchorage, disappeared and her body was never found.

The shock waves that moved through the darkened room with each added story slowly began to morph into a sorrowing, silent lament. I caught my breath and continued scribbling as fast as I could for fear of losing any of these precious words. Others seemed to stop breathing as well. The tension intensified. Finally, the young woman with a Bible open on her lap began to softly pray, *come Lord Jesus, come Lord Jesus, come Lord Jesus, come.*

My stomach convulsed and cramped as I hunched over the papers in my lap. Similar stories were familiar to me from teaching at the women's jail in Anchorage. Now the stories weren't being told by inmates, they were being told by the faithful people who were leaders in the very institutions that were complicit in the great wounding. The pain in my stomach moved into the center of my chest, and then migrated to my throat. I couldn't contain the sorrow any longer; tears slipped down my cheeks and onto the pages.

At last, it was time to rejoin the larger group and report back what we had shared. One by one the scribes stood and read off a litany of alcohol related accidents prevalent in their villages. As the time drew nearer for me to share, I began to tremble. I looked at my paper, at our list of tragedies, and I knew I had to start our report with James's words about what the old days were like and what had happened to cause things to change as they did. *White people come, they began to teach about God from books… the Elders fell silent… all the water has gone out… the people are thirsty.*

There was a long silence. James stood at last and said, "Now, the elders are speaking again." The tension broke and people began to squirm in their chairs, then turn to their neighbors and whisper in small groups.

When dinner was announced, everyone gladly moved to the

buffet. The delegates had brought their favorite subsistence foods: fresh and smoked salmon, moose meat, dry meat, muktuk, the skin and blubber of the whale, and seal oil for a traditional dinner. Quiet voices filled the dining room. The exhaustion was palpable. We had all worked hard. As the time drew near for Evening Prayer, even the quiet voices trailed off.

Suddenly a door swished open and a flutter of energy rippled through the gathering. James entered the room wearing skin boots and his traditional kuspuk, a short, hooded parka usually worn for celebrations. His hair was slicked down, and his face radiant. He carried his walrus-gut drum in front of his chest like a breastplate. Following James were The Rev. William Tyson and his wife, Marie; William was the Deacon from Emmonak, a village on the Yukon River Delta 100 miles as the crow flies from Hooper Bay. They were also wearing traditional kuspuks and skin boots and carrying dance fans. Marie's kuspuk was knee length with a wide ruffle around the bottom and sewn from bright flowered cotton fabric. The excitement and sharing grew louder and louder. I asked the Elder next to me what was happening.

"This is the first new dance and song made from Hooper Bay in a long, long time. Maybe since boarding school days," she said.

James sat on the floor with his legs stretched out in front of him. William knelt on the floor facing James, and Marie stood several feet behind William with her hands poised, ready to embody the words. We gathered around them as James swirled his stick on the underside of his drum creating a rhythmic shush-shush, shush-shush, shush-shush. James closed his eyes and seemed to be listening. William and Marie began to move their bodies and hands in time with the shush-shushing. I closed my eyes, too, and noticed a pulsing, starting in my hands and quickly moving to my belly and feet. Finally, I surrendered to the drum and let my whole body join the steady undulation.

At last James began quietly striking the underside of the rim and singing his new song. William's hands began to express the Yup'ik words. We were drawn into the heart of the story even though the words were unfamiliar to us. Marie kept time with steady, repetitive hand movements that seemed to mimic the supporting role of the wind or perhaps the earth. There was a pause and then the story began again, a little louder and faster this time. William's gestures were more pronounced. He seemed to be hunting a wild animal. Marie's movements were livelier, too, with more bounce in her knees, more distinct hand gestures. People were smiling broadly now. Many of us were caught up in the rhythm of the drum and kept time with our shoulders and feet. This pattern repeated itself several times. It was over too soon.

I was just about to say something to my neighbor when suddenly a tumult like thunder and lightning broke loose in the center of the room. James had begun to beat his drum so loudly it sounded like rifle shots ringing out. His deep baritone voice filled the dining hall, leaving no space for anything else. William reared up on his knee and thrust his hands into the sky the better to kill this wild thing, and Marie seemed to be single-handedly holding the universe in place. The hair stood up on the back of my neck. Several Yup'ik people joined in singing, and the rest of us leaped into the dance without ever leaving our chairs! It was as though the bad spirits and lurid images from the afternoon were exorcized and we were set free, at last, to dance. Later James interpreted the words for me.

> My life: I hunt for my descendants so I can feed them.
> I hope they can do the same as I do. Ya-ah-ga-ya.
>
> I beat my drum and sing. I beat my drum and sing.
> I dance, potlatch, fire bath, that's what I do. Ya-ah-ga-ya.
>
> My descendants, I tell you want you to use my word
> So you can go safe way and no trouble. Ya-ah-ga-ya.
>
> I beat my drum and sing. I beat my drum and sing.
> I dance, potlatch, fire bath, that's what I do. Ya-ah-ga-ya.

The Native delegates seemed completely revived by the dance and were standing in small groups laughing and talking loudly. Me? I was nearly comatose. I just wanted to find my sleeping bag and climb in. The two Roman Catholic Sisters from Tanana stopped me as I was heading out the door.

"The report from your circle sounded like a parable," said one.

"Yes, The Parable of Two Buckets of Water," said the other. I smiled weakly and thanked them.

"Tomorrow we can talk more," I said. I was just beginning to understand the effects of complicated grief and loss on generations of Alaskans and the church's complicity in it. I had never looked at death up close before and didn't yet know that death was to become my constant companion.

During a break in activities the next morning, I took a cup of coffee and headed for the lake where an old wooden boat dock rocked gently in the breeze. The air was filled with the dewy scent of the cottonwood trees that grew around the lake. I shivered and wrapped my shawl more tightly around my shoulders as I sat down cross-legged on the dock, facing the lake. The sun crested the Chugach Mountains to the east and sent ripples of sunlight skittering across the water. The birch and cottonwood trees circling the lake shush-shushed in time with the lapping of the water and the faint clunking of the dock hardware. Everything reminded me of the dance last night.

Hearing voices coming from the lodge, I turn to see Pauli Simmonds, Bessie Titus, and Robin Sherry walking towards me. They were worship leaders from St. Barnabas Episcopal Church in Minto. The Athabascan village sits on a bluff above the Tolovana River flats at the end of the Minto Spur Road off the Elliot Highway, 126 miles from Fairbanks. As part of the Gospel Mission Team, we had traveled together to Point Lay, on the Arctic Coast, and Chalkyitsik, in the upper Tanana Valley north and west of Fairbanks. They waved and smiled and joined me on the wobbly dock.

"What does that mean, 'would you rather be yellow or be red'?" asked Pauli.

Bishop Harris had asked me to lead an icebreaker that morning that would help us see ourselves and others differently. I had talked about my work as a volunteer at the women's jail in Anchorage and how I had been using values clarification exercises to help the women see themselves in a more positive light. Questions like *would you rather be yellow or red, a king salmon or a rainbow trout, a swan or an eagle* can be a playful way of revealing our unconscious values because the answers reveal a certain love for or attraction to the qualities of that color, or animal or bird. The premise of values clarification is that human actions spring from values—those beliefs usually held most deeply inside us—that give us a sense of worth or belonging or meaning. These hidden values can be corrupted or exaggerated by abuse or neglect or the conflicting values of a dominant culture.

"What colors did you pick?" I asked.

Robin said, "Red."

"Describe red for me."

"Red is powerful. Red is passionate. Red is the color of blood and fire. Red is exciting."

"Does that sound like you?" I asked.

Everyone agreed it did, including Robin. We all laughed.

"I picked yellow," I said. "Yellow is enthusiastic. Yellow is playful. Yellow says: look at me, notice me. Yellow doesn't need a reason to feel happy."

"Why is it important to know that?" Bessie asked.

"Well, it can help us appreciate our differences. There are no wrong answers to these questions, but the answers can help us understand our strengths and how we relate to each other. Even Jesus said something about 'Where your treasure is, there your heart will be also.' I think *treasure* means values."

After a few minutes, the others were laughing and telling stories. I fell silent. They were good friends, confident and relaxed; they seemed to know everything about each other. I had traveled with them but

I still felt like an outsider. I felt a deep longing to know them better. Soon they were telling stories about praying for this person and that person. Finally, I got up the courage to ask them to pray for me. From the time I was a small child, I'd suffered from stomach aches. I seemed to have swallowed my feelings when I heard all the stories from the night before, and I was in pain. They didn't hesitate. They gathered around me and laid their hands on different parts of my body. I felt warmth coming from their hands, and the tightness in my shoulders, chest, and gut began to release as I began to let go. Each, in turn, prayed for healing for my stomach. Then Robin and Pauli started praying in a language that I didn't recognize. Certain phrases seemed to repeat over and over, penetrating deeper and deeper into my mind and body. I knew the biblical teaching about speaking in tongues, and I'd heard them praying for others during our Gospel Mission revivals, but this was the first time I ever had anyone from the Episcopal Church pray for me this way. I began to experience a kind of peace and giddy happiness. My stomach ache disappeared.

"I wish we had some holy oil," said Robin. "We could anoint you."

"I think God wants us to pray and fast for the Church," said Pauli.

"I think God wants us to do it in Minto at St. Barnabas," said Bessie. "Judith can come with us."

The excitement of yellow began to collide with yellow's conflicting values: insecurity and cowardice. The idea of going to Minto to fast and pray for the condition of the world scared me. I knew how to listen to people's hearts and understand their motivations by sharing chocolate chip cookies and leading playful exercises in values clarification. I knew how to play my guitar and sing at the top of my lungs in a raucous revival. But I had no idea how to sit in silence, starving, and listening to my own heart for the voice of God. I had no idea what I was supposed to do with my life. I just knew I wanted to belong, I wanted to be liked by these three women, who represented everything wonderful about Alaska, who did pray and fast and really could hear God's voice. Good grief, I thought, I guess to get what they have I'll have to go to Minto.

WE PUT THOSE WHALE BONES BACK INTO
THE SEA. WE SING TO THOSE BONES.
WE GIVE THANKS THAT OUR PEOPLE
WILL HAVE FOOD FOR ANOTHER YEAR.

—The Rev. Patrick Atungana, Point Hope

2.
PORCUPINE

When I stepped into the sunshine at the Fairbanks airport, Robin, Bessie and Pauli were waiting at the curb in Robin's car. Robin got out and immediately ordered me to drive. I bristled, thinking, *red can be very bossy*. But I climbed in behind the wheel. Who was I to argue—I who wanted so badly to fit in? Pauli repeated her vision that we were to pray and fast and *listen for God's voice*. I had never heard God's voice, and I'd certainly only fasted when the refrigerator was ten feet away, so I had no idea what to expect.

Bessie kept saying, "Maybe we can get some traditional food like salmon or moose to break our fast." These women were born and raised in Minto and were used to living off the land. I was used to living off of Safeway and Fred Meyers.

My husband, Kris, had dropped me off at the Anchorage airport that morning with a promise to take our four sons camping while I was gone. I promised to bake an apple pie as soon as I got home. Kris worked twelve-hour days at a company he started in 1969 when he bought Alaska Fuel and Transfer. By 1980 he had acquired AAA Fuel, Peter's Creek Fuel, Ace Fuel and several lines of construction equipment: Hyster forklifts, Grove cranes, Massey Ferguson dozers and loaders, all under the corporate name Fraley Equipment, and had forty-five full-time employees. The boys were excited to spend time with their dad over the next five days. I felt like I was going on my own camping trip and I was terrified.

About three and a half hours outside of Fairbanks, I saw some kind of four-legged animal swaying side to side as it waddled across the road. Robin looked up and began to shout, "Stop the car, stop the car, stop the car! We can eat porcupine."

I slammed on the brakes, and the car skidded on the gravel. A cloud of dust billowed over us as she continued shouting.

"Get out, get out, get out!"

Did she mean me? Alarmed, I flew out of the half open door.

"Get him, get him, get him!"

I ran down the dusty road after the porcupine. He swerved over the bank and down into the boreal forest. Panting, I leaped off the embankment into a pile of brush, creating a thick cloud of dust that covered me with fine silt. Scrambling to my feet, I saw the porcupine dodging in and out of the birch and spruce trees. I followed. He scooted under cranberry bushes. I leapt over. At last, I was gaining on him, so I shouted back to the women, who were safe at the car, "Okay, I've caught up with him, now what?"

"Kill him."

"Kill him?" Fear shoved alarm out of the way; a childhood memory took its place. I'd sworn, then, never to kill another innocent animal, and here I was… But I wanted to belong.

"Yes, kill him."

"How? With what?"

"A stick, hit him with a stick."

The porcupine was still dodging in and out of the trees and bushes, nearly silent, certainly graceful, quills colliding with each other in an undulating pattern down his back. He was determined to escape, and beautiful in a heroic sort of way. Still chasing, I looked around as the trees and brush blurred past, and I stumbled, swooped down, and in mid-step grabbed the first stick I saw. It was about five feet long.

"I've got a stick, now what?"

"Hit him. Hit him on the head."

Holy crap, why aren't they coming to help me? Why am I out

here alone? This must be some kind of white woman initiation! Maybe they just want to see what I'm made of. Well, damn it, I'm a cowgirl.

"I'm sorry," I whispered to the porcupine. Clunk. The stick broke in two. "The stick broke!"

"Hit him again," came the instruction, now faint, now very far away, as I crashed deeper and deeper into the wilderness.

"Kill him!"

"I'm sorry." Clunk.

The stick broke in two again and I was left holding a piece eighteen inches long and three inches in diameter. This was the weakest damned stick I'd ever seen.

He was running for his life now.

"Kill him!"

I would never fit in if I couldn't even kill a porcupine. "I am so sorry." Ker-plunk. With my puny stick I delivered a terrible blow to his tiny head, and at last he dropped in his tracks. I began to cry. "I'm so, so sorry." I remembered William, the Deacon from Emmonak, saying, *when we go hunting for food, we must thank the animals for giving up their lives for us.*

Sobbing now, I thanked him over and over, "Thank you, thank you, thank you."

Long moments later I finally shouted, "Okay, he's dead, now what?"

"Bring him here."

"Bring him here? He's covered with quills."

"Pick him up by his paw."

"His paw?" I looked closer. A tiny front paw stretched into a patch of dwarf dogwood at the base of an old spruce tree. It looked safe enough, no quills. I grabbed that paw and held him as far away from my legs as I could, his lifeless body dangling like a sack of potatoes. He must have weighed twenty-five pounds. I trudged this way back through the forest to the car, where the real hunters and gatherers waited safely on the road. All the way I continued my mantra, "Thank you, thank you, thank you."

Covered with sweat and dust and remorse, I arrived at the car to find the women jubilant. Robin blurted out, "This is a perfect thing to break our prayer fast with. We'll get Uncle Simon to cook him for us."

Thinking more of the immediate problem—one dead porcupine and four women in a very small car—I asked, "Where do I put him?"

"Throw him on the roof."

One wild swing and he was on the roof behind the chrome rails, facing straight ahead. Sobered, I drove the last few miles into Minto to St. Barnabas Episcopal Church to pray and fast for the condition of the world, now short one member from the animal kingdom.

Word that Judith had killed a porcupine spread like wildfire—no secrets in Indian Country—and when we emerged from the church two days later, hungry, clear-eyed, and rooted to this place, Uncle Simon presented me with a small box of quills labeled with my name. Dinner roasted over the campfire. I settled into an old camp chair beside the glowing embers. The golden splendor of the sun hanging low in the northern sky blanketed everything in a deep cadmium yellow like a Fred Machetanz painting. A chubby russet-and-gray fox sparrow with bold markings on its chest streaked in and out of the shrubby bushes around Uncle Simon's camp tucked in the woods near the church. He perched at last on a low shrub, threw back his head and with a clear whistle and several short trills and churrs began to sing what sounded like one of the gospel songs we sang at the church, "*He reached down his hand—hand for me. He reached down his hand—hand for me. He reached down his hand—hand for me.*" Then he fluttered to the ground and began kicking backwards, digging small holes with his feet, foraging for seeds and insects.

I took a deep whiff of the porcupine roasting over the fire, and shuddered. I tried to smile. Somehow the rousing song and dance of Brother Sparrow, the throb of the red and yellow embers in Uncle Simon's sacred fire, the sizzle of our feast, with smoke rising as incense, and the image of Bessie, Pauli, Robin, and me anointing each other with holy oil, singing gospel songs, and praying for the world only intensified the loneliness and deep longing hidden inside of me. My chest felt heavy, my stomach churned, tears were close to the surface. I wanted happily ever after. I wanted what we were doing to morph with the image of St. Francis and his followers praising the Lord in the decaying church at Assisi. I wanted our retreat to be the beginning of a fire that would burn so fierce and intensely bright, like Francis sang in his Canticle of the Sun, that we would all be healed by its warmth and light. But I had my own secrets.

✦ ✦ ✦

I was easily overwhelmed by fear and anger and grief. I couldn't seem to hang on to my faith for more than a few days at a time. When I was five years old, I attended Vacation Bible School at the Friends Quaker Church in Homedale, Idaho. We were given blocks of pine and a wood burning tool. Our Sunday School teacher asked us to burn the message, "God Is Love" into our wood.

"What does that mean?" I had asked. Could God love children who run away from home, who talk back, who are afraid of the dark, who are always in need of clean clothes and a good scrubbing?

"Does God love me?"

"Yes."

✦ ✦ ✦

I reached into my jeans pocket and fingered a small crystal garnet hidden there. My mother loved garnets, and I often carried one in my pocket when I traveled to help me feel close to her. She died when I was twenty-two, and we never reconciled. I fingered the garnet again and decided to take my chances with Robin, Bessie, and Pauli. Somehow, I felt safe with them, and besides, when they prayed, I really did seem to hear God say, "I will always be with you."

(L to R) Dan, young Kris, Kris, Bill, Tim, camping on the Susitna River.

IN THE OLD DAYS BEFORE
THE PREACHERS COME IN, THE OLD
PEOPLE TELL US HOW TO LIVE GOOD.
THEY ARE OUR PREACHERS.

—Ellen Savage, Holy Cross

3.

A TANGLE OF YELLOW

Homedale, Idaho, 1955

I slowly rolled the window down in my father's black 1952 Chevy Coupe as we pulled away from our white frame house on the corner of Washington and Third. My father gripped the steering wheel with both hands and looked straight ahead. A Lucky Strike dangled from his lips, sending a curl of smoke around the rim of his gray fedora. My mother lit her own cigarette and made grumbling noises under her breath. My older and younger brothers, Billy and Johnny, who shared the back seat with me, shoved and called names declaring they were hot, and hungry, and couldn't breathe from all the smoke. I ignored them as I strained to catch one last glimpse of my Grandma and Grandpa Pence.

Grandpa was sitting in a faded green garden chair in front of their cottage. Grandma was standing behind him with her hands on his shoulders, as though holding tight to the man who had been her rock for over fifty years could change what was about to happen. He didn't look very rock-like; in fact, he looked miserable in his pale blue shirt tucked into baggy trousers. His suspenders stretched across his boney shoulders. His cane rested in his lap. A whisp of gray hair lifted and fell in the warm wind. Grandma looked like she was about to host a family picnic in her mauve suite and summer hat. I knew she was devastated by our move. I'd heard her raised voice that morning and knew she was arguing with grandpa. At last, she lifted a hand acknowledging our departure. Neither of them smiled. My chest began to swell as I gulped down their sadness. They looked like their world had just come to an end. I knew mine had.

My grandparents sold the Hot Springs ranch in the Bruneau Valley and moved into their two-room cottage across the street from us after my parents were married. My grandma said I cried incessantly when I was born. She was the only one who could console me. She would jostle me in her arms as she sang Irish hymns and fed me bottles of warm milk. As I grew older, she taught me to make apple pie at her kitchen table. As I rolled out the flakey crust, she would read me the poems she had written about the pioneers who settled the Bruneau Valley. Grandpa would recount stories of his father and mother, who came into the Bruneau Valley from the Oregon Trail. My favorite told how a Shoshone Indian, Bruneau John, saved them from the Great Bannock Uprising in 1878 when a war party of Bannock Indians rode into the valley killing white settlers and stealing horses in retaliation for depredations by the U. S. Army and the immigrants who stole their land. Real heroes weren't the rich and powerful, Grandpa would say; real heroes were the ones who risk their lives for others, and who showed generosity and kindness to strangers.

My mother was born Rosalind Pence on the Hot Springs Ranch in Bruneau, Idaho in 1907. She was no stranger to sagebrush and rattlesnakes. Her parents had taken her to sheep camp every summer from the time she was born. Grandma Pence would cook biscuits and beans in a cast iron Dutch oven over a campfire, and wash up in the little creek that flowed out of the mountains. Grandpa Pence would tend the sheep and horses, and come back to camp at supper time and fill the evenings with stories and cowboy songs. My mother grew up singing and became a teacher when she was eighteen years old.

In 1940, my mother was a young widow working hard to support her two daughters. She was lonely and wanted to have fun and dance at the Pastime Club. She met my dad there. He was handsome and loved to laugh. Dad was the oldest son from a family of six children, and had been working hard his whole life. He was smitten by this older woman, who was settled with a home and a car and a career. They both needed something that was impossible for the other to give—security, sanctuary, and fidelity. They'd been fighting all morning.

✦ ✦ ✦

I turned and looked again at our garden, a tangle of yellow and pink and purple from the daffodils and roses and tulips my mother had planted. Her prize forsythia bush blazed golden near a tall lilac tree that brushed the peak of the roof. The lilac's thick jade green leaves blocked the sunlight and created the perfect hiding place whenever I wanted to be alone. My dad turned the corner and I lost sight of the only home I'd ever known.

Grandpa Pence sitting in his front lawn, Homedale, Idaho 1955.

Grandma and Grandpa Pence, Homedale, Idaho.

The Arthur and Edith Pence two room cottage, Homedale, Idaho, 1955.

SALMON AND SEAL AND ALL
THE ANIMALS ARE OUR BROTHERS
AND SISTERS. THEY GIVE THEMSELVES
TO US SO WE CAN LIVE. WE MUST
THANK THEM FOR THEIR LIFE.

—The Rev. Deacon William Tyson, Emmonak

4.
PYROCLASTIC FLOW

"Volcanoes made this valley," my mother said as we topped the Thousand Creek grade and drove into the Virgin Valley. The 250-mile drive had worn the boys down, and they were sleeping. I was curious about the changing landscape and slowly a sense of adventure began to replace the pain of leaving grandparents behind.

"Pyroclastic flow," she added.

The Sheldon National Wildlife Refuge is located in the Virgin Valley, a large basin high in the Black Rock Desert in the northwestern corner of Nevada, surrounded by low hills formed millions of years ago when hot rock and ash met gases from the earth's belly and exploded burying everything in their path. Looking closely at the hills, you could see the layers of ash laid down when the earth was roiling in prehistoric struggle.

The spring before we moved, my father had heard about an outcropping of rose-colored sandstone on the Refuge that was suitable for making building facades, fireplaces, and flower boxes. He took a lease on the claim with his two brothers, Theron and Bob Wegman. The lease came with a camp: a scattering of tin buildings on the edge of an old Civilian Conservation Corps camp built in the 1930s. The CCC boys had built a swimming pool, truck ramp, and shower house from 2 x 3-foot blocks of hand-chiseled sandstone from the same quarry my father would mine. Both camps were surrounded by a smattering of ponds fed from the warm artesian springs that bubbled up from a deep underground volcanic formation.

The place we settled in 1955 had a main cabin with two bedrooms and a living room, and two smaller two-room cabins that were used as housing for Uncle Bob and his family, and a bunkhouse for the men. The cook shack, where everyone gathered for meals and to play cards after supper, was just to the left of the main cabin. The wash station, three yards from the cook shack, was a weathered table of rough wood about five feet long, which supported a one-inch steel pipe that came out of the ground and flowed continuously from the artesian spring below. The men would come in from the quarry, dusty and tired, and stop at the wash station outside the cook shack. The very act of scooping hands full of water over their heads seemed to erase the grime and exhaustion from their shoulders, and soon they would be laughing and joking and teasing the cook.

My mother was a substantial woman, tall like her own mother and heavy-set, with large pendulous breasts. She was shy about her body, so she always wore navy blue (dark colors make you look smaller, she would say) and a large hat that nearly covered her eyes. Because of her weight, she wore sensible shoes, the kind that could take you over the desert in search of petrified wood or agates or opals. She loved rocks and would spend hours in the desert before the heat of the day made it impossible for anything but jackrabbits and horned toads to survive. She'd come home from a day at the Rainbow Ridge Opal Mine with fragments of fire opals in her pockets—brilliant green and orange—and put them in a pint mason jar filled with oil in the middle of the table in the cook shack. Then she'd tell us about ancient forests that once lived there, maybe sequoias or hemlock that got covered in the ash and slowly turned to stone.

I learned later that fallen trees must lie in a stable, quiet environment for millions of years before opals are formed. This stillness allows cristobalite spheres to line up in formation until mineral-rich water fills all the empty spaces after the tree matter rots away. Then, when everything lines up just right, the light creates reflection and refraction as it passes through the opal and reveals the fire.

When we first moved to the Virgin Valley the melodious sounds of the burbling water that splashed onto the ground and meandered from the wash station to the marshy pond behind the cook shack enthralled and drew me into a world of make believe. I fashioned the outline of a playhouse with porous black volcanic stones and marked the outlines of doorways, and passageways and rooms, spending hours there every day. I began to find small creatures—lizards and horned toads—and soon had jars filled with wildflowers and sagebrush and my new-found friends. Frog's eggs glistened like bits of jellied candy with little black dots that grew into tadpoles in their protected sac; small black water snakes hid in their own jars filled with marsh grasses. Most of the wild creatures I would keep for a few days then turn them loose where I'd found them. But one day I caught a four-foot bullsnake. He was my prize catch. I kept him in a gallon-sized Best Foods mayonnaise jar, taking him out often to hold him and speak to him as though he understood me.

My mother stapled a small booklet for me out of soft brown paper, and gave me a sharpened #2 pencil, so that I could draw the shapes and patterns of the reptiles I kept. My father told stories of the fiery colors of the sky at dawn that he'd seen while running his diesel truck into Winnemucca from the stone quarry. I wanted to experience the beauty and the wildness of the sunrise for myself, so I began to slip out of my warm quilts and gallop into the hills above our camp while the sky was still a deep indigo and rippled with stars.

Predawn in the high desert is often freezing, even in June, but the artesian well that flowed in a steady stream, driven by the heat of the molten rock far below, created a micro-climate for the vesper sparrow and the gray flycatcher and the sage thrasher that gathered to drink and scratch and search the marshy grasses for worms and bugs and seeds, and the horned lizard and the collared lizard that warmed themselves there from the night's chill air.

Morning, and the earth's stillness as she trembled awake, became my favorite time of day. In a sense it became my spiritual home as well, the place where peace was most palpable to me. By the time I reached the foothills, the mountains to the east would be clearly etched against a turquoise sky. A golden yellow would begin to push out the turquoise and quickly melt into orange with striations of peach. If the sky was cloudless, the orange would give way to pure yellow, the color of light itself. It's then the Western meadowlark would let go a trill so clear the other birds would look up, heads cocked and eyes fixed on the horizon, and wait for the deep crimson to begin to burn the very spot where the sun would peak the mountains. At last, a pin-prick of pure gold would pierce the horizon and flood the valley. Blinded by the light, I would turn and watch the golden hue creep down the hills across the valley west of me. The frost fled in patterns cut from the very hills themselves. The sagebrush, awash in diamonds one moment, softened into the greens and grays of the high desert in the next, let loose a burst of acrid perfume that hung like incense in the still air. The earth seemed to breathe in the tiny droplets of dew, sustaining life in this place that would be a furnace by midmorning. I drank in the cold, moist bouquet, too, knowing I would soon be sweltering as I loped across the desert searching for horned toads and bullsnakes.

A bullsnake is a great pretender. The gray and rusty brown markings that undulate down its back as it glides effortlessly through the sand and underbrush resemble the diamond pattern of the rattlesnake, and its hiss even mimics the rattle of its noxious cousin. At 11 years old I knew the difference. My father and my uncles would shoot the head off any rattlesnake that came into our camp, or chop its head off with a shovel if they had one handy. I'd watched them do it any number of times. A rattlesnake's venom helps it capture and kill small animals and birds for its survival, but it is just as deadly to humans. A bullsnake, on the other hand, is helpful; bullsnakes eat pack rats and voles and gophers that are a nuisance to the ranchers and the miners who live and work among the rocky outcroppings in the high desert. They were welcome in our camp.

One day I carried my fat bullsnake by the tail into the cook shack, jiggling his body so it couldn't gather the tension needed to strike. Its smooth, scaled flesh was dry and supple in my small hands, its skeleton rippling as it lunged again and again in an attempt to escape. Aunt Dorothy and the cook, frying potatoes and venison steaks for the crew screamed, and I laughed, tickled by their reaction, and jostled the snake back to my menagerie of wild things behind the wash station.

Looking back now I realize that exotic animals or reptiles awaken a place so primitive inside us that once we begin to catch them or play with them, we are forever changed. From ancient times the snake has been thought to symbolize immortality, healing, rebirth, and transformation; what was this young girl searching for? A chance to satisfy her curiosity about wild things? The pure joy of being in touch with nature? Or was she simply trying to gain some mastery over her disordered life?

✦ ✦ ✦

Life in the Virgin Valley was eerily quiet compared to my chaotic life in Homedale, where I had the steady presence of my grandparents to help me make sense of it. When I was born, my mother owned and operated the Rosalind Theatre. In 1944 you didn't have babysitters, you either had a relative watch after you or you went with your mother wherever she went. I went to the theater every night from the time I was able to sit up in the back row on a board stretched across the arm rests so I could see over the heads of those in front of me. Carmen Miranda, Danny Kaye, Judy Canova, Judy Garland, Doris Day, Debbie Reynolds, and Gene Kelly were my favorite babysitters. But I also watched Marilyn Monroe, scantily clad, flirt with some handsome cowboy, and Bette Davis slap her leading man because she felt some insult or slight or jealousy. When the movie was over, my sisters would walk me home and put me to bed. It was difficult to sort out the drama on the silver screen and what was happening at home—my own parents argued relentlessly—raised voices, accusations of flirting and infidelity, screen door slamming, and the sound of my father's diesel truck rattling awake and rumbling off into the night.

My mother would cry behind a closed bedroom door, and I would stand in the hallway until the sobs subsided and she fell asleep, then creep back to my bed. I never questioned what was going on. I absorbed the cacophony of sounds and images the way a thirsty cottonwood absorbs water from the river on a hot summer's day.

✦ ✦ ✦

One summer morning I found myself alone. The cook shack was empty, so I crept in hoping to find something sweet. I scanned the table in the center of the shack: lipstick-stained coffee mugs from my mother and the cook, an ashtray choked with Lucky Strike cigarette butts, and a jar of opals confused the flowered oilcloth. I looked beyond to the makeshift cupboards that lined the back wall, seeking chocolate chip cookies or Sugar Daddies hidden there. Then I saw the teapot simmering on the back of the propane stove. I carried it to my playhouse and set it down as I unscrewed the lid on the jar holding the bullsnake. Then I poured the steaming water into the jar.

The bullsnake roiled and twisted and convulsed halfway out of the jar as I looked on in stunned disbelief. In a split second the stench of boiled flesh filled my nose. My stomach convulsed into a knot. I dropped the teapot and knocked the jar over with my foot. The half-dead creature slithered out into the marsh-mud and twitched and rolled and finally lay still. I stopped breathing as I watched and waited for some sign that this was not true, that I had not really done such a thoughtless, catastrophic thing to something I loved so much.

I retched and gulped the acrid bile as wave after wave of nausea undulated from my gut. The steady burble and thrum of water—clear, clean water splashing into the rocks from the steel pipe at the wash station—stood in sharp contrast to the deep lament that moved through me, like the moan of the wind moving at a steady 25 knots up through Thousand Creek Canyon at sunset, driving the shame of what I'd done into some darkening underground cavern.

Startled from my shock by voices coming from the bunk house, I looked again at the place where the snake lay twisted and blistered, its body beginning to swell, and I picked up a shovel and carried the corpse behind the cook shack. As the full impact of my actions settled over me, I began to whisper, "I am so sorry." Then I dug a shallow hole and buried it in the hot sand.

✦ ✦ ✦

It was easy to steal the cigarettes. I had noticed them lying on the table in the cook shack earlier. Now I slipped two Lucky Strikes into the pocket of my jeans and headed for the hillock outcropping near the stone quarry on the road to the cow trail that veered off to the right, down the bank and past the pond. I started to trot, covering a lot of ground, all the time looking back to see if the cook shack was still visible. When I could no longer be seen, I slowed down and looked for the rock where I kept my cache. The rock was the size of a loaf of the cook's homemade bread and similarly shaped, but common, melding with the rosy scree. I found it and sat down and took the two now slightly bent Lucky Strikes out of my pocket. I cached one and lit the other like a cowboy, gently placing the sweet-smelling cigarette between my lips, striking the match on the box away from my face so I wouldn't get the sulfur smell up my nose, and then, when the flame and hiss settled down, bringing the flame to the end of the cigarette and sucking in until my mouth filled with the acrid-sweet smoke, and I felt the bite of the nicotine on my tongue.

Small flitting movements in the sagebrush drew my attention and I got up to search the rocks and dried grasses for the familiar slithering that used to give me such joy. I kicked the dull red clay, obliterating the pattern, the dusty trail that reminded me of what I wanted to forget. Over time the memory of that day became buried, like so many sequoias and hemlock under layers of ash. The summer heat shimmered across the hot springs pond and rose like phantoms jeering across space and days and the divide between innocence and guilt.

✦ ✦ ✦

My mother didn't talk about our sudden move from Homedale to the Virgin Valley. She didn't talk about why my oldest sister Pat left college and came to live with us, suffering from wild emotional swings of euphoria and depression. She didn't talk about Grandpa and Grandma Pence being left alone in Homedale even though they were getting old and less able to take care of themselves. She didn't talk about closing the Rosalind Theatre after television was invented and people stopped coming, or moving from the home she had built after her first husband died. She didn't talk about the hardship of moving into a tin shack in the Black Rock Desert devoid of flowers with no running water or indoor plumbing. She didn't talk about why suffering has to be made visible, or why complicated grief and secrets can't be buried.

✦ ✦ ✦

I knew I had to go home. I crushed the cigarette butt and scattered the remains in the wind. Back at camp I stopped at the wash station, carefully avoiding the overturned jar and abandoned teapot, and began to scoop great hands full of tepid water over my face. Again, and again, I held my hands under the flowing stream, and swished the purifying liquid over my face. *I'm so sorry. I'm so so sorry.*

"Can I peel the spuds?" I asked the cook nonchalantly as I entered the cook shack. She looked surprised, then moved away from the sink. I set to work scrubbing and peeling the skins from the Idaho Russet potatoes until all the ugliness was gone.

Aunt Dorothy came in to help make lunch. "Look what I found at the wash station. Our teapot. It was just lying in the dirt. Now how do you suppose it got there?"

I shrugged and jabbed the peeler into an eye on the potato and cut it out clean, then let the artesian water wash over my trembling hands.

Foreground, a stone bridge connecting two artesian ponds. Teri Goodloe Peters (L) and Beverly Slack Goodloe (R) visited the Refuge in 1994 with the author. Background, the old stone shower house. Warm water flows continuously from a pipe in the ground.

IN 1927 MY DADDY FLOATED THE LOGS FOR THE MISSION FROM THE ANVIK RIVER. HE RAN THE SAWMILL OVER ON THE ISLAND AND BROUGHT THE LOGS ACROSS THE WATER ON A CABLE. IT TOOK THE MEN THREE YEARS TO FINISH THE MISSION.

—Alta Jerue, Anvik

5.
DO YOU LOVE ME?

Two months after the Ecumenical Consultation in Wasilla, the Rev. Scott Fisher called from the bishop's office and asked if Bev Dodge and I wanted to fly with him out to Anvik, a small Athabascan village at the confluence of the Anvik and Yukon Rivers in Western Alaska, three hundred and fifty miles from Anchorage, to help with services at Christ Church. We arrived just ahead of an Arctic storm blowing in over the Nulato Hills from Norton Sound on the Bering Sea. After dropping off our duffle bags and my guitar at the tribal office, we spent the afternoon walking up and down the narrow dirt roads, visiting the elders to tell them we'd have Holy Communion the following evening.

We stopped at Grandma Alta's house to pick up the church register, the beaded altar frontal, and the key, then we headed to the church to check the barrel stove and the wood supply. While Scott poked about the sacristy, I sat quietly and listened for the murmur of prayers that surely soaked the handmade pews, and the laughter of water that must have filled the stone baptismal font over and over again as the people who had inhabited this land for thousands of years promised to follow Jesus. I imagined what it would be like to be the priest in this place. Already, I felt a deep connection to the landscape and the people, but I didn't know why.

We picked up our gear and walked up the long hill to the school. The teachers and children were gone, and Angela Young was just locking up. Born and raised in Anvik, Angela worked at the school as the teacher's aide. She was a member of Christ Church and often helped with services. She had invited us to stay with her in a log cabin back in the trees. We were thankful for her hospitality.

When it was time to turn in, Angela gestured to a small bed in a room off the living room. My heart dropped. Bev and I were expected to share the bed. I thought I would have a private corner to throw my sleeping bag in. I'd always said I was like the *Princess and the Pea*, hyper-vigilant, unable to sleep if there was the slightest noise, and uncomfortable taking my clothes off in front of other people. I took a deep breath and unrolled my sleeping bag on the edge of the bed, then quickly climbed in fully dressed. I was awake for hours, listening to the unfamiliar noises of the others sleeping and comforted by the crackling sounds coming from the wood stove. As the fire burned low and the cold settled in, I cocooned deeper into my sleeping bag, letting my breath escape through the small hole I'd cinched around my face. It seemed like only a moment later that I woke with a start at the sound of the plank door whishing open and shut.

I crept out of bed and quickly assessed the situation. Angela had gone to school early to supervise breakfast for the children. The fire had gone out and there was a skim of ice on the water barrel near the kitchen counter. I chopped the water free with an ax from the wood-box and took a small glass from the counter and dipped it in the water. I stepped onto the porch and looked east to see if there was any hint of a sunrise. Not today. The promised storm was here, and crystalline snowflakes were beginning to coat the spruce trees. I said good morning to the small chickadee chittering in the brush, and then splashed the icy water on my face, gasped, then whispered, "Thank you, thank you, thank you God, for today." Okay, I was almost prepared for whatever adventure lay ahead. I just needed some coffee.

Stepping back inside the cabin ready to start a fire and make coffee, I was stopped by Scott's gentle voice. "No good to burn someone else's wood or use their supplies."

Bev backed him up, "Makes sense."

"Don't worry, we'll find something to eat," he assured me.

They were probably right. But I couldn't remember the last time I'd been this hungry or this cold. I knew I'd be in withdrawal by noon if I didn't have any caffeine. Damn.

I'd wanted to bring coffee and food with us, but Scott traveled in the footsteps of Jesus—*take nothing for the journey… no staff, no bag, no bread*. My stomach rumbled, but I kept my mouth shut. Instead, I tortured myself imagining Angela in the cafeteria serving stacks of golden-brown pancakes to the children with melted butter and maple syrup pooling around the edges. I could almost smell the steaming mugs of coffee swirling with cream. I was pretty sure I was going to freeze into a lump of ice or starve to death or die of full-blown caffeine withdrawal, but what did I know?

We resumed our knocking on doors and inviting families to church until we stumbled into Whitey's Café about noon. After we ordered burgers, fries and coffee, I surveyed my two companions sitting across from me. Scott was a little like a frugal friar who lived on tobacco and Compline prayers whispered at midnight, but he did have a kind way about him, even when he was correcting me or telling me I couldn't burn someone else's wood. Bev and I had been in an adult Sunday school class together at St. Mary's. A retired civil servant, single, no kids, she approached every dilemma with a rational, logical, questioning mind. I was married, had four half-grown sons, surrounded myself with children, loved wearing shawls and hats, played the guitar and sang loudly, and laughed easily. We were an unlikely trio.

I was just starting to warm up and feel alive again with Whitey's strong coffee when my companions began arguing over who came down the Yukon River first, the Anglicans or the Episcopalians. I tuned them out and turned my attention to Whitey and the café he had built into the corner of the Mission. The old log building had anchored this spot on the bank of the Yukon River for nearly a century. It was built as a dormitory for the Christ Church Mission and Orphanage by the Rev. Dr. John Chapman and the local men between 1887 and 1889. A sawmill stood on the sandbar at the mouth of the Anvik River where the local men had cut logs for the Mission. Slash-marks from the saw teeth were still visible on the floor and walls. Some of the windows looked original, with seed bubbles and a faint blue tinge.

Bob Marley wailed a song from his *Exodus* album on the radio behind the counter, One Love! I sang along, letting the Jamaican rhythm carry me into a kind of Island reverie. I'd been part of the folk revival of the 1960's, singing in a Peter, Paul and Mary style band at the University of Nevada at Reno. I loved all kinds of music: country, folk, reggae, gospel, rock, and even hymns from the new 1980 Hymnal. Marley was a folk hero to everyone influenced by the Vietnam War, the desire for political change, and Rastafarian spirituality. I had the perfect hair for dread-locks, and I secretly wanted them. The sizzle of the French fries and the smell of the burgers on the grill were intoxicating. Now I was pretty sure I was going to survive… great music, endless coffee, and giant burgers on their way.

The door flew open and a flurry of snow filled the café as a tall, older man stepped in out of the storm. His eyes fastened on me rocking out with Bob Marley. The old man was handsome, in a rugged sort of way. Just the sort of man I could imagine mushing down the Yukon River with a team of dogs, or roaring up the trail on a powerful snowmachine. He carried himself a lot like my father: six feet tall, erect posture, strong shoulders that looked like they could chop enough wood for winter or slog a 40-pound king salmon out of the Yukon River or lug the hind quarter of a bull moose out of the forest. He raged out of the storm like he belonged here, and, of course, he did; this was his country, his river, his village. Maybe his parents or grandparents were raised in this orphanage after the influenza epidemic of 1917–18. I felt a flutter of excitement; finally, some action, finally someone interesting to talk to.

He lurched toward me. I stood up, smiled, and held out my hand in greeting. In one explosive movement the old man grabbed my hand and jerked me towards him.

"Do you love me?" he snarled.

Startled, I pulled back and tried to get my hand loose. His grip was like a wolf trap, steely cold and brutal. *What the hell*, I thought, completely discombobulated. *Do I love this guy?* My mind whipped through a book I'd been reading by C. S. Lewis, *The Four Loves*—Eros, passion; Storge, affection; Philia, friendship; Agape, charity or God's divine love. It's got to be one of those, I thought, beginning to panic.

Marley didn't miss a beat. I took a deep breath, met the old man's gaze, and leaned in close enough to smell alcohol on his breath and see his broken teeth and the stubble of his graying beard. "Yes, I do love you," I said as earnestly as I could, praying C. S. Lewis knew what he was talking about.

He jerked me closer and growled in my face, "My wife, she gonna *keeeell* you when she find out you love me."

Sweet Jesus, I whispered under my breath. I wrenched my hand back and forth again, trying to escape. It was no use; my assailant wouldn't let go. My companions were still arguing while I was being confronted with life and death and the meaning of love. I threw kindness out the window, leaned closer, and growled back, "Well, I love your wife too, but I hate alcohol, and alcohol is going to *keeeell* you if you don't stop drinking."

Just then, Whitey exploded from behind the sizzling burgers and had the old man by the shoulders and out the door in seconds with a promise of delivering his burger in a few.

I slumped into my chair. What the hell just happened? Was the old man real or was he some sort of messenger? Then I remembered a dream I'd had years earlier. I was standing at the kitchen sink washing dishes. A beautiful woman stood behind me, reading a list of questions: do you hide your drinking from others? Do you drink to relax or feel better? Do you drink when you promised yourself that you wouldn't? Once you start drinking, do you drink more than you intended to? She was talking to me, but I didn't turn around.

To say I hated alcohol was a lie. I drank my whiskey straight up and had since I was sixteen years old. What I hated was the brutality of being trapped. I hated that my storybook-idea of life in the bush was being turned upside down. I hated that my companions were engaged in a dense argument that didn't seem to have any bearing on what was happening in Whitey's Café. I hated the irony of Bob Marley singing about love, and this old man and I misunderstanding what love was all about.

I had no idea, then, how much my own childhood influenced my understanding of life on the Yukon. I grew up with three larger-than-life sources of information about people and what was expected of them: My Grandpa Pence, my mother and the Rosalind Theater, and adventure books by Jack London and James Oliver Curwood.

My grandfather filled my days with hero stories about Bruneau John, and how my great grandparents were able to hide in the Roberson Caves near the Bruneau River and survived the Great Bannock Uprising. Stories about Bruneau John and how he saved his white friends were a family legend. My own grandfather was a gentleman, kind and generous. He rarely smoked, or drank whiskey, or cussed, and never in front of the children. I often heard him say, "We're alive today because of the generosity and kindness of Bruneau John." I wanted to be a hero like Bruneau John, to please my grandfather.

My mother's passion was the movie theater my father built for her after they married and moved to Homedale. It was a wondrous place filled with popcorn and ice cream, John Wayne and Betty Hutton, Loretta Young and Clark Gable. It didn't matter if the movie was "Fort Apache," "Annie Get Your Gun," or a rerun of "Call of the Wild," there was always action, suspense, bravery, and, of course, romance and happily ever after. I dreamed of living such an adventure.

The books of Jack London, *The Call of the Wild* and *White Fang*, and James Oliver Curwood, *Kazan* and *Baree, The Son of Kazan*, cemented my desire to live surrounded by dogs and snow in the wilderness of Alaska. Danger? Bring it on. Storms? No problem. But the reality was much more difficult than I'd imagined.

✦ ✦ ✦

Sitting in the café I tried to figure out what had just happened. When I met Scott, I wanted to be like him—kind, soft spoken, humble, faithful. Now I was angry at him and Bev and their stupid argument about Anglicans and Episcopalians. Who cares? I wanted to shout. Can't you see that this man had a hold of me and wouldn't let go? I wanted to love this man, like I imagined Scott or my grandfather might love him—in spite of his looks or smells or what he said or did—instead, I'd found myself frightened and then reacting by stepping into his personal space and matching his anger. My cheeks were burning.

Whitey put warm platters of burgers and fries on the table in front of us, then refilled our cups. I stared at my food and wondered—can I love myself? When I'm cold and hungry? When I'm drinking? When I'm frightened and mean? Is it possible to love a stranger if you don't love yourself?

The old Christ Church Mission on the banks of the Yukon River, Anvik, Alaska.

Old Anvik Mission.

Old car at Anvik Mission.

Christ Church, Anvik.

Old Anvik Mission log work.

WE DO WHAT WE HAVE TO DO.

—Esther Wegman, Grandview, Idaho

6.

WOMEN'S WORK

"Tanana is called Nuchalawoyya in the Koyukon Athabascan language of the people," said Scott. "It means 'where the two rivers meet,' the Tanana and the Yukon Rivers." Scott and I were on our way to the village of Tanana, 130 miles west of Fairbanks, for confirmation training. The Rev. Andy Fairfield, assistant to Bishop Harris and the chief pilot for the Diocese, loaded our gear into the red and white Cessna 206 that my husband Kris had just donated to the Diocese. Kris and I had been married twenty years by this time, and I had urged him to attend a men's retreat at Meier Lake Conference Center with the blind evangelist, Bill Hickenbotham, so he could better understand my passion for Native ministry. He came away with his own faith renewed and responded by donating our airplane to the Diocese. He also made several other large donations to the Boy Scouts of America, Midnight Sun Council.

Andy was obviously delighted with a beautiful airplane that could carry five passengers and a payload of 1,400 pounds; he hummed under his breath as he checked the oil, wiggled the flaps, cleaned the windshield, and ran his finger along the propeller checking for possible chips from take offs and landings on the gravel village runways. I liked Andy from the first time I met him, with his easy smile and kind eyes. When it was time to untie the airplane, I deftly uncurled the double half-hitch and coiled the rope over the parking cone. I was taking ground school training at the King Center in Anchorage and wanted to show off.

Andy would fly us out to Tanana, drop us off, and then fly on to Ft. Yukon, Arctic Village, Allakaket, and Beaver to bring in church leaders for confirmation training and leadership development along with three Native priests, the Rev. David Salmon from Chalkyitsik, the Rev. Titus Peter from Birch Creek, and the Rev. Bergman Silas from Minto.

It was my first trip to Tanana and I didn't know Titus Peter or Bergman Silas very well but I was excited to be working again with David Salmon. Besides traveling with David on the Gospel Mission team, I had participated with him several times at St. Matthew's in Fairbanks when Bill Hickenbotham came to lead healing services. David was to become one of my most beloved mentors, and Nuchalawoyya would come to mean much more to me than a place; it felt more like the coming together of two cultures, or two ways of understanding the world. As the days progressed, Nuchalawoyya even began to feel more personal, like the coming together of two parts of myself.

I had been assigned to stay with Grandma Mary Dick in her new two-bedroom log cabin, a good walk to our meeting place at St. James Episcopal Church. Grandma Mary's cabin was one of several built on higher ground after the last ice jam flooded the low areas. She kept a wood fire burning all the time, and I thought I could earn my keep by carrying in an armload of split birch for the wood box every time I came in from the outhouse. Being useful helped me feel less unsure of myself. The quietness of the Native people still unnerved me. They were so unassuming, so easy in their environment. Growing up, my own father had chided me for singing too loudly and always getting in the last word; *who do you think you are*, he would say, or *what will the neighbors think?* I compensated by being overly prepared, jamming my duffle bag with everything I could possibly need: a sleeping bag, towel, clean clothes, toiletry items, mascara, rouge and lipstick, a stack of books including Johannes Tauler's *Spiritual Conferences*, the selected writings of Meister Eckhart, and a well-worn copy of *Values Clarification*, my Bible, Prayer Book, and gospel song book, and a stash of peanuts and chocolate Hershey bars. God forbid I would have a moment without something to read or eat.

An elder had died just before we arrived. The men of the village had gone hunting for a moose, and the elder's granddaughter was handing out bags of moose fat to make the traditional Indian Ice cream for the potlatch. Grandma Mary had been given a sack of moose fat and when I asked her how she made it, she invited me to come home early from my meeting and she would teach me.

As I walked up the snowy path, I caught a whiff of the most wild, woodsy smoke coming from inside the cabin and knew immediately what it was. My father and my uncles hunted white-tail and mule deer in Nevada, and we always had fresh steak during hunting season. As I pulled the heavy plank door open, I could see a cast iron skillet of moose fat sizzling on the stove—Grandma Mary had been cooking the fat over the wood stove all morning, rendering out the oil. She nodded and showed me the three-pound coffee can she had filled with hot fat.

Grandma Mary's recipe came from Maggie Elia, whose ice cream was reported to be the best in the Tanana Valley. While the fat cooled, she gathered the rest of the ingredients and recited the recipe out loud:

>Wesson oil: *six cups*
>
>Ice water: *six cups*
>
>Sugar: *three cups*
>
>Low bush cranberries: *half a gallon*
>
>Oreo cookies: *one package, broken*
>
>Bread: *one loaf, cubed*
>
>Sailor Boy Pilot Bread: *one box, broken*
>
>Raisins: *one box*
>
>Walnuts: *two pounds, chopped*

"Whip the fat twenty minutes, then when it begins to turn white, add the Wesson oil and ice water one cup at a time, alternating oil and water, beating five or ten minutes between additions. The fat will begin to turn white and fluffy." She watched me closely to make sure I was paying attention. I smiled and nodded, remembering my own grandmother teaching me to make apple pie. "When you have whipped the ice cream for one hour and fifteen minutes total, you add the sugar and the berries and the other things from the list."

"Okay, I think I can do it," I assured her.

"You got to sing to that ice cream when you stir it," added Grandma Mary.

"Sing, Mary? What kind of song?"

"You know, Indian song—ya-ya, ya-ya, hi-ya—like that."

"Okay," I whispered. I loved to sing, but singing an Indian song felt like a privilege, and I wasn't sure I'd earned it.

"And don't let no mans come into the kitchen," she said.

"No men?"

"No, they will spoil that ice cream. This is women's work. Always turn the spoon in one direction, like that," she said. "And don't stop stirring until it's done."

Mary began to turn the wooden spoon in a clockwise direction, the direction of the rising sun, just above the large stainless-steel bowl, and then she motioned me to take over. I took the spoon in mid-turn, plunged it into the warm fat, closed my eyes, and began a soft murmur, "Ya-ya, ya-ya, hi-ya. Ya-ya, ya-ya, hi-ya."

The rhythm and repetition of the song carried me back to an incident from the day before. The Rev. Bergman Silas, the Native priest from Minto, came to the meeting with his wife, Sarah. I was attracted to them immediately. They seemed so happy. They smiled all the time and greeted everyone warmly. During that first day's meeting, Sarah had her Bible open on her lap and kept saying, "Praise God! If it's the Lord's will, it will happen." Each time, Bergman nodded and agreed, then said something funny to make everyone laugh. They were like Minto's own version of comedians

George Burns and Gracie Allen.

I started to follow Bergman around during the breaks. For every problem or concern voiced at the meeting, I had some big idea how to solve it. "Why don't you do this, why don't you do that," I'd say. I was full of advice and solutions. Exasperated, Bergman stopped and looked at me and said, "You white womans talk too much."

I stared at him in disbelief. There wasn't a shred of humor in his voice. He was mad. I felt hurt, then I felt my cowgirl temper rising and my cheeks beginning to burn. I decided to show him a thing or two. I'd keep my mouth shut and not speak again until God told me to. The rest of that day I didn't open my mouth. During the Bible study I kept my head down and my finger on the verse we were discussing. No one even noticed I wasn't participating. When it was time to sing, I handed my guitar to one of the younger men from Ft. Yukon. He led the singing.

The granddaughter who had been caring for the elder before he died came over and asked Bergman and the other priests if they would officiate at the funeral in two days. I heard them talking, but I didn't get involved. I mostly sat in the corner and read my Bible so I wouldn't be tempted to talk.

Bergman came over to the corner where I was sitting and said, "I want you to read the Old Testament lesson at the funeral, Isaiah 61: 1–3."

I looked up and hesitated a minute, then said in a flat voice, "I'm not speaking until God tells me to."

Bergman began to shout, "Well, who do you think told me to ask you?"

"Okay," I said, "I'll do it."

We both started to laugh. George Burns had just disarmed the cowgirl.

After Bergman and I reconciled, I went for a long walk on the road near the river. The day was clear and cold, the temperature hovered around minus six degrees, and the wind gusted to twenty knots off the river. I was meditating on the lesson Bergman had given me to read at the funeral. "*The spirit of the Lord God is upon me, because the Lord has anointed me… to bring good news to the poor… to bind up the broken hearted… to proclaim release to the captives…*"

A door opened and Grandma Ruth stepped out on her porch and hollered. "Judith, want soup?" I waved and smiled and followed her into her warm cabin and sat down at the table under the window opposite an old man, Joe, whom I'd met the first evening at the Mission House. He was eating soup too. I smiled and said hello and added how nice it was to come in and warm up. Ruth put a bowl of moose soup in front of me. Plump noodles swam in the clear fat. I realized I hadn't eaten all day. I was ravenous. Two blue-speckled enamel bowls with Pilot Bread and butter sat on the table between us within easy reach. I helped myself and thanked her again for inviting me in.

✦ ✦ ✦

At the Mission House, the first night of our gathering, I was leading introductions using one of my values clarification exercises, "If you could be any animal or bird what would you be?" Joe had playfully imagined that if he could be any animal or bird, he would be a little baby duckling. We had all laughed with him when he said this. He did resemble a baby duckling even at 89 years of age, with his shy, awkward smile. His wife, Sarah, had confided that she would be a swan. We all responded with oohs and ahhs. She did look rather swanlike as she sat beside her husband on the sofa: strong, confident black eyes that seemed filled with wisdom. She had a long thin neck, and translucent skin that hung loose over high cheekbones.

After the introductions, the bible study, and gospel singing, we invited people to recall any uncomfortable memories from the past. The younger people shared stories of grief and loss but most of the elders sat perfectly still, listening. Sarah had gone on to share that she and Joe had gotten together when they were both fifteen years old. They were out on the trail when Joe, chopping wood with his hatchet, had accidently chopped into his leg. They had no one around to help them, so she gathered spruce pitch from an old tree and covered the deep wound with the pitch. His leg healed completely. Joe had lifted his pant leg, not even a scar.

✦ ✦ ✦

Now Joe, sitting across from me, said, "You make me think of my mama. When I was twelve years old, my mama died. I never cried for her."

Startled by his words, I looked up and put down my spoon. The memories shared by the younger people must have helped Joe access this memory from somewhere very far away. Or maybe the warm soup at Ruth's table helped him feel comfortable enough to speak. I lowered my eyes for a moment out of respect for his words. When I looked up, his eyes were red rimmed and full of water.

"I had a dream the night she died," Joe continued. "I saw her standing at the top of the long stairway at the Mission House, with the night sky and the stars behind her, and all the people from our village who had died, walking past. I started to go up those stairs to her, but she held up her hand, like that, then shook her head and said, no. You can't come here. You have to go home. I turned around and walked down the stairs and out the door."

Joe's lower lip began to tremble. I felt my stomach turn upside down. I knew I had to pray for him in the Episcopal tradition of laying-on-of-hands, the way I had learned from the Rev. Mal Miner and the Order of St. Luke's at All Saint's in Anchorage, and the Rev. David Salmon and Bill Hickenbotham at the revival at St. Matthews, but where were those mentors now when I needed them? *Lord have mercy.* Then I remembered a healing retreat at Holy Spirit Retreat House in Anchorage years earlier. I had watched a Counselor support the lower body of a person who had buried tears from some long-ago loss. I got up and knelt beside Joe, and put my left hand on his belly and my right hand on his lower back, then gently pressed my hands into his frail body. Silently I prayed for the release of those tears that had been held in for a lifetime. He began to sob. I began to sob with him.

Ruth was at the stove stirring the soup. I heard her quietly begin to pray in tongues. Then she began to sing in Indian, "Ya-ya, ya-ya, hi-ya."

"Your mother loved you very much," I said at last. "She wanted you to go on living."

"Yes," he said. "She loved me so much she used to put her dry tit in my mouth to let me suck long after she had no more milk."

✦ ✦ ✦

"Ya-ya, ya-ya, hi-ya."

The smell of the warm rendered moose fat filled my nostrils and brought me back to Grandma Mary's kitchen. I continued to stir the ice cream and sing, "ya-ya, ya-ya, hi-ya."

Another memory wafted up from somewhere deep as I sang to that ice cream. It was a picture of Grandpa and Grandma Wegman standing together in front of the little cottage on the banks of the Snake River in Grandview, Idaho, where they lived all their married lives. I see a small dark-skinned man dressed in old bib overalls standing beside a taller fair woman with honey brown hair. She's wearing a polka dot dress with a lace collar held down with a small broach. Grandma has dusty blue eyes the color of the sky, and she's standing with her hands behind her back looking pleased with herself. Grandpa is wearing a fedora pushed back so you can see his black hair and piercing black eyes; his hands are on his hips and his smile reveals his spirited nature. He and his brothers would often play for dances around the valley. They could all play the harmonica, fiddle, banjo, and guitar.

Grandma and Grandpa Wegman raised six children in their tiny two-bedroom cottage. Grandma and Grandpa slept in one bedroom and the two daughters, Geraldine and Roberta, slept in the other. The four boys—Bill, Clayton, Thereon, and Bob—slept in a canvas wall tent outside the back door. In the winter Grandma would heat bricks on the wood stove and send each boy to bed with a hot brick, and Grandpa would sleep on a cot by the woodstove in the kitchen so he could keep the fire burning all night.

My father, Bill, was the oldest child. He was fourteen in 1929 when the stock market crashed in New York. He worked to help support the family. Looking back, I wonder if the experiences that followed were what made those brothers so tight. My father looked out for his younger brothers all his life. The two youngest, Thereon and Bob, stayed with us off and on in Homedale and together with my father they became Wegman Brothers when they started mining Owyhee Rose building stone in the Virgin Valley.

Grandpa Wegman raised a pig every summer and slaughtered it in the fall. He smoked the hams and sides of bacon and Grandma made sausages out of the rest. She would circle the long links of sausages into a large stone-ware crock, and then cover them with rendered pig fat to preserve them. She made head cheese out of the gelatinous snout, ears, and jowls, and pickled the feet with spices and onions and apple cider vinegar. Sixty-two years after Grandpa died, the new owners of the cottage found a smoked ham still hanging in the attic. When I heard about that ham, I wanted it! I'm sure it was stone-hard, but I wanted to heft it and smell it and think of Grandpa and Grandma, and remember what hardworking people they were.

Grandma Wegman attended the Congregational Church and sang gospel hymns and read her King James Bible every day. She would recite the Lord's Prayer and the Twenty-Third Psalm in the evening as she washed up in her bedroom before bed. On a low dresser she kept a large white porcelain bowl with a matching white pitcher filled with water and a clean washcloth. I can still hear the water gently splashing and the thrum of her beautiful alto voice, "*The Lord is my shepherd, I shall not want...*"

Now, reflecting on Joe's story about his mother, I knew why the picture of my grandparents had come to me in that moment. It was the end of June, 1952. I was seven years old. Grandpa Wegman had died of a heart attack. My father gathered us all into our brand-new, black Chevy coupe and drove the seventy miles to Grandview for the funeral. The casket was nearly invisible under a garland of red roses, yellow chrysanthemums, pink gladiolas, and white carnations. Grandma looked sad, like she wanted to cry. But she wasn't crying and neither was anyone else.

Just then, Grandma sighed and said what I'd heard her say so many times before, "We do what we have to do." She wore her stoicism like a cloak that both comforted and protected her from despair, a courage I didn't fully understand as a child.

I only knew Grandpa was in that casket, and all that spirited playfulness was gone, and no one was crying. The women from the Congregational Church began to sing, "What a friend we have in Jesus, all our sin and grief to bear." And I began to wail.

"Stop crying," whispered my sister Pat.

I couldn't stop.

She squeezed my hand and glared at me.

I cried louder.

Others around me began to stir uncomfortably. Several looked at me, frowned, and then looked away. Grandma's head dropped to her chest and she squeezed her lips between her teeth, and closed her eyes. My father glanced at me vacantly, then back at the flowers blanketing the casket.

Pat tightened the grip on my hand and jerked my arm upward.

"Stop it," she said, then gave my face a stinging slap. "You have to be strong."

I stifled my crying. I stifled it for forty years—we do what we have to do, Grandmother—until an Elder at Nuchalawoyya reminded me that children need to cry for their mothers and grandfathers no matter how rheumy their eyes, or brittle their bones, or wrinkled their skin.

❖ ❖ ❖

I cried then, in earnest, as I stirred the ice cream. I cried like my very life depended on it. At last, I took a deep breath and started to sing again, ya-ya, ya-ya, hi-ya. I thought again of Bergman's request that I read the lesson from Isaiah at the funeral for the elder the next day, "*To comfort all who mourn... to give them garlands instead of ashes... oil of gladness instead of mourning... they shall be called oaks... oaks.*"

I raised my voice, feeling a new lightness in my body, until it echoed off the cupboards—Ya-ya, ya-ya, hi-ya—as I sang to that ice cream, and stirred in the direction of the rising sun, and let no mans come into the kitchen, for this is women's work.

Esther Nelson Wegman, John Henry Wegman standing in front of their cottage in Grandview, Idaho 1950.

My father Bill Wegman and old Ford on his 15th birthday, Grandview, Idaho.

Theron, Bob, and Birdie Wegman, Grandview, Idaho.

My father Bill Wegman on the right, and his brother Clayton, Grandview, Idaho.

ON THE DAY OF RECONCILIATION,
WE GO TO EACH PERSON IN THE
VILLAGE AND SAY 'IF I HAVE HURT YOU
IN ANY WAY, I AM DEEPLY SORRY.'

—Walter Meganack, Chief, Port Graham

7.
IS ANYTHING BROKEN?

Snow was deep and the days, though short, were sunny and crisp. Nighttime temperatures averaged 25 to 30 below zero. Scott and I were gathered in the Mission House with church leaders for training the afternoon of the first day when the door opened and a man stepped inside. "I want to see Judith," he said to the people sitting close to the door.

I looked up. The man stood very still. He glanced at the person he had spoken to and then fastened his gaze on the door post as if maybe he wished he hadn't come. I stepped forward and introduced myself.

"Can we talk?" he asked, almost inaudibly.

The pocket on his gray coat was torn, and the right sleeve was streaked with soot, probably from a campfire or stoking his wood stove. I'd been traveling with Scott and David Salmon almost monthly doing healing services, and people were beginning to ask for me by name when they wanted prayer.

I motioned to Scott to join us, and together we went into the back room. I pulled a chair up for the man and asked him to sit down.

I sat facing him and the priest sat in the ragged stuffed chair propped against the wall. "The night my old lady died we had a fight. She went out, and I didn't stop her. I knew she was drunk, but I didn't stop her. All this time, I can't sleep. I wish I had stopped her. Can you pray for me?"

Everyone was talking about the young woman and her partner

who had been drinking. The woman had stumbled out of the cabin they shared and wandered through the dark forest until she'd become hypothermic, then lay down and never got up. Her clothes were dropped along the trail, a grim witness to her delirium.

I felt my stomach recoil. I wanted to run away. I wanted to shout, "Why didn't you go after her? Why didn't you find her and take her home to her mother?" Instead, in that dingy back room in the Mission House on the Yukon River, I looked into this man's eyes and saw only shame and regret. Something in me began to shift and soften. But I didn't want to soften. I wanted to stay angry. I wanted to blame.

At last, I stood up and laid my hands on the man's head and began to pray that someday he would find the God whose property is always to have mercy. That he would, in time, find the forgiveness he sought. That he would one day forgive himself. Then I prayed for the woman and for her life cut short by alcohol. My hands trembled. The man began to sniffle and then tears began to flow down his cheeks. My stomach felt as if it was full of biting snakes; something inside me broke and I too began to cry. I pulled the vial of holy oil from my pocket and anointed the man's forehead with the sign of the cross and said, at last, "Jesus has forgiven your sins by the grace of the Holy Spirit. Go in peace."

After the man left, Scott turned to me and said, "You know what just happened here?" I waited for him to answer his own question.

"He gave you his confession."

"Why me? I growled. "I'm not the priest."

All my angst at the inadequacy of the men priests to squarely face the suffering of the people and do something concrete about it came flooding back. Years earlier, when the National Church voted to ordain women to the Priesthood, I'd stormed into the office of my priest, Chuck Eddy, and declared, "We already do everything else, and now we have to be the priests too?" Now I felt that same anger again, "Why me?"

"I don't know. He asked for you by name. He must have felt safe with you."

I didn't sleep much that night or for the next 10 nights. I felt inadequate to meet the needs of the people, and I couldn't stop asking why. Why did alcohol have such a hold on people? Why didn't the police do more to stop violence against Native women? Why were there so many stories about sexual abuse and neglect of children? Why didn't the church do more to help people heal?

"I want to walk on the trail where the girl died and say prayers," I told Scott.

"We can do that," he said.

The trail wound through the spruce forest. Deep dry snow blanketed everything, muffling all sounds except the scrunch-scrunch of our boots. A boreal chickadee began flitting in and out of the trees with her bright *chick-a-dee-dee-dee*, bidding us come. I gladly followed her flight to the base of an old gnarled spruce at the edge of the trail. Hardened pitch had oozed out of a gouge in his scarred trunk when the wound was fresh and now looked like a crystalline waterfall. I fished in my pocket for the bottle of holy oil, took off the lid and filled it with chunks of pitch. I inhaled deeply and let the tree medicine fill my throat and lungs, *thank you, thank you, thank you*, I whispered.

✦ ✦ ✦

By the time I was 17 years old drinking with my school friends at the sand dunes outside Winnemucca was a regular occurrence. One night, when it was time to go home, Lenny picked up the half-full bottle of Jim Beam and asked what we should do with it. I grabbed it from him and drank it straight down. I passed out. My friends trundled me into the car, drove me home, shoved me in the front door, and drove off before my mother got up. I woke up with her slapping my face over and over again, and shouting "How much did you have to drink?"

"I only had one beer."

The following weekend I wanted to spend the night with my best friend Holly. My mother thought I was lying again and said no. I took off up the road to Highway 95 and stuck out my thumb. A dark blue sedan stopped; I climbed in, then realized my mistake.

"Where ya headed little lady?" the old man purred. His shifty eyes narrowed as his nicotine-stained fingers did a slow tap tap on the steering wheel. He smelled like piss and diesel fuel.

"I got family in Denio. You heading that way?"

"You bet." He grinned then; his teeth were the color of shit.

I didn't smile. I didn't look at him again. I kept up a tough girl persona until he turned down the straight stretch off 95 to Denio. At the bottom of the hill, I saw a truck at Sod House.

"Let me out here. I've got friends that live at this place."

I slammed the door, then waited for him to drive off before I took a deep breath.

I trotted to the house. No one was home. I circled the house trying doors and windows. It was Friday and getting dark fast. I found the bathroom window at the back of the house unlatched. I rolled an empty gas drum up to the window and climbed up and jimmied the window open as far as I could—about 16 inches. It was just getting dark. It would be a damned cold night if I didn't get in.

I slipped my feet through the opening and sat with my butt on the sill as I tried my grip on the inside of the sill. I was slim and strong from playing volleyball. I figured I could just pull my back side through the narrow opening and step down onto the toilet. I pulled my butt and shoulders through in one movement. My feet glanced off the toilet and the full weight of my body dropped as my neck was coming through the opening. The sharp crack of vertebrae as my chin hung up on the window was like a pistol shot. I pawed the air with my hands and feet as I fought to tighten my back and take the pressure off my neck. Somehow in all the flailing, I touched the toilet and pushing up with my legs and tucking my chin under the window frame, I got free and fell to the floor.

The silence of the dark house, the fight with my mother and her not trusting me, and the fright with the shitty toothed old man swept over me all at once. My chest began to heave, and I let out a cry.

✦ ✦ ✦

Every day I prayed for the young woman who died from alcohol abuse. Every day I prayed for her partner and other family members who were still drinking. Every day someone new came with a painful story of abuse or neglect. I continued to ask *why me*, not recognizing the call that was becoming clear to those around me. I didn't connect my own brokenness with what was happening to others. I didn't know anything about alcoholism or intergenerational trauma leading to high-risk behavior. I was running on caffeine and adrenaline, and I was wide open to the suffering of others. By the time I got back to Anchorage, I was exhausted and could only lie on the sofa in the family room and watch the ice on Cook Inlet flow out with the tide. In the stillness, the sound of glass shattering startled me. I looked at the windows, then at the ice on Cook Inlet. *My imagination*, I thought.

No, there It was again, a sharp crack, then tinkling like a crystal goblet falling to the floor and shattering. I wondered if this was the iconic *crack in the cosmic egg*. The sound wasn't coming from the room, and it wasn't the great plates of sheet ice on the Inlet swirling and chafing their sharp edges smooth. It seemed to be coming from inside my head. I sat straight up. *Good grief, I'm having some sort of breakdown.* I reached for the phone and called my husband, Kris, at work.

"Come home," I said. "I think I'm cracking open."

"What?" he said.

"I heard the sound of glass shattering. I think I'm going crazy. I need you to come home." Then I collapsed on the sofa and waited.

"Is anything broken?" I asked Kris when he got there. "I thought I heard glass shattering and scattering on the floor in the dining room." He looked at me blankly as he sat down beside me and cradled my head in his lap. He gently placed one hand on the top of my head and the other on my belly. Feeling a steady thrum of energy course through my body, I knew he was praying for me. We stayed like that for a long time.

"There is so much suffering, so much shame, so much violence and death."

"You have to stop going," Kris said.

I looked at him long and hard. I'd often said he was like the rock in our marriage and I was like the wind. He was strong, steady, anchored in the here and now. I was the risk taker. I loved being in the middle of action, storms, and possibilities.

"No," I said flatly.

"It's hurting you,"

"You don't understand. I will not abandon the women and children. I'm going to figure this out."

"Let's go for a walk." He stood up and lifted me from the sofa. He helped me into my warm coat and then wrapped a shawl around my shoulders. We walked up and down McCollie Avenue until I could feel my body begin to relax and my breathing become steady. Twinkle lights outlined birch and spruce trees, and red and green and blue Christmas lights encircled windows and doorways, heralds of a peace on earth that I knew wasn't real for everyone. We walked home and I slept until supper time.

The next morning, I headed downtown to the after-Christmas sale at Nordstrom. I began absentmindedly going through every dress on the sale rack. I didn't need clothes. I needed to be around beauty, and smiling faces and young sales clerks who didn't seem to have a care in the world. A familiar voice said hello and asked me how I was doing. I looked up and saw a counselor friend from the university standing on the other side of the rack.

"Terrible," I said.

"In what way?" she asked.

"I've been volunteering with the church, and every time I come home from the Yukon, I'm overwhelmed with exhaustion and sadness from all the stories I've heard. My husband wants me to quit, but I have to figure this out. There is so much alcohol abuse and violence, so much promiscuity and sexual abuse." My friend moved around to my side of the rack.

"Is it alcoholism or sexual abuse you don't understand?"

"Maybe both. They seem to be connected, but I don't think I have a clear idea of what healthy sexuality is anymore either," I confided. "I'm 40 years old, and I feel like I don't understand my own sexual feelings or the feelings and behaviors of others," I whispered. *Maybe I've never known what healthy sexuality is*, I thought, remembering how hurt and angry I was when an old man propositioned me on the steps of the community hall in one of the villages the summer before.

"If I were 40 years old and wanting to learn everything I could about sex and sexuality, I'd head for San Francisco and take a workshop at the Institute for Advanced Study of Human Sexuality."

"What?" I'd never heard of the place.

"If you're being overwhelmed by everyone else's stories, it may be about needing to strengthen your own emotional boundaries. At 40 it's time to make peace with your past, revisit the values you learned from your parents and either accept them as true for you or let them go. Take the proverbial trip home, examine all the old childhood issues and relationships, bless everyone and say goodbye. Let it all go and get on with your life," she said, as though she were reading my mind.

"You're right," I said. "This is about me, not other people. I need to find out if I'm okay." I grew up in an alcoholic family with major issues around sexuality, fidelity, and trust; now these same issues were in my face. My mother's father seldom drank. My father's family used alcohol to laugh, cry, cuss, fight, unwind after a brutal day of work, run away from problems and feelings, you name it. If you were man enough to take the cork out of the bottle, you'd better be man enough to drink the whole thing. I learned to hide my feelings and fears of inadequacy by drinking and cussing from my father. I learned to hide my grief and loss with compulsive overeating from my mother.

"I just need to know if I'm okay."

"Oh, don't worry, you're okay," my friend said. We both laughed. My friend had been teaching a class based on Thomas Harris's book, *"I'm Okay, You're Okay."*

I walked out of the store, drove home, and called information for the Institute for Advanced Study of Human Sexuality in San Francisco. When the Institute answered, they recommended I start with the basics, so I signed up for Sexuality 101. When I hung up the phone, I felt mildly euphoric. And terrified.

YOU CAN SET LIMITS
TO PROTECT YOURSELF.

—The Rev. Chuck Eddy, Anchorage

8.

DAFFODILS & CHRYSANTHEMUMS

The next three weeks were a blur. Scheduling my trip to San Francisco and the class on Human Sexuality catapulted me into action. I enrolled in the spring semester at Alaska Pacific University with a whopping seventeen credits, so I could graduate in May. Next, I joined the Diet Center to get my overeating under control. I tackled a bunch of unfinished projects: cleaned out my closet, balanced my checkbook, designed a journal writing workshop for the Lutheran Women at Amazing Grace Lutheran Church, and ordered and picked up my plane tickets for San Francisco.

I'd been keeping an Intensive Journal as part of the Personal Growth and Creativity Program of Dialogue House in New York City for several years, and I was in the habit of recording my dreams and analyzing them to help me integrate material that was hidden in the unconscious. Not this time. I was so focused on getting myself, the family, and the house in order for my trip, I simply wrote them in my journal and moved on.

> Dream Log
> *January 16, 1985*
>
> *Kris and I are in the upstairs bedroom. I look over and see our artist friend is lying on the floor dead. His wife is making up his face with eye liner pencil and eye shadow. She draws a second set of eyes on his forehead. I wonder why no one is talking about it. Just then one of our children walks*

in and asks, "What's the matter with our friend?" The wife says, "It's hard to pretend he's not dead with his body laying right here."

Dream Log
January 23, 1985

The Major received hundreds of daffodils that were to be planted in all the public places. I asked if I should plant any in front of my place and the Major gives me two huge bundles. I look and see a rocky path and no soil at my place. I keep looking and see a mountain slope covered with grass that looks good. I decide to plant the daffodils in a mass so they will be really showy.

❖ ❖ ❖

It was below freezing the morning I boarded the Alaska Airlines flight from Anchorage to San Francisco. The date, February 1, 1985. It was five years since I'd begun volunteering on a regular basis with the Episcopal Church, and it was the day before my father's seventieth birthday. I was 40 years old and I wanted to make peace with this shame-based view of morality and sexuality that I was raised with.

I got my luggage and found the bus to the hotel. On the way out of the airport, I saw an enormous sculpture of Mary and Jesus. The child was standing barefoot in his mother's womb with his palms turned out in a classic gesture of peace. *Oh God, Jesus has two eyes painted above his eyes just like my dream image.* I caught my breath. My dream, just two weeks earlier, must have some special meaning for me now. At the time I recorded it, I knew the dream was important, and here it was in the daylight. The bus driver said the thirty-foot steel and granite mosaic sculpture of Jesus and Mary by Beniamino Bufano was titled "Peace."

Trembling, I closed my eyes and tried to center myself by counting my breaths—inhale, two, three, four, exhale, two, three, four—my God, what will I see next? Daffodils? No, it's February, I thought. I won't see daffodils, but with any luck I will find some peace.

I checked into the hotel and decided to take a walk to locate the Institute building so I'd know where to go the following day. I didn't want any more surprises. I had walked several blocks down Franklin Street when I became aware that someone was whistling a Broadway show tune. I stepped off the sidewalk and into the middle of the cross street at Austin and Franklin then stopped. A man with shoulder-length graying hair was riding a bicycle. He wore a red beanie cap with a propeller that twirled in the wind as he rode—a yellow daffodil was pinned to his sweatshirt. I froze, utterly transfixed, and watched as he rode by—only he didn't ride by, he turned down Austin and came straight for me. I hollered as the front wheel of his bicycle went between my legs and the basket hit my belly, knocking me flat. My head made a dull thud as it hit the pavement and I was momentarily stunned. When I caught my breath, I started patting my front and back searching for anything broken. The man leaped off his bicycle, pulled me to my feet, and hugged me to his chest, his hair nearly smothering me.

"Are you alright? I'm so sorry. Are you hurt? I'm really sorry. Is anything broken?" He kept apologizing over and over again.

"I'm absolutely fine. You don't need to worry. It was an accident," I insisted, still checking for injuries.

He seemed genuinely frightened that he had hurt me. He asked my name and said his was Craig. I again insisted that I was fine. Reluctantly he rode off. I walked to the sidewalk and saw a door and window labeled Done Rite Cleaners. I peered through the window and saw an old woman and an old man sitting on straight chairs watching television. The sign on the door said *Knock First,* so I knocked and the woman opened the door a crack. She hesitated. I wasn't one of her customers so she probably wondered what I wanted. I felt helpless and suddenly frightened and I burst into tears and said that I had just been knocked down by an old hippie on a bicycle. I cried and cried, all the while trying not to cry; gulping and fighting to hold back the tears and wiping my eyes and the snot off my nose with the edge of my wool shawl.

The old woman immediately opened the door wide and asked if she could get me some water. She had soft blue eyes and a fluff of gray hair. Several lower teeth were missing in front, which caused her to lisp. Her kindness renewed my crying and attempts not to cry, and I said, thank you and yes, and did she happen to have a tissue. She produced a box of Kleenex, led me to an old oak chair with arms, made comforting sounds, and then disappeared behind the clean clothes to fetch the water.

While she was gone, the old man took over my care and chastised the likes of all careless bicyclists and accused Craig of knocking me down on purpose and speeding away. At that point I had to come to Craig's defense. I assured the ruddy-faced gentleman that Craig had indeed stopped, helped me up, made sure I wasn't hurt and only left at my urging. Then I managed a half smile and said, "Perhaps I just needed a good cry anyway."

The old man looked confused by my words, but I drank my water, dabbed my eyes and said offhandedly, "I'm looking for 1523 Franklin Street, the location of the Institute for Advanced Study of Human Sexuality."

The old man's jaw dropped and he said, "Why, that's just across the street. We wondered what went on there—we see the most interesting people coming and going."

"Well, yes," I prevaricated. "I'm an educator and I've come to learn about human sexuality."

Reluctant to dodge the truth again or do any more explaining, I stood up, thanked them for their kindness and hospitality, and walked out the door. As I crossed the street, I realized that except for the tiny street numbers there was no sign, nothing, to distinguish the Institute building except its color. It was painted a flat black from sidewalk to skyline. Even the glass on the door and window were painted black. I gulped hard, looked back across the street and waved at the proprietors of Done Rite Cleaners, who were still watching me, and opened the door slowly, then stepped out of the bright sunlight into a dim hallway lined with bookshelves.

Boxes with books and papers spilling out onto the floor were stacked everywhere. The floors were uneven. Small, odd-shaped doorways led off the dingy reception area. A woman in black parachute pants was looking for someone. I asked for directions but she didn't know anything, either. She pointed to a room where a man and a woman seemed to be working and I cautiously looked in. I told the man who I was and he said, yes, he'd just typed the class list and my name was on it. He showed me the list and I strained to read who else was taking the workshop. I don't know who I expected to see—Dr. Jekyll and Mr. Hyde, or Dr. Watson, I presume.

I left the dark building and stepped back into the sunshine; the light was blinding. I shivered at the contrast and began walking back to the hotel. I couldn't shake the vulnerability I felt. I spotted a flower shop near the corner and ducked inside. The smell of summer foliage and grasses and flowers in February had an intoxicating effect. I hoped for daffodils, but found none. I gravitated to a large vase of yellow pom-pom chrysanthemums on a round table near the center of the small crowded space. I picked the largest mum from the vase and paid for it. The clerk wrapped it carefully with a sprig of fern in a tissue, to protect it from the wind, she said. Yes, I smiled—from the wind. I'd hardly noticed the wind.

I sheltered my mum under my shawl and continued to the hotel. Once inside my room, I filled a glass with water, seated my beautiful floral icon of peace on the desk, picked up the telephone and called my prayer partner, Ladoña Anderson, from St. Mary's in Anchorage. At the sound of her voice, I began to sob. I told her everything that had happened since I arrived in the city. Finally, when I stopped sputtering and said I wanted to come home she said, "Why did you go?"

"I wanted to know if I'm okay," I said.

"Have you found that out yet?"

"No."

"Are you sure you want to come home?"

"No."

I hung up the telephone and stretched out on the bed. My neck and back were beginning to seize up from being body-slammed on the pavement. I put my journal beside the bed so I would be ready to record any new dreams or insights. Carl Jung says there are no accidents, only synchronicity, a mysterious interrelatedness in events that, if paid attention to, reveal information about our place and purpose in the universe. The synchronicity of the two dreams and the two symbols repeated in San Francisco was important. It was as if coming to San Francisco was the way to peace. Well, Dr. Jung, I'm awake, I'm paying attention. I'm terrified, but I'm not running away.

I could hardly get out of bed the next morning. My neck and back were so stiff I could only look straight ahead. This was a sign, I thought: look straight ahead, stay the course. I remembered a dream and reached for my journal.

Dream Log
Feb. 2, 1985

I am looking for fabric in a tiny fabric store. A black mother and her daughter come in looking for fabric to make the daughter a new dress. They find what they want in a black fabric with pink rose buds on it. Then they want some pink fabric to coordinate with it. They search and search and make all kinds of noise. I ask to see what they are trying to match. They show me the rosebud that they've cut out of the fabric. I say it looks more salmon or orange colored to me instead of pink, so they go off in search of salmon colored fabric. I see a truck parked in the alley, lots of kids and fabric and I climb up into it and begin straightening up the fabric, still trying to find something for me. I look over and see the girl's car and smile. It is old and little, like a 1948 Plymouth, painted black with scallops of salmon-colored rosebuds on it. I realize she wants her new dress to match her car.

I knew from studying dreams the past several years that all the dream images represented different parts of me. It was as if the dream were showing me, I needed a new set of clothes, or a new way of being in the world. The mother and child could be disowned parts of me, or shadow parts of me. Somehow pink was too soft, too feminine. The disowned parts of me needed something stronger like salmon or orange. I smiled then. Orange is considered a power color, and is one of the healing colors. Orange is often associated with Christ. It's the color of creativity, courage, and commitment. As I thought about all this, I realized my yellow mum with its long stem looked ridiculous in the water glass, but somehow that long neck pleased me, reminded me of myself—I was sticking my neck out, too—so I gave her more water, dressed, and went out the door to find some breakfast.

Tables in the hotel restaurant were full, so I took an empty seat at the counter. A nice-looking older man next to me poured coffee from his carafe into my cup and we began to chat. He was in town on business. I said I was in town for a workshop. We both had the morning free—his first appointment wasn't until 1 o'clock and my workshop started at noon. He suggested we go Dutch in a cab to Ghirardelli Square and play tourist. He knew all the lore about the city and by mid-morning he had taken me to the Buena Vista, a pub overlooking San Francisco Bay that he said served the best Irish coffee in California. He took his without the whiskey, saying he didn't drink any more. My father loved his coffee laced with a shot of whiskey first thing in the morning; he would laugh and say, for *medicinal purposes.* "Sure, why not?" I said.

Sufficiently relaxed from the whiskey, I let slip that my workshop was at the Institute for Advanced Study of Human Sexuality. He blinked, but didn't comment. When we parted for our respective appointments, he said, "Pearl's has the best jazz in San Francisco. Why don't we meet back at the hotel for dinner and take a cab to Pearl's?"

"Great," I said, pleased that I had made a nice friend and had a plan for the evening. It didn't occur to me that my trusting naiveté could be a problem.

I walked up the street to the Institute, assured of my destination (the shot of Irish whiskey probably had something to do with my self-confidence). This time I knew to pause upon entering the dark hallway, and let my eyes adjust. The door at the end of the hall was open and people were going in. I followed. The room seemed even darker than the hallway. Pasha pillows were scattered around the floor and people were seated in groups of two and three. I suddenly felt cold and scared. I found a pillow on the edge of the gathering and set about making a nest for myself. I had my book bag. I took out my journal and pen and sat down cross-legged with my shawl wrapped snugly around me, opened the journal and occupied myself with reading the dream I'd written down that morning.

A man and woman stood up and introduced themselves as our leaders. They would not ask us to introduce ourselves, they said, out of respect for our anonymity. They gave an overview of the course and then launched into the first topic: masturbation and fantasy. Nervous titters came from several people in the group closest to me. I wanted to melt into my pillow. I'm sure my face turned red; it certainly was burning. After the lecture, we were shown a film with the most ordinary-looking naked people touching themselves and talking about their fantasies at the same time. Now the darkness seemed a relief; the anonymity, a godsend. There wasn't a sound in the room as a white-haired granny awash in wrinkles talked about the importance of pleasuring your partner and yourself as you grow old. When the film ended, we were asked to share with those sitting closest to us our experiences with masturbation and fantasy. I tried to listen politely to the people near me, but didn't hear a word they said.

The awkward silence took me back to another place and time when I felt equally stunned. I was sixteen years old and working as a waitress on the graveyard shift in a restaurant-casino in Winnemucca. I was naïve and conflicted. Part of me wanted to be a nightclub singer, and part of me wanted to be a school teacher like my mother. At the end of my shift, I would often flirt with the bartender to get a free perfect triple martini, or with Bobby Gibson, a traveling musician, who would let me sing with his band when I didn't have any customers. I thought I knew what I was doing, after all, I felt very grown up—old, almost.

One Sunday morning, after finishing my shift and my triple martini, I accepted an invitation to go for a ride with Bobby to watch the sunrise over Battle Mountain. He pulled off the road. I thought he was going to turn around but he stopped the car, turned off the engine, began fiddling with his belt, then opened his pants. I started talking fast.

"I have to get home in time to get ready for church," I said. "I'm the Sunday school teacher for the kindergarteners."

His anger exploded. "You come on like the other girls who hang around the band, and now you're spouting some shit about Sunday school."

"I teach five-year-olds," I pleaded.

He took my hand and forced my fingers around his penis. Then he began pumping in and out, in and out. I stopped breathing. I wanted to throw up. My stomach jammed with all the words I didn't say, couldn't say. Light began to flood the car; I turned my face to the light and saw the sun just beginning to peak Battle Mountain. I did the only thing I could do at that moment, I escaped into the sunrise where there was only beauty and light. The ugliness inside the car disappeared. I stayed there until I heard the engine roar back to life.

❖ ❖ ❖

The rest of the afternoon was rapid-fire: Alfred Kinsey's research, Masters and Johnson's therapeutic approach, female and male anatomy. Images were explicit. Information was given in a straightforward manner, no giggling from the presenters, no made-up words. A penis was a penis, not a ding-dong or a thunder club or a salami. Breasts were breasts, not boobs or num-nums or knockers. The process was referred to as a sexual attitude reassessment or restructuring. Students were invited to be honest about their experiences and beliefs. The leaders covered the history of sexual understanding in our culture, and where the values and attitudes and biases came from that sparked both sexual repression and the sexual revolution.

The facilitator of our small group was a United Methodist pastor, and he talked about the culpability of the churches in perpetuating sexual repression and shame. He seemed at ease with every topic, and, more especially, with the experiences of each person in the group. I was completely outside my comfort zone. My heart was pounding, but I knew I was safe.

As the day progressed, I learned that healthy sex is natural and necessary to good mental health. But sex is also complicated, and being able to move from sexual repression to sexual freedom requires, as my counselor friend from the university had said, taking the proverbial trip home and gaining some understanding of the values you were raised with. I decided to start with my mother. My mother had been raised in a socially conservative home; if any cowboy so much as cussed or made risqué remarks in front of Grandma Pence or my mother and her sister, Grandpa Pence sent them packing. Mother attended St. Teresa's Academy, a Catholic boarding high school in Boise run by the Sisters of the Holy Cross, and I'm sure those same strict values were reinforced there.

By the age of twenty, my mother had eloped with a young rancher, John Slack. They had two daughters together, Patricia and Beverly. Six years later John died in Mother's arms from a painful kidney disease, and within six months of that John's father and grandfather were also dead. My mother had not only her two young daughters to financially support, but Grandma Slack and Grandma Crocheron, as well as the T Ranch to manage. That must have been terrifying enough to a twenty-six-year-old widow, but a few months later Mother's first cousin and best friend, Alta, died in a house fire on their ranch. That was more than she could bear. She let the ranch go and used John's life insurance money to buy a movie circuit, a car, and build two houses next door to each other in Bruneau—one for her and the girls, and one for the two grandmothers. She basically ran away from home.

By the time my mother married my father and had three more children, the National Legion of Decency and sex and marriage manuals were giving dire warnings about female sexuality and promiscuity outside of marriage. Even inside of marriage, sex was primarily for the procreation of children. At the same time, the movies and popular literature were pushing the boundaries declaring that feminine sexuality and pleasure were not only desirable for their own sake, but were also acceptable outside of marriage. By this time my father had built the Rosalind Theater in Homedale, and my mother was showing movies starring Marilyn Monroe flirting, sassy, and wearing skimpy clothes. My mother must have been very conflicted, and here I was years later, equally so.

Finally, we were introduced to the Sexual Bill of Rights, which included the freedom of any sexual thought, fantasy, and desire; the right to sexual entertainment, freely available in the marketplace, including sexually explicit materials dealing with the full range of sexual behavior; and the right *not* to be exposed to sexual material or behavior. We were reminded that sexual rights are human rights, and that all persons should have the right to sexual self-determination, the right to seek out and engage in consensual sexual activity.

Okay, I thought, *there are a lot of ideas beyond my imagination here, but I need to be open, and I need to be honest if I hope to heal myself or be helpful when I go home and not remain part of the shaming culture.*

"What about children," I blurted out.

"Say more," the pastor encouraged.

I shared my concerns about incest and rape against women and children in Alaska, and the devastation that it has caused in whole villages. The pastor assured me non-consensual acts—violence, constraint, coercion, fraud—were not sanctioned by the Sexual Bill of Rights.

I finally took a deep breath—the first really full breath since I'd arrived.

After the workshop, I walked back to the hotel where my new friend was already in the dining room waiting for me. He waved. I sat down and then noticed a double martini in front of him. I ordered a single and he ordered another double. My antennae went up. That morning at the most famous Irish pub in California he *wasn't drinking anymore.* I ate my olive but didn't touch my drink. After dinner he insisted on paying the check. My antennae began to beep.

All morning we'd gone Dutch-treat. He insisted on paying for the cab to Pearl's and ordered another double martini when we were seated. I began to squirm in my chair. What should I do? I didn't want to be rude or seem ungrateful. Then I heard the words of my priest, Chuck Eddy, running through my head like a ticker-tape, *Judith, you can set limits to protect yourself.*

I stood up, pushed my chair back, smiled, and said, "Thanks for a great dinner." Then I turned and walked out of the best jazz club in San Francisco and hailed the taxi that was waiting at the curb. I jumped in, gave the address of the hotel and said, "Hurry, please." Back in my room I double-locked the door and fell onto the bed, took a deep breath, and then noticed the yellow chrysanthemum with its neck sticking out of the water. "Well, Dr. Jung," I said aloud. "I'm still awake, still paying attention, and still alive."

The next morning, I packed my suitcase and tucked the stem of the yellow Chrysanthemum into my book bag, leaving her yellow head poking out. As the door to the room swung shut, I noticed several yellow petals on the desk where she had kept watch. I smiled. After paying my bill, I noticed a few petals on the floor where my book bag had rested. I smiled again. I had just enough time for breakfast at a little restaurant near the workshop, so I tugged my rolling bag behind me down the street. As I turned the corner, I glanced back up the sidewalk. There, like crumbs from Hansel and Gretel, I saw a scattering of yellow petals marking my trail. This time I laughed out loud and remembered a story about Native American trackers who can follow a trail left by someone's spirit, even if all footprints or other physical evidence had vanished. I realized that, like the yellow chrysanthemum petals, I'm leaving a part of my spirit everywhere I go, a revelation that showed me I have a choice whether to leave a trail of light and beauty or darkness and shame.

This time, even accompanied by my suitcase, I was slightly more comfortable entering the darkened room. People seemed to be sitting in the same groups so I pushed my pasha pillow into the circle with those closest to me the day before. The same format defined the day: information, erotic films, small group sharing. The presenter began to speak about the sexual needs of paraplegics and quadriplegics and others with physical disabilities and special needs. He talked about the medical aspects of sexuality, such as the effects on sexual functioning of drugs and hypertension, psychiatric disorders, spinal cord injuries and endocrine disorders. He covered the impact of chronic illness, visual impairment, and mental retardation on sexual experience. My thoughts were again running wild. How did this affect my friend's child who was born with mild retardation? What about my brother who fell out of a pickup truck when he was a child and sustained a head injury?

Finally, the presenters examined what they called the *underbelly of the dragon*: violence, abuse, betrayal, grief, and loss. Almost immediately I was awash in sadness. During our lunch break I slipped out and began to walk around the block so I could think in private. On the back side of the block, I saw an Episcopal church with the front door standing open. I mounted the steps; no one was in the sanctuary, but I heard murmuring voices and laughter coming from a distant room, so I went in and sat in the choir pew near the altar. I opened a hymnal to one of my favorite hymns and began to sing quietly.

> *Fairest Lord Jesus, ruler of all nature,*
> *O thou of God and Man, the Son.*
>
> *Thee will I cherish, thee will I honor,*
> *Thou, my soul's glory, joy and crown.*

The underbelly of the dragon, I thought. No wonder all this grief and loss is so hard on me, I've always been *yellow*, meaning: happy, playful, an extrovert, interested in everything that's going on around me, a story-teller, a singer, an actor, a person who loves to host a party, is generous, and funny. Maybe all this *yellow* is just a cover-up for shame. I'd come to San Francisco to find out if I was okay—not if the people I'm serving are okay—but how do you separate what has happened to you from what is happening to those around you. Am I part of the problem?

I remembered a little girl in one of the villages on the Yukon Flats I had visited after Thanksgiving confiding, "Uncle said I'm bad. He said the devil lives inside of me." This child seemed so innocent, dreamy really. She kept throwing her baby doll almost to the ceiling, punctuating every word, catching the doll by the leg or arm or neck. I wondered now if he was abusing her and blaming her for his behavior. Children are powerless over their parents and the other adults in their lives. They often learn to adapt to survive, using sugar or alcohol or sex or make believe or dancing or singing or performing in some way for the love and support they need to thrive. Oh why didn't I ask to speak to her mother or her grandmother?

> *Fair are the meadows, fairer still the woodlands,*
>   *robed in the blooming garb of spring.*
>
> *Jesus is fairer, Jesus is purer,*
>   *who makes the woeful heart to sing.*

Children are innocent. Children deserve to be protected and cherished. Even teenagers need protection—especially from themselves when they exhibit high-risk behavior. By the time I was 16, running away had become reflexive: boom, conflict with my mother, jump in the car, run. One particular night, the argument started after dark. She said no about something and I cussed, ran out the door, and was in the '57 Chevy headed for highway 95 before she could stop me. This time I made up my mind I would go to Bruneau and find the cemetery where my Grandpa and Grandma Pence were buried. The car topped out at 110 miles an hour so I blew through McDermott in less than 40 minutes.

It was midnight by the time I hit the Jordan Valley grade into the Boise Valley. A diesel truck in front of me had every light blazing. I followed the trucker all the way to the bottom of the grade. I pulled into Marsing after 1:00 a.m. bleary eyed, so I decided to pull off the road and sleep until dawn. Sometime after 2:00 a.m. I heard a tap on the window and a light scanned the inside of the car. The Sheriff for Owyhee County and Marsing had stopped to investigate and suspected I was a runaway.

I'm not sure why, but he didn't take me to jail; he took me home, and his wife, in her housecoat, met us at the front door. She led me into the kitchen and pulled out a chair.

"I'm going to call the District Attorney in Caldwell," said the Sheriff.

"I'll make us some cocoa," she said, managing a smile.

"I've got Judy Wegman here. I think she's a runaway. She says she's sixteen. Should I bring her into the Caldwell jail?" he asked.

The D.A. yelled loud enough for the Sheriff's wife and me to hear from the kitchen. "Hell no, I know her dad. I'll call him in Winnemucca; he'll come and get her. Can she stay with you until morning?"

"My wife is up. We'll keep her here until her dad comes," the Sheriff said.

"Honey, have you ever thought of going to Sunday School?" said the wife leaning towards me.

"Listen lady, I *teach* Sunday School," I growled.

She looked away and gasped. All the rage I felt towards my mother flooded the space between this sweet old woman who was trying to be kind, and myself. We sat in that little yellow kitchen with the white eyelet curtains framing the window for the next three hours in silence.

My father cried when he saw me. He loaded the car on the back of the diesel truck and we rode back to Winnemucca without speaking a word. How could I tell him all I ever wanted was to feel loved and to hear him say he was proud of me?

Fair is the sunshine, fairer still the moonlight,
*   and all the twinkling, starry host;*

Jesus shines brighter, Jesus shines purer, than
*   all the angels heaven can boast.*

✦ ✦ ✦

I'd come to San Francisco to understand and make peace with the shame-based moral issues from my own life, but what really motivated me? I knew the suffering of others kept me awake at night as I recalled their stories over and over again, but what was it I was working so hard to repress in myself? I didn't fully understand the disease of alcoholism, or the intergenerational aspects of abuse, but I was beginning to see that my own volatile temper and larger-than-life-personality grew to fill the hole formed by shame, and the fear of abandonment that I had experienced as a child. This fear of abandonment clearly prevented me from abandoning others once they shared their stories with me and asked for prayer.

The choir director came in and began to straighten the sheets of music on the organ. I swallowed hard, trying to choke back my tears. He glanced at me from time to time, frowned, and finally said, "You can't stay there. I have to lock the church, and you must go."

What the hell! I felt betrayed—I needed prayer and this churchman didn't offer a word of comfort, or show the least bit of kindness or concern. I could feel my temper rising. The Methodist pastor was right, *the church is part of the problem*. I stood up, glowered at him, and marched out.

Walking back to the workshop I remembered the Rev. Bob Nelson, my confessor, saying, "Judith, you wait too long to ask for help. By the time you finally ask for help, you are at the end of your rope and the other person doesn't have the freedom to say no. You need to ask for help sooner, so if the first person says no you can ask someone else."

I walked into the workshop and announced, "I need a ride to the airport at 7 p.m." A little man wearing a Zorba the Greek hat and jeans, too tight and too short, said he was driving past the airport on his way home and would be happy to drop me off. He didn't look like an ax murderer or a rapist, so I accepted, then spent the next six hours wondering if I would be fish bait at the bottom of San Francisco Bay or make it safely onto my plane for the return to Alaska.

My nervous fantasy was cut short by the final desensitization exercise, which the presenters called the *fuck-o-rama*. It was immediately apparent why: multiple TV screens mounted on the walls were playing graphic videos of yes, you guessed it, fucking—men and women, men and men, women and women, blacks, whites, blacks and whites, groups, old people, horses, dogs, elephants. So much was happening in that pitch-black, completely silent room I didn't know what to attend to first. My eyes darted from one scene to the next and back again, until I slipped into a warm haze of acceptance. All this was natural, credible and normal; there was no alcohol, no coercion, no violence, and no children.

When the workshop ended, I gathered up my book bag and suitcase. There on the floor where I'd been camped for two days having my sensibilities shifted were yellow chrysanthemum petals. Yes, I was leaving a part of myself here. I followed the man out to his car. Good grief, he was driving a forest green MG. I looked at him with new interest; he now seemed shy and even smaller than before. He wedged my suitcase in somehow and I put my book bag at my feet. As we drove away, I glanced back. The sidewalk was dotted with yellow petals.

"How will you be different when you go home?" I asked, filling the awkward space between us.

"I don't know," he said. "I'm nervous. I live in an apartment complex with an outdoor Jacuzzi. Every night beautiful people gather there, laughing and talking. I watch from my window, too scared to go out."

"What's the worst thing that can happen?"

"I guess they'll laugh at me."

"Just be kind. Even beautiful women love kind men."

Something soft fluttered past my ankle.

We rode in silence the rest of the way to the airport. Near the entrance I strained to see if the Peace sculpture was visible, but I couldn't see it in the maze of ramps and buildings. Well, I thought, I know she's there somewhere, with the barefoot Christ child standing upright in her womb, eyes looking both out at the world and into the secret places of the heart, with hands turned, palms out, in a simple gesture of peace. I got out of the car and thanked my classmate, then said, "I'm going to picture you sitting in the Jacuzzi, laughing and talking, one of the beautiful people."

The flight to Anchorage was bumpy. A winter storm was brewing in the Gulf of Alaska and the turbulence and rattling of the aircraft kept me awake and thinking about what I'd learned and how I would be different going forward. Kris and I had such different ideas of what was desirable or even normal when it came to sex. The most important thing I learned was that healthy sex is mutual, and natural, and even playful. Everyone is different. One partner might like whipped cream, the other cheese and crackers (metaphorically speaking, of course). The important thing is to respect your own sexual needs and the needs of your partner while you work out your differences. I knew it would require total honesty and kindness. I could do kindness. I'd learned from the best: my grandparents and great aunts and uncles; my priests, Chuck Eddy, and Bob Nelson; my mentors, Scott Fisher, and David Salmon. What I wasn't good at was honesty.

When I began this journey, I really wanted other people to change: my parents, my husband, the villagers, the church. I had no idea it was me who had to change. I needed to learn to express my needs, and set limits to protect myself. My fear of rejection kept me silent many times when I should have spoken out. Kris was kind, but he was also honest and a man of action. He had come home when I called him, held me, prayed for me, took me for a walk, wanted to protect me… *you have to stop going. No… I will figure this out…* Then he let me go. True healing and integration required action. I was ready.

I took a taxi home, and as I fumbled for my keys the front door opened. Kris was standing there in his underwear looking bewildered. "I was afraid you wouldn't come home," he blurted.

I smiled mischievously and threw my arms around his neck. "Not a chance," I said. We held each other for a long time.

Finally, he took my suitcase and book bag and asked quietly, "How are you?" Then before I could answer he motioned to the naked stem sticking out of my bag. "What's this?"

I shook my head, "How am I? I'm okay, and you're okay!" Then I stepped over the last remaining yellow petals that lay scattered across the threshold and followed him inside.

Rosalind Pence Slack, widowed, with her first two daughters, Patricia and Beverly in front of the home she had built after her husband, John Slack, died. Bruneau, Idaho, 1934.

WHEN EACH OF US BOYS LEFT HOME, OUR MOM TELL US 'DON'T SMOKE, DON'T DRINK, GO TO CHURCH.'

—Clinton Chase, Anvik

9.

SHATTERED DREAMS

By the following spring, the Anchorage business community was beginning to get nervous. The Alaska economy ran on oil, and crude oil prices from the North Slope oil producers were dropping fast. Kris said we were sure to have a recession. Our company, Fraley Equipment, had millions of dollars in Grove Cranes leased to the oil companies. Before we could make a plan, the leases were canceled and we were left with machines we couldn't pay for. We went into survival mode.

Kris did everything he could to soften the blow and make good on our debts. We'd spent twenty-three years building a dream life for our family. Now we were dismantling it piece by piece. He returned as much iron as possible to the manufacturers. My Mercedes Benz would go back to the dealer. I bought a huge bouquet of flowers for the cleaning lady, and told her I could no longer pay her to clean for me. The Cessna Skymaster 337 airplane, Tucker Sno-Cat, two snowmachines, and two four-wheelers would need to be sold. Our home on McCollie Avenue went on the market at a $300,000 loss.

Well-meaning friends told us we were young; we could rebuild our fortune, but we knew we weren't prepared to sacrifice what it took to do it over again, ever again—Kris working long hours, worrying about meeting the payroll for so many employees, always negotiating for a larger and larger line of credit to meet the needs of our customers, coming home late at night after the kids were in bed too tired to laugh or play. We knew the recession was beyond our control, but the shame of our financial loss was isolating. We needed a safe place to vent our feelings, but all our business and banking friends were in the same boat. We couldn't even talk to each other about it; after all, we didn't just lose our material goods, we lost many of our dreams for the future. As we moved forward, we both agreed the two most important things were to pay as many of our debts as possible, and to protect the children from the harsh reality of bankruptcy.

Our oldest son, Bill, was in the Marine Corps, and financially independent from us. Our second son, Dan, was at the University of Washington on a rowing scholarship. They could be protected a little longer from our new reality, but our youngest sons, young Kris and Tim, were thirteen and eleven and needed to know what was happening. Driving down Northern Lights Boulevard with the boys in late April I decided the time was right to offer a little context.

"When Bill and Dan were little, we were very poor," I began. "We bought them used bicycles and ice skates at the Salvation Army, and skis at the Arctic Valley Ski Club swap meet. When you two were little, we had lots of money. We bought you brand-new bicycles at the Bicycle Shop, and new ice skates and skis from REI. Now, we are going to be very poor again."

"If I had my way," said young Kris, "I'd rather be poor when I was little."

No kidding, I thought.

A week later Kris took my beautiful chocolate brown Mercedes back to the dealer and brought a twenty-five-year-old Ford station wagon home for me to drive. When I drove to school to pick up the boys, I felt like I was in stealth mode. The usual appreciative glances from other drivers, especially men, when I pulled up beside them at the stop light didn't happen. Nobody looks at you when you're driving an old beat-up beige station wagon. Nobody. I had become invisible. I didn't know whether to cuss or cry.

In mid-May Kris brought home two old flat-bed trucks, and I began packing boxes. We would move the children to our summer home in Seldovia so they wouldn't have to watch our world collapse. Seldovia is a fishing village on the end of the Kenai Peninsula that is only accessible from Homer by boat or small airplane. Mountains and spruce forests rise effortlessly out of Seldovia Bay and Kachemak Bay and are home to black bear, coyote, mink, eagle, raven, great blue heron, and a host of migratory birds. King, Sockeye, Pink, and Dog salmon flood the bays in spring and summer, providing sustenance for sea otters, river otters, seals, and local residents. It was a perfect place to raise the children.

The plan was to put the kids in Susan B. English School at the end of August. Kris would stay in the city in an old rental house we still owned on the Fraley property, continue to dispose of our assets and pay off debts, then fly down on weekends. The flying weather was lousy most of the time, so weeks went by without seeing him.

For the first time in our marriage, I needed to get a job. Bishop Harris brought Richard Bolles to Meier Lake Conference Center to do a workshop on his well-known book, *What Color Is Your Parachute*, and Kris and I both attended. I signed up for Richard's two-week Life Work Planning seminar in Bend, Oregon. When I returned to Seldovia, I tried to implement everything I'd learned in Bend. I talked to Carol Swartz at the Kenai Peninsula Community Collage about teaching Life-Work Planning through the college. I also talked to the principal at Susan B. English school about substitute teaching and teaching a career workshop for the juniors. I was still writing my letter to the bishop about becoming a postulant for Holy Orders. Then Mildred Boesser called and asked me to be the music director for an upcoming Cursillo at Meier Lake. I loved this three-day retreat developed by the Roman Catholic Church that focused on prayer, daily holy communion, and the rite of reconciliation: all elements to help us become more effective leaders in the church. I was trying to be responsible and get a job, but I couldn't resist running off for a weekend to play my guitar and sing.

As the business of summer ended, a quietness settled over Seldovia Bay, and so did an unbearable sense of loneliness. No one told me life in a remote Alaskan village could be so isolating. There were various social circles in the community: the bar crowd, the Bible Chapel members, the fishermen, the school teachers, the Natives, older people who had retired and just wanted peace and quiet, and young people living in dry cabins with no running water or electricity. Some people managed to have a foot in two or three circles, but I didn't fit comfortably into any of them.

In the evenings I would read *Treasure Island* or *Robinson Crusoe* or *The Chronicles of Narnia* to the children for hours, or we would watch *Harry and the Hendersons* or *Ferris Bueller's Day Off* until bedtime. After the kids were in bed, I'd sneak a shot of whiskey alone in my unheated bedroom, ostensibly so I could sleep. One shot soon became two, and two shots always lead to compulsive overeating, with my sugar drug of choice being an old-timey coffee mug filled with chocolate chips, raisins, and almonds. I'd wake up with a sugar hangover and swear off my compulsive behavior until the next time, which might be weeks or months later.

In late fall Scott called from Fairbanks and said a professed English solitary under vows to the Archbishop of Canterbury, Maggie Ross, was traveling around Alaska and was looking for a quiet place to pray for a week. Would I be able to put her up in Seldovia? Sure. I had just the place upstairs in the old house the children and I lived in. It was my private studio, with a desk, chair, and a bed, that overlooked Seldovia Slough. I didn't mind sharing it, in fact, I was intrigued with the idea of a professed solitary who prayed all the time.

Maggie flew into Seldovia on the local bush plane, and moved into her temporary quarters with no fanfare. She slipped in and out of her room without a sound. I'm not sure she ate or drank much. Towards the end of her visit, she invited me into her room and presented me with an Anglican rosary that she had knotted from a single piece of cording. She inquired about my experience with the church, and did I think I had a vocation. I explained that I had spoken to Bishop Harris about postulancy for holy orders, and he said there was still a lot of resistance from the church for women in the priesthood and that we should move slowly. When I blurted this out, I became aware of my intense anger at the institutional church. My anger confused me, but I didn't have time to sort it out. I needed a job. I was wrestling with our bankruptcy. I was still trying to keep my ministry on track. After Maggie left, my anger boiled to the surface and I penned this letter to Bishop Cox, whom I'd met at the Diocesan convention three years earlier.

> October 22, 1986
>
> Dear Bishop Cox,
>
> It's been three years since the Diocesan Convention at Meier Lake Conference Center when you were the guest speaker. You may not remember me; however, I have never forgotten you or Mrs. Cox. You made a very powerful impression on me with your talks, which were on submission. I think I've been wrestling with God my whole life, however, the past ten years have been an open battle.
>
> Twenty-two years ago, when Bishop William Gordon laid his hands on me at Confirmation I had a premonition of ordination, but because my husband Kris was kneeling beside me (and women were not being ordained then) I immediately projected the premonition onto him. I told no one, but was so tickled! Yipee! My husband was going to be a priest. Of course, he hardly ever went to church, so I, who went every Sunday without fail, would come home and quote the lessons and sermon word-for-word to him—after all, if he was going to be a priest there were things he needed to know!!
>
> When the General Convention voted to ordain women in 1976, I was dumbfounded and angry. *Well, one more area where men weren't pulling their load—now women had to be priests too* was my attitude. On the day Jean Dementi, the first woman ordained in Alaska, was to be ordained, I decided not to go. I really did not agree with women's ordination and saw no point in attending something I didn't agree with. Suddenly I was lifted out of my chair. I walked out the door, got into my car and drove straight down town. I pulled into

the parking lot of the Methodist Church where Jean's ordination was being held, and walked in just as the singing started. I was immediately zapped... goose bumps all over... Every question, every response, every hymn, I was filled with a new shot of electricity, fire, the Holy Spirit, I don't know what you call it, but it was as though my spirit said over and over, "Yes, yes, yes." My mind was stunned.

That day marked the beginning of my open, conscious fight with God. Shortly after that I had a dream: *I was skipping down a tree lined boulevard on my way to the cathedral. I passed three Roman Catholic nuns and I laughed and said, "Look, I'm married to Christ, too." And I held out my hand to show them my gold ring.*

Over the past twelve years I have wept and bargained and run away from God—all to no avail. Finally last Good Friday I wrote to Bishop George Harris and asked if I could enter the postulancy process. I wept and wept that morning. I sealed the letter in an envelope and went downtown to All Saints to their ecumenical Good Friday service. When the Orthodox priest got up to speak about Theotokos, Mary, the Mother of God, I began to weep again. The pain she experienced at witnessing the crucifixion of her son! How can women be in a public ministry—we experience pain so deeply! And then there's me. I'm not only sensitive, I'm outspoken. Do you recall at the convention I spoke out passionately against one resolution and promptly punished myself with a migraine headache (which was healed instantly when you prayed for me at the healing service at St. Mary's. Praise God!)

I did mail the letter to Bishop Harris and I immediately experienced a sense of peace, which has lasted until now. The Ministry Committee at St. Mary's has recently given me permission to begin a public pre-postulancy period of prayer, listening, questioning, and discernment. I do want to do God's will and not my own. Why am I writing to you, you may be wondering. I want your blessing and wisdom.

Why ordination? That may sound naughty and irreverent but let me tell you why I need an answer to that question. I stood on the shore of the Pacific Ocean when the surf was high two years ago at sunset, and as the wind howled and the waves crashed, I shouted, "Do I have to be ordained to pronounce the absolution?" And then I remembered time after time hearing confessions and being asked to pray for forgiveness for folks. It certainly felt like absolution! Then I shouted, "Do I have to be ordained to call down the Blessing?" And then I remembered visiting a Pentecostal church and at the close of the service the preacher said, "Sister, would you ask God's blessing on us." And it certainly felt like a blessing. Then I shouted, "Do I have to be ordained to read the Gospel?" And then I remembered being at the children's service at the National Cathedral in Washington, D.C. the Sunday after Easter in 1984 and having the priest come up to our children after a few warm-up choruses and asking, "If your mother can sing that good, do you suppose she can read good, too?"

"Oh yes, yes, yes," they said. "She reads really good."

He handed me a mimeographed page and when I looked down, I saw the Gospel of John 20:19–31 (the story known as doubting Thomas). My legs got weak and I felt like I was going to faint. When it came time for the Gospel, I stood up and was filled with power. It certainly felt like the Gospel had been proclaimed.

I got in my car and drove back to my friend's home. As I drove, and thought, and remembered I finally said, "No, I don't have to be ordained to do these things, God has already given me permission." Just then the church bells began to ring. Coincidence? Affirmation? Delusion? Synchronicity?

I could go on and on with stories and dreams and prophecies. What do they all mean? Why me? Why isn't a focused ministry enough? What does ordination really mean anyway? Is ordination for the priest, the church, or non-believers? In my case, was it just a case of my will fighting with God's will? Now that I have submitted and said yes to whatever God would have me do, how do I determine if, in fact, that really is the priesthood? Maybe I've had all these spiritual experiences because I'm just naturally a spiritually sensitive person.

I do know God's love does not rest on my being ordained or not being ordained. I know without a doubt that I am unconditionally loved by Almighty God, but there must be a reason why I have been struggling for twelve years over this issue.

✦ ✦ ✦

I never mailed this letter, but writing it helped clarify some of the fight that was going on inside of me. I was certainly being called into ministry but the route was circuitous and serendipitous. The hierarchy of the church wasn't necessarily welcoming my call to ordination, either, but the people were.

Fraley Equipment, with the author's chocolate brown Mercedes Benz in the foreground. Anchorage, 1986.

THE LONGEST JOURNEY IN THE WORLD
IS FROM THE HEAD TO THE HEART.

—Ernie Turner, Shageluk and Anchorage

10.
NO TIME TO GRIEVE

My father had suffered from a nervous stomach most of his life, and the doctors had found cancer. My step-mother, Sofia, called from Mountain Home, Idaho with the news. I made arrangements to fly into Boise. Sofia picked me up and as we drove to Mountain Home, she said, "You're the only one who can help him now. He won't talk to us. Find out if he wants to take a little trip, or see any place again before he goes."

I felt smug. "I'm sure I can get him to talk," I said.

Several days later Dad and I were walking through the neighborhood. "Dad, is there anything you'd like to do while you can still get out and about?"

"Look at those dahlias. Aren't they beautiful?"

I persisted, "Dad, if you are dying, is there any place you'd like to go before you go?"

"Have you ever seen such bright yellow chrysanthemums?"

"Yes," I said, remembering my trip to San Francisco. He wouldn't go any further; he was ready for a rest, he said. Reluctantly, I followed him home. I had failed Sofia. I had failed my father.

When we got home, Dad took a nap and I cornered Sofia in the kitchen. "I am not his doctor. I am not his counselor. I am not his priest. I am his daughter, and that's all I can be."

I got out the large Dutch-oven and put two cups of cannellini beans to quick soak, then I gathered the rests of the ingredients for minestrone soup: olive oil, mild chorizo sausages, onion, carrot, celery, garlic, thyme, bay leaf, diced tomatoes, spinach, salt, pepper, and parmesan cheese for garnish. I was humming and singing quietly as I sautéed and stirred the soup and drank coffee. Sofia's daughter Joanne came in. Sofia asked, "Who does she remind you of?"

"Her dad."

I felt myself stiffen. How could this singing, soup-making, happy person be like her dad? Yes, he was the storyteller, the soup maker, the one who loved to laugh when he read the jokes out of the *Reader's Digest*, but he was also the one who criticized me for singing too loudly. *Who do you think you are? What will the neighbors think?* He would say. He could never tell me he was proud of me. He was never home when I needed him. He was like a little boy who never grew up. He led a provisional life—believing everything was going to be alright tomorrow, or someday. The singer-soup-maker was the part of me I liked the best. How could I be like him? I took my journal and went for a walk in the large open field behind the house. The late afternoon sun was searing, the sagebrush releasing her acrid perfume even as I tried to release a lifetime of hurt and anger.

Several days later Dad confided, "Well, Sister, all my life I've worked hard, and I've played hard. Now, it looks like I'm going to die hard." He never spoke of his suffering again. I returned to Seldovia without having resolved this schism between the fantasy dad who looked like Clark Gable in *Gone with the Wind*—tall, handsome, and romantic—and the dad who was tender-hearted and became moody and depressed when criticized, the dad who ran away instead of staying and fighting for the happiness he deserved with my own mother.

After I returned to Seldovia, I got a call from Andy Fairfield at the Diocesan office in Fairbanks. "Judith, how are you?"

"I'm great. How wonderful to hear from you," I said cheerily, hoping he had called to invite me to another church training in the interior.

"No," he said. "I know your father is dying, and I want to know how you are."

His words were a gut punch. I collapsed on a chair and began to cry. After I hung up the phone, I called Sofia and asked how Dad was doing. She apologized for not being able to keep him at home any longer. She had moved him to the Mountain Home hospital. Weak and still smoking in his chair, she was afraid he would burn himself up.

"Tell me what he's doing," I asked.

"Your dad can't seem to get comfortable," she said. "He sits on his bed for three or four minutes, then wants to sit in the chair. We get him into the chair, and he's only comfortable for a few minutes, then he wants to walk down the hall. Three or four minutes of walking and he wants to be back in his bed."

In my mind's eye I saw a raggedy old lion slowly pacing in a circus cage—back and forth, one side, then the other, never at rest, always pacing, trapped, an animal longing to be free. I thanked her and hung up the phone. I sat quietly for a while, and then began to pray, "Dad, it's time to go. Your spirit is restless. It's okay to go. I'll be okay. We will all be okay."

Several minutes later Sofia called back. "Your dad is gone. He died peacefully in his bed."

"Yes," I said. "Thank you for taking such good care of him."

I got on the plane Thanksgiving Day to help bury my dad. Sofia asked if I would sing and tell stories at the funeral. She rarely asked me to do anything, so I felt I had to do this much. When we went to see the pastor, he said, "Oh, we never let the family speak at the service. Why, they could cry or run out of the room."

"Well, I'll tell you this," I said leaning forward. "I may cry, because I don't believe in stoicism, but I will not run out of the room."

The following day, when it was time for me to speak, I stood up, and looked around the sanctuary. Four hundred people had gathered to say goodbye to my dad. My siblings and half-sisters had driven over from Nevada, and Sofia's three daughters were there as well. I marveled at how many children my dad had helped raise, and how many relatives and friends had come to say good-bye. Just then the scene from *On Golden Pond*, when Katherine Hepburn said to Jane Fonda, "You've had a chip on your shoulder about your dad your whole life," popped into my head. I knew it was true. On the walk from the pew to the lectern I could feel that chip begin to loosen and slip away.

William Wegman, Sr. in 1940 when he married Rosalind Pence Slack.

A WOMAN CAN GO ANYWHERE
IN A BEAUTIFUL COAT.

—Rosalind Pence Wegman, Bruneau, Idaho
and Winnemucca, Nevada

11.

SAM HOUSTON

The second winter in Seldovia I was offered a job as the Director of South Kachemak, Inc. Alcohol Program, known as SKIAP. Darlene Crawford was on the Board of SKIAP and was working for the Seldovia Native Association. She had taken one of my values clarification classes and thought I could run the program. SKIAP was a village-based treatment program with funding from both the Indian Health Service (IHS) and the State of Alaska that allowed it to serve both the Alutiiq Native people and white people living in Seldovia, Nanwalek, and Port Graham.

The State and IHS oversight staff were alarmed that the Board had hired someone with no alcohol treatment experience, so they flew into town to interview me. After following me around for several days and watching me interact with the community, they decided I could learn what was needed to do the job. They approved my hire with the caveat that I attend every training event that came along. Of course, they didn't know that I loved whiskey, so I tried very hard not to drink. I had no idea that sobriety means much more than simply not drinking.

The first week on the job my IHS contract advisor, Roseanne Turner, called to say our grant proposal was due in five days. I had no idea how to write a grant. I read the RFP over and over and then realized I needed to interview the elders in Port Graham, Nanwalek, and Seldovia to find out what they wanted the program to accomplish before I could write a proposal. The elders were eager to share their hopes for their villages.

> "I want the parents to take care of their kids."
>
> "I want the kids to be safe."
>
> "Why can't everyone just be sober."
>
> "I want to hear laughter instead of fighting."
>
> "Nobody goes to church anymore; I want the church to be filled with singing again."
>
> "I hope people buy food and cook for their kids, instead of buying booze."
>
> "I hope the kids don't grow up and drink."
>
> "I want the young girls to not drink when they are pregnant."

It was clear the elders wanted the children to be taken care of. I wanted that too; besides, I'd met a couple of the people known as "public inebriates," who had been to treatment many times and relapsed as soon as they got back home. They were pretty scary. I took this information to Jim Miller and Mack Kvasnikoff, my two village counselors, and we began to brainstorm program ideas: Elder-Youth conferences, women's retreats, children and youth prevention activities, Alutiiq values, Alutiiq dancing, drum making, drug and alcohol education, to name just a few. We would still offer counseling for court ordered clients and any adults who wanted it. I wrote this all up just in time, and the proposal was accepted and approved. We were off and running.

I hired a prevention coordinator, Dee Dee Higman, to work in the school and run the after-school programs educating children and families about the disease of alcoholism and doing prevention activities. Peni Moritor, would keep the books and pay the bills. Sandee Elvsaas, would run women's groups and do one-on-one counseling. I focused on writing the grants, managing the grants, managing the village staff from Nanwalek and Port Graham, and counseling the court ordered clients.

Counseling the court ordered clients meant watching endless educational videos with the clients and running a weekly group.

Alcoholism was not a respecter of persons. Really good people, well known people, people with important jobs in the community managed to end up in my office for alcohol and other drug infractions—driving under the influence, fighting in bars, neglecting their children and having the children taken from them by the child protective services, wrecking their car or four-wheeler, underage drinking, staying drunk for weeks at a time, only sobering up when it was time to go fishing—to name just a few.

I'd never had a job before. Soon I was exhausted from the constant pressure of running an agency, managing office and village staff, balancing a budget, writing reports, networking with other agencies, trying to keep my postulancy for Holy Orders with the church moving forward even though we no longer lived in Anchorage. I'd never had to keep a house warm with a wood stove. I'd never had to climb under a house with a blow-dryer and thaw the water pipes. I'd never had to single parent two teenage boys who were constantly taking a twelve-foot skiff out into Seldovia Bay in all kinds of wind and weather or reassure two little boys that their dad would be home soon. I filled a stack of rainbow-colored spiral notebooks with "She, Judith, can do this. You, Judith, can do this. I, Judith, can do this."

One of the village counselors suggested a women's drum making retreat at Harmony Point, a wilderness lodge near the head of Seldovia Bay. I jumped at the idea. We had drum making supplies left from a youth prevention workshop in Port Graham. We could make drums and do some inner healing work with just women. Perfect. We sent out the invitation to women in Nanwalek, Port Graham and Seldovia.

I knew Barbara Flaherty from my women's retreat work in Anchorage. Barbara agreed to come and suggested inviting Rose Beck, a mental health counselor who had been doing some exciting work helping women heal the shattered connection between the physical, emotional, intellectual, and spiritual components of the self after experiencing trauma. It was a great team.

Rose brought her massage table and announced that anyone who would like to do body work could lay on the table and just see what came up for them. By Saturday evening no one had taken her up on her offer, so I volunteered to give it a try. I got on the table fully clothed. The other women sat in a circle on the floor around me. I knew them all personally and trusted them completely. I had shared many cups of tea at their kitchen tables, I knew their children's names, I had heard their stories. They trusted me, too.

Rose invited me to relax and just begin to breathe normally. Then she led me in a deep relaxation exercise. My breathing became deeper and slower until I felt like I was floating. About fifteen minutes into the relaxation response, I began to moan and groan. Quietly, at first, then louder and louder. The sounds were purely involuntary, I didn't invent them or try to stop them, I just trusted Rose and the process, and let them develop. All of a sudden, I felt like I was having a baby. My abdomen began to cramp terribly and I began to have bearing-down pains.

Rose quietly asked, "What's happening?"

"I'm giving birth," I said, and just kept moaning. I became so focused on myself and my pain I lost all awareness of my surroundings or the women sitting near me. I was completely focused on the task at hand. I didn't feel self-conscious, or embarrassed, or idiotic.

At last Rose asked, "To whom?"

"Myself."

"What is your name?" She asked.

"Sam Houston." I moaned.

"What!?" she bellowed.

I'm sure she had expected me to say something like Amelia Earhart, or Eleanor Roosevelt, or some icon of the women's movement, but instead, this ridiculous name exploded from my unconscious mind.

"Why Sam Houston?" she demanded.

"Because, he could jump on his fucking horse and ride off anytime he wanted."

And with that I jumped off the table and began to beat my

drum and dance around the table singing at the top of my lungs. The women rose up off the floor in one fluid movement with their drums and followed me. The yowling racket was godawful. When we'd exorcised every doubt and demon, we collapsed on our pillows howling in laughter. I did want to run away from the stress and crush of running a village-based treatment program, and single parenting four sons, but I didn't. I persevered. I asked for help and I got it. I slept like a baby that night.

WE MAKE SIGN OVER THE FOOD SO
THE PEOPLE WHO HAVE ALREADY GONE
INTO THE LIGHT CAN EAT WITH US.

—Katherine Hamilton, Shageluk

12.
A PLACE COME TO LIFE

The in-village trainings were so successful that in 1989 Jim Miller asked me to plan and organize a village-based treatment program for families from four villages from Kachemak Bay and Prince William Sound. We would host it in Port Graham and invite Native families from Nanwalek, Tatitlek, and Chenega Bay to participate.

Walter Meganack, the Chief of Port Graham and also the Chairman of the South Kachemak Inc., Alcohol Program Board of Directors, was in favor of the idea, and the Board approved the funding. When I asked Walter for a Sugpiaq name for the treatment program he said, "Ungwirwiiliik. It means *a place to come to life.*" I smiled broadly. What a perfect name for the first ever in-village treatment program for Native families in Alaska. Walter smiled too, and kept nodding his head. I had a B.A. in Human Resource Development from Alaska Pacific University, so I called the university and asked if I could do a Masters of Arts in Teaching by directed study. I would use the course work to help me design Ungwirwiiliik. They agreed.

By the spring of 1990 we were ready: twenty-seven adults and ten children from Port Graham, Nanwalek, Chenega Bay, and Tatitlek signed up to participate. The program would run from Monday through Friday for two weeks. Families would arrive at the community hall first thing in the morning for breakfast and not go back to their beds until 9:00 p.m. at night. Ernie Turner, Jim Miller, Mack Kvasnikoff, Nancy Yaw-Davis, Barbara Flaherty, Sheila

Seetomona, Stephen Staubes, Maggie Napoleon, and several other presenters agreed to be staff.

On one of the first mornings of Ungwirwiiliik, Walter came to welcome us and give his customary morning prayer. He stood and looked thoughtfully around the circle, then extended his hands in a gesture of peace and said at last, "Today is the Day of Reconciliation in the Russian Orthodox Church. If I have hurt you in any way, I am deeply sorry." I looked up, surprise, but before I could respond a stillness fell over the room. Every face turned towards this small commanding figure and waited.

Walter raised his hands a few inches and every person stood up. Then he turned to me, standing on his left, took my hand, looked intently into my eyes, and said, "If I have hurt you in any way, I am deeply sorry." The sincerity of his apology was so real and heartfelt, I could feel *my* heart begin to open—Walter had never hurt me, or disrespected me. He had never made me feel like an outsider, even though I had never worked with Sugpiaq people before. Yet here he was apologizing to me; making himself vulnerable to me. Before I could reply he stepped to face the person standing on my left, and repeated his words, and on and on around the circle from one person to the next—*if I have hurt you in any way, I am deeply sorry.*

Walter's energy was magnetic; I turned and followed him around the circle, repeating his words and gestures to the person on my left. The circle began to turn in on itself, like an enormous snake; each person following in turn, echoing Walter's sincerity until every person had apologized and received an apology from every other person. The soft murmuring of voices flowed like living water, first one person began to cry, then another, until every adult in the circle was released from whatever demons or resentments they had been bound by; the children's faces were glowing.

We began each day with a talking circle, a spiritual way of greeting, sharing feelings, and debriefing that I had learned from Doug and Amy Modig at the Rural Provider's Conferences. It was a lesson in deep listening and trust. The circle opened with a prayer from the oldest elder, and then a sacred object (a feather, stone, candle, drum, or any other symbolic object) was passed from person to person. As long as a person held the sacred object, they had the floor to speak. I felt like I was being immersed in the Native way of being; people were free to share whatever was on their heart, and speak, uninterrupted, for as long as they wanted to. When they finished, they passed the object on to the left. There was to be no cross-talking or commenting on what others said. This was very difficult for me in the beginning. I was so impatient and opinionated. I wanted to control the pace and content of the sharing. Gradually, I came to understand that healing came when each person could take as much time as they needed. There was no rushing, no shushing. And people didn't *have* to share. They could simply say hello or thank you, and pass the sacred object on. I learned to rest in the circle; trust that what was being shared would find its mark, and what was being heard would be held tenderly, and with respect. Eventually, I learned to share myself. After everyone spoke, an elder would say a blessing to close the circle, and then what was shared was not spoken of again outside the circle.

We then moved on to activities that centered on healing from alcohol and other drug addictions: Jim and Mack taught the disease model of addiction, breaking the cycle of shame, and issues for adult children of alcoholics. Nancy Yaw-Davis taught a class on kinship. Maggie and Sheila taught healthy lifestyles, nutrition and exercise. Stephen taught a class in anger management, knowing the difference between healthy anger and violence, grief and loss, and parenting skills. Barbara taught us about healthy communication, and using art and creativity instead of drugs for relaxation and play. I led us in values clarification exercises, and we made a poster of Alutiiq Sugpiaq Values (see page 121). Then I drew on my training from San Francisco and led a session in healthy touch and healthy sexuality. I was running on pure adrenaline, only getting three or four hours of sleep a night.

We laughed, we cried, we made drums, we *rocked* each other, we learned to confront each other without violence, we learned to forgive each other, and say what we needed from each other, we held AA meetings every day. All this was done with grandparents, parents, and children. For many it was the first time they had played a game and laughed with a sober parent or grandparent. It was transformational. The children were the true heroes because they told the truth, and were so quick to forgive.

At one of the AA meetings, someone talked about hiding her drinking from her family, in other words, being a closet drinker. I was stunned. So far, I had only heard stories of tragedy, and grief related to alcohol. I had never heard anyone tell *my* story. I felt so vulnerable, I was ready to do whatever it took to heal from this cunning and baffling disease. That night I called Kris in Seldovia and said, "Hi, I'm Judith and I'm an alcoholic." He was silent for several minutes, and then he said in a pitying tone that immediately set off my cowgirl temper, "I'm sorry."

"Damn you, I'm not bad, I'm sick." I shouted, and I hung up the phone. I called a friend who was in Al-Anon. She listened. She understood. I sobbed.

Week two of Ungwirwiiliik brought us Ernie Turner, the well-known Athabascan treatment director from the Ernie Turner Center in Anchorage. Ernie wanted to do some inner-child healing work, saying *the longest journey in the world is from the head to the heart*. He gave everyone two 3 x 5 cards and asked us to write on one card what we always wanted to hear our fathers say to us, and to write on the other card what we always wanted to hear our mothers say to us. Then half the group sat in a circle with their backs to the outside, holding their cards in front of them so the other half could read the cards aloud as they walked behind them—the men reading what we wanted our fathers to say, and the women reading what we wanted our mothers to say.

I realized I wanted to hear my mother say, "I trust you." And to hear my father say, "I'm proud of you." I underestimated the power of those words spoken quietly in my ear as the outer circle turned round the inner circle. My mother had died when I was 22, and I never had a chance to earn back her trust as an adult. To hear the women say, "Judith, I trust you," was deeply liberating. I could feel the presence of my mother and two grandmothers behind me. Hearing the men say, "Judith, I'm proud of you," caused me to completely break down in sobs, but I was not alone. The entire inner circle was sobbing. The cacophony of common grief was somehow consoling. I was not alone.

The next afternoon Ernie took all the men and boys into a room by themselves, and I took all the women and girls into a room. We invited the participants to name what they most wanted to hear from others. We formed two circles, half in each circle, facing each other. I was still feeling vulnerable from the day before, but I wanted to model the power of affirmations and to build on what I had started in the circle the day before, so I began the group exercise by saying, "Hello, I'm a white woman, and I'm proud of myself and I trust myself." The response from the person facing me was, "Hello, I see you are a white woman, and you are proud of yourself and trust yourself." Then the woman in front of me stated her affirmation, "Hello, I'm proud to be a beautiful Alutiiq woman." I responded, "Hello, I see that you are proud to be a beautiful Alutiiq woman." It was electrifying. Around the circle we went, stating our affirmation, hearing it back, and then listening to a new affirmation, and speaking it back. Thirty years later, the woman who stated that *she was proud to be a beautiful Alutiiq woman* still greets me with those words when she sees me.

After Ungwirwiiliik, I returned to Seldovia with a renewed commitment to put my sobriety first and to continue my inner-child healing work. For the next year I woke up every morning and said to myself, *I am powerless over alcohol, and my life is unmanageable. There is a power greater than myself that can restore me to sanity. I turn my life and my will over to God as I understand God.* My desire to drink was gone, but I felt sad and wondered if I would ever be able to play again.

One afternoon, I headed down the boardwalk to visit a friend that I used to drink tequila with. He was in the boathouse working on his artwork. Another friend was fiddling with an old record player and a stack of 33-rpm records in the back room. Suddenly a Viennese waltz blasted from the record player. My friend jumped to his feet. He bowed, I curtsied, and then we waltzed around and around the boathouse, then he stopped, bowed, I curtsied, said goodbye and walked home. I was elated. I had played with my friend and there wasn't a drop of tequila involved. My sadness vanished.

I didn't drink for a year. Then one day I heard myself say, *well, maybe I'm not really an alcoholic*. I knew from teaching my court ordered clients about issues in long-term recovery that one of the first steps in relapse is denial—not accepting that I really had a problem. I'd been a closet alcoholic and now I was being a closet recoverer. I knew I needed to go to AA and work the 12-steps in order to have real sobriety, and to stay sober. I didn't know who I could talk to about this in Alaska because all the treatment directors were my colleagues and I felt ashamed to admit I didn't know what to do. I jumped on a plane for Seattle, and went to one of the Milan treatment programs and asked for an assessment. "Yes, you are an alcoholic," said the young counselor who saw me, "But you're getting off at the fourteenth floor instead of the basement."

When I returned to Anchorage, I went to the AA meeting at St. Mary's Episcopal Church on the corner of Tudor and Lake Otis. I hid in the back row by the window. I kept looking away every time the speaker looked in my direction.

"I want to hear from the woman in the back row who keeps looking away." Laughter and smiles from those near me.

"Hello, my name is Judith and I'm an alcoholic. I'm an alcohol program director, and I've been sober a year. I was a closet alcoholic and recently I realized I was being a closet recoverer. I don't want to do that anymore."

"Well," he said. "You're not the first alcohol program director we've had here, and you won't be the last." This time the entire room erupted in belly laughter. My shame evaporated and I laughed louder than anyone.

"Thank you."

I got a sponsor and began to work the 12-steps. She asked me to meditate every day on Psalm 139.

Every morning I would make coffee, open my Book of Common Prayer, light a candle, and read line by line the words of the Psalmist, pausing after each line to listen both outwardly and inwardly for the word that stood out that day. In the beginning all I felt was a vague uneasiness. Holy cow, everywhere I go, God is already there; He knows everything I'm saying; darkness and light are both alike to Him. This doesn't even make sense, but I trusted my sponsor so I stuck with it.

Gradually, I began to focus on the idea that God created me in my mother's womb; the same God who created the universe and our world knit me together, causing the Psalmist to declare, "I am marvelously made." When I told my sponsor I didn't believe it really meant me, she said it was time to move on to Step Four—make a searching and fearless moral inventory of my life.

I had no idea how to begin. Then I remembered the work of Agnes Sanford, the Episcopal author and healer who taught me and a group of friends from St. Mary's to divide our lives into five-year segments, meditate on each segment in turn, and write down any uncomfortable memories that came to mind. Uncomfortable memories were a lot easier to recall than weaknesses and moral defects, so I started Step 4 there. When I finished, I had filled fifteen pages of my journal with uncomfortable memories, one line for every memory. I was dragging around a chain heavier than the ghost of old Marley.

My sponsor wouldn't let me read my Step Four inventory to her as my Step Five. Too easy, she said. She insisted I go to St. Mary's, my own church, and read it to one of the priests there. I felt embarrassed to read all this stuff to someone I knew well, but I had to do it. I chose Bob Nelson, the associate rector, a warm and gentle man who had always been kind to me. We opened our Prayer Books to page 447.

"Bless me, for I have sinned."

One by one I read every uncomfortable memory aloud, clothed in the sanctity of that sacred ritual; little by little, fear, confusion, hurt, disappointment, shame, anger, grief, loss, betrayal, sadness began to slip away. I didn't gloss over it. I didn't look up. I didn't try and guess what Bob was thinking. I didn't stop until I'd finished.

"The Lord has put away all your sins," said Bob. "Go in Peace, and pray for me, a sinner."

When I walked out of Bob's office, I felt buoyant, like a red balloon tethered to the bell tower. I didn't know anything about endorphins or trauma recovery work, but in that moment I believed I was not alone. I was forgiven. Everywhere I'd gone, and everywhere I would ever go, I would be in the company of the one who made me and loved me, and who declared that I am marvelously made, already, just as I am.

❖ ❖ ❖

The next few years continued to be a financial scramble for us. Kris and I moved the family back to Anchorage. Kris had been hired as the CEO for the Aleut Corporation, one of the thirteen Native Regional Corporations formed after the Alaska Native Claims Settlement Act was signed into law in 1971. He was deeply involved in lobbying Congress, and the United States Navy, to secure title to the Adak Naval Base for the Aleut people. Kris was not Alaska Native, but he had been elected to the Alaska State House of Representatives for the 1977–78 term and had a good understanding of how government worked. He knew all the key players in Washington, DC.

I took a job with Human Affairs of Alaska (HAA) as a level II alcohol counselor serving the Kotzebue contract. Once again, I found myself working with men and women who suffered from severe sexual abuse trauma. My weekend course in San Francisco barely scratched the surface. I headed for the Women's Book Store on Tudor and bought every book on sexual trauma that they had. This began a rigorous course of self-study.

About that same time, John Bradshaw, the well-known speaker and author in the recovery community, came to Anchorage for a two-day workshop based on his book *Home Coming: Reclaiming and Healing Your Inner Child*. Hundreds of participants were expected to attend. My boss at HAA volunteered me to be one of the counselors to be on hand if people became overwhelmed by their feelings and wanted to talk to someone. "Original pain work involves actually experiencing the original repressed feelings… It is the only thing that will bring about 'second order change', the kind of deep change that truly resolves feelings. In first-order change, you change one compulsion for another compulsion. In second-order change, you stop being compulsive," said Bradshaw.

The truth of his words snuck up on me. I had stopped drinking and compulsively overeating, but I had become a workaholic. In Kotzebue I couldn't turn anyone away. I saw twenty clients in two days, often working through my lunch hour, and into the night. One night I even disarmed a man who shared he wanted to harm himself. After doing a suicide assessment, and determining he had a plan, the means, and the opportunity, I quietly informed him I was a mandatory reporter, and that I was going to call the police. He begged me not to. I walked back to the hotel with his revolver in my pocket, shaking like a leaf.

Bradshaw invited the participants to tell their story as if it were a fairy tale and they were the prince or princess. He urged them to embrace their "heartbroken little boy's (or girl's) loneliness and unresolved grief about their lost father, lost family, and lost childhood." He called embracing the original pain the legitimate suffering Carl Jung spoke about. Walking home from the workshop that afternoon I saw a rag doll in a store window. I stopped and bought her. Later that evening I got out my journal and began, "*Once upon a time, in a land far, far away lived a king and queen… they had a beautiful daughter who had hair the color of straw in sunlight, the color of salt water toffee after a night of pulling, the color of moonlight glistening on the pond in Virgin Valley, Nevada when winter coated the rim with frost and a mist shimmered just above the surface. Her grandmother said she had Shirley Temple curls. She said they were the color of tapioca pudding made with egg yolks from old hens that roamed the back yard scratching for worms and bugs…"*

I made a stab at grieving my lost childhood, but it was just too painful. The doll went on the shelf, and I went back to work. When my contract with Human Affairs ended, I took a job as Executive Director of STAR, Stand Together Against Rape. Again, I was thrown into a high learning curve: grant writing, lobbying for State funding, liaising with the Anchorage Police Department's Sexual Assault Response Team, supporting our counseling staff, and advocating for our clients.

Four months later I was hired as the Intervention Analyst for the United States Postal Service for Alaska. By this time, I had been accepted as a postulant for Holy Orders and began my studies for a Masters of Divinity degree by directed study in the Native Ministries Program at Vancouver School of Theology in British Columbia. Bishop Mark MacDonald appointed me Missioner for the Lower Yukon, and I began serving the villages of Anvik, Shageluk, and Grayling on weekends, or when I took leave without pay. I continued my sobriety in a women's 12-step program with my sponsor. Our two oldest sons were married and the two youngest sons were in college.

Yes, I'd traded my compulsive eating and drinking for compulsive working, and I still didn't understand my need to reclaim and heal my inner child, but that would all change when I began to walk up and down the hills of Anvik, Shageluk, and Grayling with some of the most remarkable people I would ever meet.

UNGUIRNAQ
Cuqllimtenek tawaten uyguillrapet litnaurluki asirqanek luumacinek

AGA' UCIMEK
LING' AKLLUKI CUQLLIPET
TAANGANIRLUTA
IQLLUNGAINERMEK
MAKUT CACAT ITAKLLUKI NUNAMTEHNI
PICA' AKLLUKI UYGUILLRAPET
AKIRTUINERMEK
CACAQIINAQ TANGERLLUKU
UK' ERTATLUTEN
ASIRLUTEN
ASIKILUTEN
PICAKILUTEN
ANGUARKUNAK
TUKNIGLUTEN
ALINGTAILLUTEN
ILIULUTEN

Elluta picimcestun taumi aga' ucimcestun mani ilamtehni taumi nunamtehni

NUPUGNERPET NALLUGKUNAKU
ALL' INGULUTA
CUQLLIMCESTUN ELL' UTA
PISURLAUCIMCESTUN
ILAMCESTUN ELL' UTA
QAILLUN UNGUCIQAMANI NUNAMI TAUMI SUNGCAUTNEK
QAILLUN LUUMACIRPET ELL' ARTA
KINANKUT ILAKECESTA
QAILLUN NUNAGPET ENGUARLARTA

Tawaten um quliruutakut kalikam kinaukauceta

Translation by Feona Sawden

UNGWIRWIILIIK
A PLACE TO COME TO LIFE

With guidance and support from Elders, we teach our children these Alutiiq Values.

SPIRITUALITY
RESPECT FOR ELDERS
GROWING SOBRIETY
HONESTY
RESPECT AND WISE USE OF NATURAL RESOURCES
LOVE FOR CHILDREN
FORGIVENESS
OPENNESS
TRUSTING
SHARING
LOYALTY
UNCONDITIONAL LOVE
CARING
TENDERNESS
HUMILITY
STRENGTH
COURAGE
HELPFULNESS

In living our Traditional and Spiritual Values with our family and community we practice

KNOWLEDGE OF LANGUAGE
UNITY
HERITAGE
SUBSISTENCE
FAMILY ROLES
SURVIVAL SKILLS, LIFE SKILLS, MEDICINAL HERBS
ARTISTIC EXPRESSION
KNOWLEDGE OF FAMILY TREE
COMMUNITY UNIQUENESS

And this makes us who we are

MY DADDY TELL US WHEN YOU SHAKE
THE HAND OF SOMEONE WHO HAS DIED,
THEIR STRENGTH COMES INTO YOU.

—Edna Deacon, Grayling

13.

POTLATCH

On Christmas Day 1998, a call came in from Shageluk; a log cabin fire had claimed the lives of a father and his son, and the family wanted me to officiate the funeral. I'd been serving the village of Shageluk for a year. I had assisted at several funerals over the last ten years, but I'd never officiated one myself. This shift in responsibility and expectations from the village felt enormous. I was scared, but I knew I needed to go.

Getting to Shageluk involved flying in a Beechcraft 1900 to the hub-village of Aniak on the Kuskokwim River, and then transferring to a single engine Cessna for the forty-minute flight over the mountains to the Innoko River. After grabbing the first seat available on December 26th, I called Katherine Hamilton, my new ministry partner from Shageluk, to tell her my arrival time and to ask for more details about the fire.

In the very early hours of December 24th, Harvey Benjamin was walking home through the dark streets when he heard glass shatter and then saw flames shooting up the log walls of the tiny cabin shared by Tommy Dutchman and his son Tommy Jr. Harvey ran to St. Luke's and began banging on the old bell that sat in a wooden crib in front of the Mission House. By the time the villagers arrived, flames had engulfed the cabin, and all anyone could do was watch in stunned silence.

The temperature hovered at minus twenty the morning I flew into Aniak. The winter sun was no match for the ground haze blanketing the tundra, and I could just make out the gentle folds of the Kuskokwim River below us as we made our approach.

The small flight shack was filled with travelers waiting for their airplane to Crooked Creek, Red Devil, and Stony River, and the floor was puddled with the snow we had all tracked in. The home bound passengers carried totes of groceries and supplies from the Alaska Commercial Company store. Everyone had on their Arctic-style snow pants, parkas, and boots. I groaned as I realized my snow pants were too thin to be much good, and my boots weren't adequate either. At least my red down parka would be warm to 20 below zero, I thought, as I reached up and stroked the beaver and Russian raccoon fur ruff that my friend Harriet Maillelle had insisted on sewing for me. "You'll need fur on your parka when you travel down to help my people," she had said when she sent me off to the Alaska Fur Exchange to find supplies. "The weather is much colder there, and I don't want you to freeze to death."

Finally, it was time for my flight to the Yukon. The plane was filled with freight bumped from an earlier manifest by family and friends coming to help with the funeral preparations. I pulled my wool hat down, snugged my fur ruff around my face, plunged my hands into the pockets of my parka, and closed my eyes. By the time the plane arrived in Shageluk, I was chilled to the bone. Arnold, the village agent for the airlines, picked me up at the airstrip and took me to the Kashim, the octagonal building in the center of the community where everything important happened. Arnold didn't talk much, and I didn't either.

In the Kashim I saw Herman, Arnold's uncle and a village elder, sitting on the bench near the coffee pot; the ready light flashed red, so I dropped my duffle bag and guitar on the bench behind the barrel stove and fixed a cup. The coffee was hot and strong and gave me an excuse to just nod my head, and grunt, "Good, good," to Herman, who looked like he'd been sitting in vigil for his friends all night.

A strange silence hung over the Kashim, not a hushed silence—the boom-box in the corner was blaring country and western—but a silence that felt empty and frozen. A quick glance revealed the yellow body bags lying side by side in the far corner where the Christmas tree had stood; in the half-light I could see a trail of tinsel and shattered lights in the drag marks on the wood floor leading from the corner to the door. Death stopped every celebration, it seemed.

Chairs were lined up in front of Tommy and Tommy, Jr., so I took my coffee and moved toward them. A nagging curiosity followed me and began to fill the silence. What caused the fire? I wondered if it was alcohol related. I wondered if the wood stove overheated and the red-hot chimney caught the roof on fire. I shook my head, as if answering myself: I may never know. I slipped into a chair with my coffee and closed my eyes, hoping to gather my thoughts, hoping to hear a word or phrase that would help me make sense of the uneasy feelings lingering just below the surface. Words of scripture or song usually filled my mind when I took a moment to be still, but today presented only an uneasiness I couldn't understand.

A memory seemed to be lodged just below the surface, like permafrost ready to melt, ready to flood the Innoko lowlands that, moments before, had lain hidden beneath the tundra and bogs, forgotten. I'd learned a long time ago that when one memory is released, other memories quickly follow until the water, locked away millennia ago, busts free and flash floods saturate the earth. I knew I would have to sit awhile in this place far from my home—a place with unfamiliar customs, where grief is raw and laid bare, and death and sorrow live side by side with ritual and grace—before I could understand and make peace, and then surrender those memories into that braided river of my own culture and faith. Only then could the flood waters retreat, the river rest easy in her banks, and the purple iris spring up, new, again.

The last time I'd seen Tommy alive he was drumming at the school with Raymond, Phillip, and Harvey as the children practiced their traditional dances. His shock of white hair reminded me of Albert Einstein. I remembered his strong arms beating the drum, and the foot he kept time with, and his clear voice as he sang the ancient

Athabascan songs he'd learned as a young man. I'd seen vitality like that one other time, in the Inupiaq village of Point Lay on the Arctic coast, when two old men came into the school at midnight to play their drums for the Eskimo dancing after Bishop George Harris had celebrated Baptism and Confirmation. The old men looked so frail before they began to drum, but once the walrus gut skins began to sing, the old men were filled with power and shot through with life. Tommy was like that the day I saw him drumming at the school—shot through with life. Tommy Jr. hung back and didn't talk much, but I remembered a sweetness about him and a kindness in the way he spoke when we were introduced.

I opened my eyes and began to take in the scene in front of me. Something wasn't right. What was I seeing? Oh God, two lumps; all that was left of their bodies were the torsos now forming two lumps in the yellow body bags, two lumps, and all that vitality and kindness gone. I began to cry.

❖ ❖ ❖

"Mother, why does the skin on Barbara's neck and hands look twisted and melted like candle wax spilled out on the table cloth?" I cried.

The year was 1954. I was 10 years old. Mother had brought our cousin Barbara to live with us when she was eighteen, and gave her a job at the Rosalind Theatre. Barbara had been working in the potato fields and Mother wanted her to go to business school so she could earn a better living.

"There was a fire when she was a little girl… she tried to save her mother," said my mother, then she turned away, walked into her bedroom and closed the door. I heard her begin to cry. I wanted to take care of my mother. I wanted to comfort her, but she hated crying, and sickness, and any kind of weakness, so she would never cry in front of us; always only behind a closed door.

❖ ❖ ❖

Katherine, my new friend, came into the Kashim and poured a sack of candy into a tin bowl that rested on the floor just in front of the body bags. "We make sign over the food so they can eat with us," she said as she pinched the air above the candy with her thumb and first finger, pulling away three times, in a quick, flicking motion. We hugged, and then sat together in silence. I wanted to ask her what caused the fire, but I couldn't find my voice. Probing to satisfy my own curiosity seemed disrespectful. The door banged open, and Harvey came in carrying several cases of soda pop. He set them on the floor next to the bowl of candy, and then he took a soda, cracked the top, made sign, and sat with us for a few minutes. The door opened again, and the Kashim filled with children. The candy and pop were magnets. The children helped themselves, made sign, nodded respectfully to Tommy and Tommy Jr., then filled the folding chairs in front of the body bags. A kind of sweetness began to fill the Kashim and nudged out the dread. I took a long breath and felt myself relax into the chair. Several of the boys giggled and squirmed visibly, then reached for more candy. Katherine teased them as they stuffed the candy in their pockets and headed outside to play.

"In the old days, children weren't allowed in the Kashim like that," she said. "Too much bad things can happen."

I didn't know what she meant, but, again, I couldn't seem to ask why.

"Are the bodies always put in this corner?"

"Ya, we always put them that way, facing the light."

I was pleased to have Katherine as my guide this trip. Her mother, Lena Phillips, was raised in the Anvik Mission after her parents died in one of the great flu epidemics early in the last century. She married Charlie Dementi when she was old enough, and they moved to Swiftwater. Katherine was born in Swiftwater in 1932. Lena moved the family to Shageluk after her husband died of tuberculosis in 1946. Katherine's mother taught her to read and write and to weave baskets and trays from spruce and willow roots. Katherine had worn her teeth to brown stubs cleaning the roots in the traditional way.

"It was our job to gather wood when we were just little," she had said one day as we hiked the narrow trail to visit grandma Elizabeth Workman. "Jimmy was too big, but Gilbert and Louise and me would go out before the sun come up, when the snow still had a thick crust on it. We were small so we wouldn't break through. If we broke through, we'd get stuck in the deep snow and there'd be no one to come for us. Daddy would go out on his trap line and we would stay with mama in our cabin and wait. Three families lived around Swiftwater. We never knew death until my daddy died. People don't have accidents then."

"What did you do when your daddy died?" I had asked.

"We moved down here to Shageluk. We live in a little cabin near the old village. Mama would trade spruce root trays and baskets to the old storekeeper for food. I sold my first spruce root tray to that old man. He gave me a dollar for it."

Later we would stop at Katherine's cabin for tea and Pilot Bread. She had a curious way of pulling her hair back into a pencil-thin ponytail. Her hair was waxy and yellow and so thin you could see her scalp where the bobby pins worked to keep it out of her face. Combing it with her fingers, she tugged it into the rubber band and dropped the loose strands on the woodpile, to be burned up when she stoked the fire the next time.

✦ ✦ ✦

My great aunt Mattie and great uncle Frank had one daughter, Alta. She and my mother were first cousins, but they acted more like sisters. I see them together in every family picture; two chubby girls playing with dolls; two fat teenagers with arms draped around each other's shoulders; two young adults, still overweight, but well dressed in the latest flapper dresses and wide brimmed hats with children playing at their feet. Alta was married to John. They had three children: Barbara, Kay, and Jack. John got up early every morning to milk the cows. He always started the fire in the kitchen before he left the house. No one knows exactly what happened that morning. Alta was found by the stove holding baby Jack. Some say the fire didn't kill them; she and the baby were electrocuted and died instantly. Barbara and Kay, eight and six years old, were outside helping with the chores. The girls heard screams and ran back to the house. Barbara hit the door with her face and hand and the paint, blisteringly hot, melted her flesh, leaving scars that lasted a lifetime.

❖ ❖ ❖

I sat in the Kashim the rest of the day, taking a break only to walk to the clinic where I watched the women sewing the fur hats and boots for the traditional burial. No one talked about what caused the fire. I circled up to the school shop and admired the progress the men were making building the coffins and spirit houses. No one there said anything about the fire either.

When I returned to the Kashim, I noticed the new placemats in front of the body bags, one for Tommy and one for Tommy Jr. A plate, with mouse-sized morsels of food on it, sat in the middle of each mat. A coffee cup, water glass, and silverware completed the place setting. A lamp filled with red kerosene sat on the bench. Other personal items adorned the placemats: a lighter and cigarettes, a deck of cards, a dollar bill, several coins, a knife, an ax, a compass, a comb and razor, a Bible, pictures drawn by the children, and plastic flowers from the store—simple icons of lives lived on the edge of the Innoko River; values made visible in wood and steel, tobacco and fire, spades and hearts.

Tommy's family came into the Kashim with boxes of sandwiches and platters of fish and moose steaks, moose soup and Pilot Bread, and bowls of fruit salad. Someone made a pot of fresh coffee and opened a five-pound bag of sugar and a new jar of nondairy creamer. Someone else put out stacks of paper plates, bowls and napkins, and plastic forks and spoons on the end of the long table. One of the elders took the plates from the placemats and cleaned the morsels of food into a bag that was kept on the bench behind the bodies. The plates were cleaned and made ready for the new food that was being brought in. The contents of the coffee cups and water glasses were poured outside on the ground, and the cups and glasses cleaned and refilled with fresh coffee and water. Katherine came in with a pot of moose soup, made sign and placed it on the table, then joined me on the folding chairs.

"This food is holy-like," said Katherine, gesturing to all the food on the table. "Tommy and Tommy Jr. are here watching and eating with us, feeling all this love from the people."

Soon the older men who had been building the coffins and spirit houses in the school shop, and the younger men who were digging the grave at the new cemetery on top of the hill, filed in. Immediately the frost and sawdust and sand mixed with baritone voices nudged out the silence of disbelief, and the Kashim took on a new character: the comfortable murmur of voices and shuffling feet, throat clearing, and the honest exhaustion from working in the bitter cold all day.

The women who had been sewing the fur boots and hats and gloves at the clinic came in and their voices raised the pitch and volume a notch. More food arrived. The children, hungry from sledding and playing in the school yard, came in for dinner, too. I was asked to say grace. The men took off their hats. With tears close to the surface, I thanked Dinaxitó for giving us family and friends to care for us, for moose and salmon and berries and fry bread to strengthen us, and for traditions that sustain us. I asked Jesus to bless the work of our hearts and hands and bring us into the way of peace. The men took their places at the front of the line, filled their plates, and sat at the long table. The women and children came next and took seats wherever they could find them.

"For four days we feed the village," said Katherine. "Everybody comes and we all eat together. If a man dies, the men eat first. If a woman dies, the women eat first."

After the men were fed, Katherine and I joined the women and sat on the bench near the barrel stove with our moose soup. I was suddenly very hungry. Everything tasted delicious.

After supper, one of the younger women shouted, "Hey Judith, get your guitar and we'll sing." Songbooks were passed out as I tuned my guitar and began to play. More coffee was made, and we sang all our favorite gospel songs until late into the night. Hamil, an elder sitting at the poker table, called out, "Number twenty-five. My favorite."

"Okay, Hamil, this one's for you," I called back. "*Farther along we'll know all about it, farther along we'll understand why. Cheer up my brothers, live in the sunshine, we'll understand it all by and by.*"

Okay, I was beginning to get it. Even though I didn't fully understand how God would take away this great sadness, I did know God could and would reveal everything necessary—in the words of Hamil's favorite song—farther along. I smiled, the first time all day, and reached for my prayer book for the vigil prayers. When people settled down, I began to read:

"Dear Friends: It was our Lord Jesus himself who said, 'Come to me, all you who labor and are burdened, and I will give you rest.' Let us pray, then, for our brothers Tommy and Tommy Jr. that they may rest from their labors and enter into the light of God's eternal Sabbath rest."

After I put my guitar away, I walked alone to the school with my duffle bag. The music and stories and prayers drifted past my wearied shoulders and floated heavenward, joining the Pleiades and Orion and Cassiopeia and all the company of heaven. It had been a long, long day. I had not fully appreciated until then that grief-work was just that—work—the work of the community. The people obviously had their own rituals, songs, and ways of proceeding through the funeral observances. They had also managed to integrate their cultural practices with their Christian faith. I couldn't help wondering why the villages needed me, a white woman and an outsider, to officiate the Christian funeral liturgy. I lay down on my gym mat and drifted into an uneasy sleep.

✦ ✦ ✦

I was twenty-two years old and already married and living in Alaska when my mother died. I arrived in Bruneau, Idaho, just before the funeral and passed the day of her funeral in a sort of numb, superficial, obligatory shuffle, one foot in front of the other, with no awareness of where I had come from or where I was going. I had a new hairdo, though, the only vestige of how to prepare for a funeral, or a wedding, or a family crisis that I remembered from my mother. She faced every major event in her life with a new hairdo, and if possible, a new hat, which, of course, made the new hairdo redundant. When I think about her hats now, I realize they provided her a private vantage point. She could gaze silently out at the world, and yet remain half hidden, herself a mystery to others. I wondered if she wanted it that way. I wondered if she had a choice. I never really knew my mother. She remained hidden from me both in her life and in her death.

✦ ✦ ✦

The women wouldn't let me cook or sew, and it was out of the question to hang out in the school shop with the men who were building the coffins, so I spent hours the two days preceding the potlatch sitting on the folding chair in front of the bodies. In the beginning, I felt exposed and vulnerable with no place to hide. After the initial shock wore off, I began to notice a shift that was happening in the Kashim. Amid the cacophony of meals and music and Katherine and the other elders coming to sit, the stillness no longer felt like the dread of unanswered questions. A peace began to fill the spaces around the bodies, like the peace that passes understanding. Somehow through all the traditional rituals of the village, death was being transformed from something shocking and hidden into something natural and visible. I don't mean that this unexpected death of a father and his son wasn't sad. It was terribly sad, but it wasn't an insurmountable tragedy. They weren't gone, really; they were somehow changed, and present in a new way.

✦ ✦ ✦

Mother retired from teaching rural school music in June of 1967. In August she went to the hospital with nausea and pain in her stomach. She thought she had the flu. Her heart, the doctor said. She must stay in bed. Dad was scheduled to take a truckload of Owyhee Rose building stone to California. Mother insisted he go; she would be fine. He called my sister Beverly to come and stay with her.

"She wanted a peanut butter milkshake," Beverly said later. "I told her, no, it was a terrible idea, but she insisted. I argued and argued with her, but it was no use."

Mother was obese. The yellow, mini school bus she drove was filled with recorders, harmonicas, other rhythm instruments, and Coca-Cola and candy. Children loved her; she always had a pocket full of butterscotch, peppermint, and root beer barrels.

There were whispered stories that my mother's uncle tried funny things with young girls. Those stories weren't spoken to me until I was a grandmother myself, but once I heard them from my older sister, all the signs—shame-driven obesity, fear of intimacy, complicated grief, and fear of abandonment—began to make sense. Child abuse is the worst kind of betrayal. It steals innocence and imprisons it in some kind of black hole that cannot be filled with expensive clothes or peanut butter milkshakes. Was it a peanut butter milkshake that killed my mother, or was it shame that could only be masked by something thick and creamy sweet? I needed to know. Can deep wounds ever be healed?

✦ ✦ ✦

It's traditional on the Lower Yukon to hold the potlatch on the fourth night after the death, and the burial the following morning. On the morning of December 28, single-engine airplanes and snowmachines began arriving from around the region. The weather was still hovering about minus twenty, which made travel marginal. The charter companies won't fly if it's colder than minus twenty, and traveling the trail by snowmachine from Anvik, Grayling, or Holy Cross in that deep cold can cost you your life if you break down or run out of gas. I marveled at the number of people who kept coming. They would all stop first at the Kashim to sit a while with Tommy and Tommy Jr., then go off to help cook or sew or build or dig; all the preparations had to be finished before the potlatch could begin.

By early evening it looked like everything was ready. A crowd had begun to gather outside the Kashim. The few old men and I, who were still inside, moved outside and joined the others. Katherine saw me empty-handed and thrust a box of Pilot Bread into my hands. She had a cardboard box filled with fry bread as her offering.

"Gee, you want your relatives to be just hungry," she teased. "Everybody brings food to the potlatch so their relatives, who have gone before, will have something to eat. Don't forget to make sign over it when you lay it down." I nodded yes and managed a smile, as I whispered, "Thank you." I had attended a number of potlatches on the Yukon and knew some of the traditions, but it was comforting to know Katherine cared enough about me to want me to follow her cultural rules.

Trucks and snowmachines towing sleds filled with potlatch food and gifts lumbered down the street towards the Kashim. The gathering parted and a path opened to the door without a word being spoken. The Christmas tree that had been dragged out of the Kashim the day of the fire still lay in the snow. The sight of it didn't seem so brutal now. Somehow I had begun to understand, a little more, the respect the Deg Hit'an people had for their dead, and the strength they received from practicing their traditional ways.

"The family goes in first with all their food and gifts," said Katherine. I followed her into the Kashim and did everything she did, safe in her care.

We settled into our seats behind the family and watched as the women repeated the ritual of emptying the plates and cups and glasses for Tommy and Tommy Jr. in preparation for the potlatch feast. Pots and bowls and boxes of food covered the entire floor in the center of the Kashim. The area behind the caskets was piled with boxes and bags of gifts that would be given away after the feast. One of the elders asked me to say a prayer over the food and gifts, and when I had finished, they began to fill Tommy and Tommy Jr.'s plates with tiny morsels of food from every single offering.

At last, when Tommy and Tommy Jr. were served and had fresh coffee and water, young men began to circle the Kashim, left to right, the direction of the rising sun, with boxes of smoked salmon strips and bowls of Indian ice cream, the most prized traditional foods. The family was served first, then the elders and others who sat on folding chairs and benches around the Kashim. Guests sat passively as the serving continued. I knew from potlatches in Tanana and Minto years before that it was not polite to ask for more of something you really liked or refuse something you'd rather not have. That same rule seemed to apply here, but that didn't stop me from saying an extra loud thank you when the bowls of ice cream came by.

I was starving and kept eating spoons full of the ice cream as it was put on my plate. Before I realized it, all my ice cream was gone. I looked over at Katherine's plate. It was piled high with ice cream and she was taking tiny nibbles with her fingers. She looked at my face, then at my plate and must have known what I was thinking (more please!). Her shoulders began to jiggle as she tried to keep from laughing. The transparency of my greed got the best of her and soon we were both laughing out loud.

The rest of the potlatch was a blur of generosity and love. My plate was piled high again with moose liver and ribs and king salmon, fry bread, cupcakes, cookies, candy and Pilot Bread. When the gifts were passed out, I was blessed with yarn and sewing needles and socks. The men received gloves and socks and many other symbols of the work they participated in. Looking around the Kashim there were no signs of sadness, only love. Only love.

✦ ✦ ✦

I wondered if Mother felt love from me. I never had a time or place to work through the shock of her death. She died in the middle of the night, alone, in the small hospital in Winnemucca, Nevada. She'd gotten out of bed, against doctor's orders, and had a heart attack. The fall and subsequent bruising left her body disfigured, and the casket was closed when I arrived. I was not allowed to see her face one last time. I was not allowed to dress her body or kiss her goodbye. I had forgotten our own cowboy traditions of sitting with her body until the dread left and peace took its place. I felt estranged from our extended Idaho family and friends who, in an earlier time, would have been sewing and hammering and preparing favorite foods. I had no time, no time, to make sense out of this most natural of life's passages—the death of my mother.

✦ ✦ ✦

The mist begins to shift. Layers of unfinished grief and loss fill the silence around me as I think about this, now. Our family traditions from the ranch in Bruneau before 1930 were to put the dead in the parlor on the table or the ironing board, and do almost exactly what these tribal people from the Innoko River are still doing. What have we done with our own cultural traditions and to this most holy work? Is there no way to recover all that we have lost?

✦ ✦ ✦

The morning of the burial I went to the Kashim early. An Arctic cold front had slammed Shageluk during the night and dropped the temperature to 57 degrees below zero. I was shivering from the cold when I arrived. The people who kept vigil playing cards all night were still there. Some were drinking coffee and eating from the food left on the tables from the potlatch, others were lining up the chairs. Family members placed the new clothes on top of the body bags as though they were dressing the spirit body. The leather gloves adorned with beadwork and fur were where the hands would have been. The new pants covered legs that were not there. The new parka and fur boots and hats were where they belonged. Country and western music still blared from the boombox in the corner.

I sat on the folding chair in front of the bodies for one last visit before the service. The brutality of the scant remains that had shocked me just days before were now transformed by beauty, and seemed perfectly natural. Beauty filled the boxes. Beauty filled the front of the Kashim. My eyes traveled down the scene and lingered over the beauty of the fur boots and fur hats and gloves, so lovingly stitched with thread with no knots.

"Knots only slow you down on your spirit journey," Katherine had said. "Knots feel just heavy when you're flying up."

I had watched an elder fill the fur boots with dry grass the day before so Tommy and Tommy Jr. would be warm and comfortable for their journey into the light. The stories and traditions of the elders had completely transformed death for me. I realized then what I must do. I must make the altar beautiful, too.

"Are you going to need a table?" asked Harvey.

"Yes, do you have anything small?"

"Just the poker table."

"That will be perfect. Round, I like that."

The table was cut from an old piece of plywood with 2 x 4 legs. It represented simplicity, what they had, and made by someone from Shageluk and used for everything from poker to potlatch, to bingo.

I walked quickly to the church. I thanked God for no wind. It was so cold I had to slam my shoulder against the church door over and over before it began to inch open. The whole place was frost covered, even the windows, but there was enough translucent light to let me make my way to the altar. The white beaded altar hanging, called a frontal, was thumb tacked to the spruce altar. Mittens off, I tried to pry the tacks holding the linen but couldn't get my nails underneath. My fingers became numb. I dared not tug on the linen; faint rust rings around the tacks indicated they had been there for years, maybe decades. I stomped my feet and pulled my mittens on and tried to warm up.

Under the altar, I saw something neatly rolled in brown paper. Unrolling it, I yelped with joy to find a red beaded frontal that looked as old as the white one. Red—the color of love and fire and saints who have been martyred and high holy days—would be perfect for Tommy and Tommy Jr.

Tucking the red beaded frontal under my arm, I picked up a box of prayer books, along with the brass prayer book holder, the brass candlesticks, and all the old linens I could find, and I headed back to the Kashim. One of the girls on her four-wheeler stopped and took the box of prayer books from me—what a relief. I paused long enough to wonder how much trouble I would get in for using the red beaded frontal—white is the traditional color used for funerals—but my need for beauty trumped my need to follow the rules.

✦ ✦ ✦

I have no proof, except the intergenerational psychic scars I bear, that my mother was molested by her uncle. When my sister Beverly and our cousin Tess were nearly eighty years old, they admitted to each other and to me that Uncle Frank had tried to molest them both when they were children. I imagine Grandma and Grandpa Pence are turning in their graves as I write this. How dare I drag this shame into the light? I'm trying to untangle this knot in my stomach, Grandfather, and to do so I must untangle my mother. It's that simple. And to be free myself, I must set my mother free. That's all. I'm trying to understand the betrayal that caused a woman to demand a peanut butter milkshake on her deathbed even though she must have known it would kill her. I don't want to die with a peanut butter milkshake on my lips because I kept silent and couldn't or wouldn't uncover the truth.

✦ ✦ ✦

The barrel stove in the Kashim couldn't keep up with the cold, but it felt so much warmer than the outside air that I took off my coat and mittens before beginning to dress the table. Elders filled the folding chairs in front of the coffins, and the younger people crowded onto the benches along the log walls. I pirated tacks from the children's artwork and anchored the red beaded frontal to the table. Several of the linens were so old they were rags, but they had been neatly ironed by someone and folded in the traditional way—in thirds, symbol of the Trinity: Father, Son, and Holy Spirit. The old linens formed a checkerboard pattern on top of the table, covering most of the bare wood.

Raymond, Tommy's brother, and the rest of the family came in and took their places in the front row of folding chairs facing the coffins. The high school teacher came in with the service booklets with Tommy and Tommy Jr.'s picture on the front, and one of the teenagers passed them out with the prayer books. I lit the candles and then realized the boom box was still blaring in the corner, so I got up and turned it off.

A silence fell over the Kashim—the first real silence since I arrived three days earlier. The silence quickened into a heaviness that caused me to slump onto the bench behind the altar. This feeling was new, and it left me confused and a little hesitant. I didn't know how or when to start the service. Then the sound of a ragged breath, a sniffle, and full-blown sob ripped a hole right through the heaviness. I looked up and saw that Raymond had begun to cry. The sound of one brother crying for another had an immediate effect—cascading sobs rippled through the gathered community. Tears began to streak down my face. The heaviness began to drain out of the Kashim like a fat belly that has finally birthed new life into the world. The heaviness, pierced by sorrow, could finally be released.

The enormity of that tragic loss had finally found a place to be poured out. It was as though the beauty of the flickering candles, and the red beaded frontal made by the great grandmothers when the gospel first came into this land, and the generosity of all the sewing and hammering and digging and honored traditions—Athabascan and Episcopal—had shaped a big enough, safe enough container for our common grief, and we were set free, at last, to cry and celebrate the life of this father and his son.

The tears subsided, and Raymond nodded for me to begin. I eased off the bench and began to intone the opening anthem. *"I am Resurrection and I am Life, says the Lord. Whoever has faith in me shall have life, even though he die."*

❖ ❖ ❖

Death demands our immediate attention, but sometimes more death intrudes. The night my mother died, a fatal car crash at the sand dunes outside of Winnemucca on Highway 95 diverted the mortician, and he was unable to pick up her body at the hospital until morning. When he finally returned for my mother, the bruising from the fall had already turned her body nearly black. I wish I'd had the courage to lift the coffin lid to look at my mother one last time. I wish I'd said goodbye. I wish I'd taken her hand and said the things that still lay tangled in my stomach 47 years later. Who are you, Mother? What was your life about? Why did we always fight? What did you hope for me? Damn it Mother, I'm old now but those questions buried long ago still rob me of the here and now.

Mother and Alta were the same age. I wondered if Alta was also molested. I wondered if she and Mother shared this secret. I didn't want to reach too far with this. I didn't want to postulate betrayal out of my own fertile imagination if there was none there. I did want answers, though, and maybe cowboy justice; that was my own shadow speaking, ready to lasso the bum and string him up on the nearest tree. Pedophiles are notorious repeat offenders. As a priest, I've never had a pedophile come for confession. I have knelt with their victims, though. I've held them as they've wept. I've wept with them plenty. No going back once innocence is shattered. Perhaps the best any of us can hope for is serenity, and maybe courage.

✦ ✦ ✦

After the prayers, I picked up my guitar and began to sing as Raymond and the family moved forward to say goodbye to Tommy and Tommy Jr. *"Amazing Grace! How sweet the sound, that saved a wretch like me! I once was lost but now am found, was blind but now I see."* One by one, the people came up to the coffins to say goodbye. One small boy picked up the glove, where the hand would have been if the fire hadn't been so hot, and shook it vigorously. Edna, an elder from Grayling, leaned in and whispered, "My daddy told me when you shake the hand of someone who has died, their strength comes into you. That's why we always do that."

When the farewells ended, Hamil and Phillip, two elders, motioned for the community to gather around the coffins and reminded everyone, "Okay everybody, we stomp four times to send their spirits into the light, then again four times, then four and four, like that." The villagers seemed to rise as one, folding chairs rasping, booted feet murmuring assent, the amorphous mass moving purposefully into a tight circle around Tommy and Tommy Jr. The children dodged between grandmas and grandpas and got as close to Hamil and Phillip as they could.

"Clear a path to the door," I heard another elder say.

I hung back at the altar, prayer book in hand, ready to snuff out the candles and follow the coffin. I wasn't prepared for the thunder or the shock wave that undulated through the Kashim, like a rifle fired four times in rapid succession, then silence, then four times, silence, four, silence, four. Shivers flooded my body and shot up my spine. I felt something release inside me. I looked around the room, others must have felt it too, there were smiles on every face.

Rudy and Arnold screwed the plywood lids on the coffins and the pallbearers headed out the door. I followed the men to the doorway, chanting the closing prayers. "The Sun of Righteousness is gloriously risen, giving light to those who sat in darkness and in the shadow of death."

Then I turned back to the pile of winter gear I had cached behind the altar, and quickly pulled on my snow pants, parka, and the gloves that Grandma Bertha had given me, tucked the prayer book into my pocket, and walked out the door. The winter sun spilled over the ridge in shafts of gold and peach and warmed the air to twenty five or thirty degrees below zero. The men had already crossed the school yard and were heading for the trail up the mountain behind the school. I knew I wasn't fit enough to hike the trail, so I stopped young Gage on his four-wheeler.

"Can you ride me up?"

"Hop on."

People scattered in all directions. Some followed the procession up the trail; others went home to put on warmer clothing. I climbed on the back of the four-wheeler and hung on. The machine wallowed in the steepest places and I offered to get off, but Gage didn't stop. This was probably his challenge for the day—getting the preacher up the mountain.

The warmer temperature buoyed my mood. The sunlight showered the path with diamond reflections. I felt like laughing as I gulped in the crisp air and hung on for dear life. Then we rounded the bend and entered the dark forest. The unexpected gloom and cold were sobering, and I buried my face in Gage's parka. When he finally stopped at the gravesite, I looked up. No one was there. Raven's guttural croak shattered the silence, and the hair on the back of my neck stood on end. I shivered noticeably. Gage looked at me.

"You'll be okay?"

"Yes, the men are coming." Their voices sounded far away as I climbed off the machine.

The four-wheeler disappeared back down the trail, and the frost-covered trees quickly muffled the engine sounds. A chickadee was chirping and foraging for birch seeds blown on top of the crusted snow, or was that my imagination searching for any friendly sound? No, there it was again. "What are you doing here? What are you doing here?" They seemed to sing.

What an idiot. What *was* I doing here? The single large hole for both coffins gaped before me. My feet felt like chunks of ice. I walked back and forth in front of the hole, flapping my arms like wings, trying to keep the circulation going. I could die up here, frozen solid like Mr. Tumnus in *The Chronicles of Narnia*. I began to flap harder. Raven announced the arrival of the procession as his croak telescoped through the trees again.

The men looked surprised to see me, and I mumbled something about getting a ride. I stopped my ridiculous flapping but kept walking back and forth, trying to get the feeling back into my toes. My feet felt like they weighed 100 pounds. I wondered if frostbite was as painful as I'd heard. I covered my cheeks with my gloved hands. The cold moved up my legs. I began to shiver. Strangely, my hands weren't cold in the thin acrylic gloves from Grandma Bertha.

People began to gather. Other four-wheelers and snowmachines arrived carrying mothers and grandmothers. The coffins were placed on fresh cut spruce poles suspended over the grave. The men stood ready, the coiled ends of rope in their hands, and looked at me expectantly. It must be time to begin. "Give rest, O Christ, to your servants with your saints, where sorrow and pain are no more, neither sighing, but life everlasting." I reached down and picked up a handful of earth from the graveside, and without looking I threw it in the direction of the coffins. "You only are immortal ... you are dust and to dust you shall return ... Alleluia, alleluia, alleluia."

I stopped short. Something was terribly wrong. The clods of earth hitting the coffins sounded loud, really loud, too loud. I looked up. The coffins were still suspended on the spruce poles above ground. The men were still looking at me, only this time their eyebrows were arched in surprise. Mortified by my obvious blunder, I looked at Raymond. He looked at the coffins and then back at me. I felt my cheeks begin to burn. I looked at the coffins and then back at him. I nodded down, he responded in the affirmative. I took a deep breath, put down my prayer book and said, "We will now lower the coffins." I looked back at Raymond. He smiled. I let out a huge breath, uuuuuhhhhh. My shoulders slumped. My blunder was forgiven.

The men with the ropes pulled as one and raised the coffins several inches. Other men pulled out the poles and laid them aside and grabbed onto the ropes behind the first men. Wordlessly, skillfully, respectfully, the men began the hand over hand work of lowering the coffins into the ground. When the coffins were firmly seated, they pulled the ropes free, coiled them, and laid them aside with the poles.

Raymond looked at me and smiled again. I inhaled deeply and began from the beginning. This time the frozen clods of earth sounded just right—distant, like thunder rumbling out of the hills, hollow, like no need to cry anymore, your loved ones are not here, they have joined the glorious company of the saints in light and all the company of heaven in that place where there are no tears, only mercy and the blessed rest of everlasting peace.

One by one people circled the grave and threw in a farewell handful of dirt. The men moved quickly with shovels to complete the work. Favorite gospel songs were sung. Smoked salmon strips and Pilot Bread were passed out, along with Oreo cookies and handfuls of wrapped candies. I could smell a campfire burning from just over the rise. I would learn much later about the tradition of burning food and clothing, but not now.

Someone broke off dried spruce twigs to mark the corners of the grave, and the men adjusted and leveled the dirt to make a flat foundation for the spirit house. The spirit house looks like a roof with short walls. The fence is made of 2 x 4's and is painted and adorned to match the spirit house. The fence is often engraved with symbols from a person's life: moose or salmon if he was a great provider, playing cards, or a skiff, or an airplane. I looked over at the waiting spirit house and fence, and wished Katherine had told me about this tradition. She hadn't but I knew it was as old as any of the burial traditions of the Deg Hit'an. Someone had whispered once that before the missionaries came the bodies were laid on the ground and the spirit house placed over the body with all the potlatch items and favorite things from the person's life.

My attention moved back to the women who were placing the placemats, dishes, and all the sacred objects from the potlatch on the grave. When they were finished, the men mounted the spirit house on top of everything and placed the fence around the whole thing. All the silk flowers and Styrofoam hearts and crosses were hung on the fence and placed against the spirit house. The icy forest bloomed like a summer day. Pictures were snapped for posterity.

✦ ✦ ✦

Mother's funeral was a blur. I was so busy pretending to be strong, the adrenaline must have erased all the feelings and memories. I came home to Juneau and Kris and our two babies and started to cry and could not stop. Alarmed, Kris finally called Mark Boesser, our priest from Holy Trinity. He came and sat with me a long time until at last I blurted out, "She never kissed me goodbye. We always kissed hello and goodbye."

I wish I'd opened her coffin. I wish I'd taken her hand so her strength could come into me. I wish I'd cooked the meals that fed the community that built the coffin that dug the hole. I wish I'd washed her body and dressed her in her favorite navy blue dress.

"If wishes were horses, hobos could ride," Mother used to say in response to one of my great howling litanies of childhood desire. I would stomp off, more hurt than angry that she wouldn't let me dream.

But maybe dreaming is dangerous. Maybe dreaming keeps little girls locked in an imaginary world of happily-ever-after. Maybe dreaming, without the hard work of building foundations under those dreams, only masquerades as soul food, but leaves us hungry, and disappointed, and wanting more and more; never satisfied.

I didn't help my mother live or die gracefully. There, I've said it. I was the runaway daughter, the one who wasn't there. Beverly was there. My brothers were there. I was nowhere in sight. Oh, how I wish I could have a do-over. I'd take my babies and go home and sit with her and say, "Gosh Mother, how did you do it? Did you ever have time to think of yourself? Did you ever dream about what you wanted or hoped? What were some of those dreams?"

❖ ❖ ❖

The young people were the first to turn from the grave site. They called to one another as they began the much easier trek down the mountain.

"Come on, Judith."

I stumbled after them, and then turned to the girls behind me. "If I freeze into a lump on the trail," I said, "just grab me by the hair and drag me down the mountain and throw me into the Kashim next to the fire."

They laughed and said they would.

We came to a spot with a vertical drop of about fifteen feet. The girls kicked out their feet and slid down on their butts. I stood at the top of the cliff in horror. It looked impossible. I was so cold and so completely exhausted I wanted to lay down right there and never get up.

"Come on Judith, you can do it."

I took a deep breath and jumped, legs splayed, arms reaching heavenward. In that brief moment I was free. I had begun to embody one of the final prayers, *"The Lord will guide our feet into the way of peace, having taken away the sin of the world."* I had also taken into myself the shot-through-with-life-vitality of Tommy, the kindness of Tommy Jr., the generosity of my mother, and, just maybe the courage of the young women who had so nimbly flung themselves into the air. The sun, cascading through the spruce and birch, caught my golden red hair and looked, some would later say, like flames shooting straight up out of my blood red parka.

Alta Hutchison, left, and Rosalind Pence were first cousins and best friends. Taken at Hot Springs school, Bruneau, Idaho, 1921.

Rosalind Pence Slack in 1940 when she married Bill Wegman.

WHEN WE WERE CHILDREN, OUR MOM TAUGHT US HOW TO PRAY. EVERY NIGHT WE PRAY IN INDIAN, 'DINAXITÓ, THANK YOU FOR THE GOOD DAY, KEEP US SAFE UNTIL TOMORROW.'

—Lucy Hamilton, Shageluk

14.

THERE IS NO DARKNESS

The early summer sunrise filled the steps and radiated off the western wall of the little cabin where I was staying. I had slipped out with a steaming cup of coffee cradled in cold hands and found this pocket of warmth. From the time I was a small child living in the Virgin Valley, sunrise has been the place where I'd felt God's presence most powerfully. I opened my Prayer Book to Psalm 139 for my morning meditation.

> *"You have searched me out and known me, you know my sitting down and my rising up; you discern my thoughts from afar."*

My piety and the silence of the sleeping village seemed mocked by the robins and little fox sparrows who were trying their best to get us all to wake up and notice the beauty of this place. I began to smile and quiet my breath. I was awash in my favorite time of day, my favorite season and my favorite Psalm. I smiled as I continued to read.

> *"You trace my journeys and my resting places and are acquainted with all my ways."*

Then suddenly, someone was running fast down the dirt road behind me. It was as though the traveler, skittering this way and that on loose gravel, was fleeing for their life. I felt a stab of fear. A dark-haired young woman came into view. I smiled in relief and raised my hand in greeting. She veered off the road and came towards me.

"Good morning. You're up early," I said cheerfully.

"You're that lady from the church, aren't you?"

"Yes," I said. "Please sit down. Would you like some coffee?"

"I'm in trouble." Tears brimmed as she slumped down on the steps beside me, covered her face with her hands, and began to cry. I closed my eyes and tried to quiet my racing heart.

> *"Where can I go then from your spirit? Where can I flee from your presence?"*

"Can you help me understand what is happening here?"

She looked up and searched my face.

"I was on my way to the river. I was going to jump in. I was going to kill myself."

I felt my whole body quicken, like I'd been hit by a seismic wave. I fought to stay present to the warmth of the sun on my cheeks, and the bright clear sound of the birds singing. I sat my coffee cup down on the steps and took a deep breath.

"I'm glad you didn't," I whispered. "I'm glad you stopped here instead. Do you want to talk about it?"

"I went to a party last night. I got drunk. I slept with someone who was not my husband." Her words came out in a torrent. "I don't know if God can ever forgive me," she wailed and then her body folded in a heap over her lap.

I looked at that young woman bent double with sorrow, and felt the knot in my stomach begin to unravel. Fidelity had been a huge issue in my family when I was growing up. My mother and sisters had always felt my father was being unfaithful. He was so handsome and funny. He loved to laugh, and women were charmed by his easy manner and the way he embodied stories, especially if whiskey was involved. I didn't know if the rumors were true or not, but I was beginning to see the parallels with what was happening here. This was alcohol, and all the damned crazy things we do when alcohol is involved—things that we'd never do if we were sober. I needed to let go of my resentment towards my father and the rumors about him if

I hoped to remain present to this young woman. I took a deep breath and simply began.

"I see how sorry you are."

"Oh yes, I am so sorry."

"Don't you know, God sees how sorry you are, too—and God has already forgiven you."

I paused a moment to let this sink in, then continued to whisper, "Your job, now, is to forgive yourself. Do you think you could do that?"

She studied my face again, and at last nodded yes.

I reached into my pocket for my holy oil, made the sign of the cross on her forehead, and laid my hands on her head, "Lord, this is your beloved daughter. She's devastated by what she's done—breaking your Commandment—and she's deeply sorry. Thank you for your assurance of forgiveness. Please Lord, now, in the name of Jesus, help her to forgive herself and turn her life around. Take this guilt and shame from her—that she may be free to love you and love her family and love herself."

I took her hands in mine and searched her face for a response. She took a deep breath and nodded yes.

"Now, promise me you will never kill yourself," I said firmly.

"I promise."

"Maybe you would like to go home and make pancakes for your children."

"Yes, I would."

I smiled broadly and felt my shoulders soften. As the young woman walked away, all the darkness I felt towards my father shattered into love.

I'M SO PROUD OF THIS VILLAGE.
EVERYONE CAME (TO THE ORDINATION)
TONIGHT AND NO ONE IS DRINKING.

—Phillip Arrow, Shageluk

15.

FIRST BEAVER

Katherine and her sister-in-law, Lucy Hamilton, came to Anchorage from Shageluk and invited me to lunch at the Sea Galley with Lucy's daughter, Bella Schjenken. I told the ladies Bishop MacDonald wanted to do the ordination in a village.

"How about Shageluk?" said Katherine.

"Well, I want a fiddle dance," quipped Lucy.

"So do I."

I'd been working nonstop holding all the pieces of my life together, and I was ready to play. The idea of a fiddle dance at the ordination made me laugh out loud. It was settled, the ordination would be on February 1, 2000, the Feast of St. Brigid of Kildare. Kris, who was also a postulant for Holy Orders, would be ordained a permanent deacon at the same time. He was still a volunteer pilot for the diocese, so he flew Bishop MacDonald, the Rev. Anna Frank, Grace Hensler, and me into Shageluk in the Cessna 206. A storm was building over the low hills from the Arctic coast, and the wind was blowing a steady fifteen knots, gusting to twenty-five when we landed. I could smell snow in the air. Arnold picked us up at the airstrip and drove us to the Kashim with all our gear. Snowmachines and a group of young men were at St. Luke's, just 300 yards from the Kashim, so I went to investigate.

I found Charlie, a tall, kind, teddy bear of a man who taught shop skills to the students from Grayling, Anvik, Shageluk, and Holy Cross putting up a bell tower on St. Luke's church with his high school students. Grandma Mary Semone had remarked every time I visited and prayed for her, "Our church has no bell tower. It doesn't even look like a church with no bell tower. I want our church to have a bell tower." I shared her concern with everyone who would listen. One day I mentioned the dream of a bell tower to Charlie. "We can do that," he'd said. He and his crew smiled and waved and helloed when they saw me. The snow began to fall and the wind picked up, but they kept at it. I shouted my thanks and headed back to the shelter of the Kashim.

The women had gathered earlier in the day and filled the Kashim with white crepe paper streamers and red and white balloons. It looked like a wedding hall. The men had collected every folding chair from the church, school, and city office. There was enough seating for the whole village. Joy had printed eight-foot banners that said, "Congratulations Judith Lethin, and God's Blessings Kris." The schoolteacher, Jeanette Dementi, arrived with the children from her class and they began adding red and white beads and ribbons to the service booklets and peeling the cellophane off of 100 red candles. Anna put the red beaded frontal on the folding table and anchored it with the ancient brass candlesticks, cross, and prayer book stand. Everyone had a job; everyone knew what to do.

Grandmas began arriving by snow machine. By this time the wind was howling and blowing the snow sideways. Everyone stopped at the door to shake the snow off their parkas and snow pants. Jeanette's students passed out service booklets and candles. Old people and young people began filling up the rows of folding chairs. Victor Rock with his fiddle, and Bernard John with his guitar had been invited to play for the fiddle dance. Jimmy Dementi brought his guitar and joined Victor and Bernard up front. They quietly played a few gospel tunes as we continued to get ready.

Bishop MacDonald and Anna vested in their clergy robes and took their places on two folding chairs facing the congregation. Bishop MacDonald wore a simple white chasuble and red stole that matched his miter, his liturgical headdress. Anna, the first Native woman ordained a priest in the Anglican Communion, wore an alb and the embroidered stole given to her by Jean Dementi, one of the first women to be ordained a priest in Alaska. Grace Hensler, a faithful friend who had been my ministry companion when I first began traveling on the lower Yukon, wore her lay reader cassock and surplice. She was to be commissioned an Evangelist. Kris and I wore simple flax albs. Kris would continue to serve the bishop as deacon and volunteer pilot.

"Blessed be God: Father, Son, and Holy Spirit," intoned Bishop MacDonald.

"And blessed be His kingdom, now and forever. AMEN," the people responded loudly.

And just like that the Kashim seemed to decompress and settle more comfortably on its foundation. Everyone looked around to try and understand what had just happened. But all we could hear was stillness. Someone got up and opened the door and looked outside. Giant snowflakes were falling straight down. The wind had stopped, and the celebration had begun.

Katherine Hamilton, Jeanette and Jimmy Dementi, Shirley and Phillip Arrow, Carolyn Workman, and Arnold Hamilton gathered close to present us to Bishop MacDonald. Questions were asked and answered, prayers were said, lessons read, gospel proclaimed and preached, more questions and more prayers, and at last, Bishop MacDonald laid his hands on our heads and prayed that God, through Jesus Christ, would give his Holy Spirit to us, fill us with grace and power, and make us deacons in his Church... *Make them, oh Lord, modest and humble, strong and constant, to observe the discipline of Christ. Let their life and teaching so reflect your commandments, that through them many may come to know you and love you.*

Katherine stepped forward and placed a deacon stole on both Kris and I, and Bishop MacDonald presented us with Bibles, the sign of the authority given to us to proclaim God's Word and to assist with the ministration of his holy Sacraments. Bishop MacDonald laid hands on Grace and commissioned her to go forth as Evangelist, proclaiming the word of God in the power of the Holy Spirit. He presented her with the Prayer Book and Bible that he had been given when he was Consecrated the Seventh Bishop of the Episcopal Diocese of Alaska.

After the Communion and blessing, we lit our candles from the altar candles and began to process to St. Luke's so the bishop could bless the bell, now resting in his new bell tower, and name him St. Michael, the Archangel. The great storm was over, in so many more ways than were obvious: I was being swept along on this river of celebration in spite of struggling 36 years against my destiny.

Flickering candles, snowflakes the size of quarters, jubilant children, and the gathered community filled the street around the church with laughter, and teasing, and yes, a few snow balls. As Grandma Mary Semone looked on, Bishop MacDonald gathered Charlie and Kris and half a dozen children onto the porch and prayed a blessing over this wonderful old bell that would call the people to worship.

"Can I ring the bell?" shouted one of the children.

Everyone laughed, then children and adults lined up to give the rope a good pull. At last, everyone headed home to fetch their potlatch food. When we returned to the Kashim, the men had set up the tables and rearranged the chairs. It was a feast fit for a wedding. Baked king salmon, smoked salmon strips, half-dried salmon with potatoes and onions, roast moose, moose stew, moose soup, spaghetti with moose red sauce, roast beaver, Jell-O salad, macaroni salad, fry bread, cakes and cupcakes, cinnamon rolls, berry pies, fish ice cream with blueberries and salmon berries. After everyone sat down with their plates piled high, the elder, Phillip, stood up to welcome everyone.

"I'm so proud of this village. Everyone came tonight and no one is drinking. Everyone is sober. Now Judith is going to talk."

My mouth flew open. I didn't expect to be called on to speak right after such a powerful revelation about everyone being sober. I stood up and took a deep breath. "Hello, I'm Judith, and I'm an alcoholic," I said. "I quit drinking ten years ago, and that is why I can stand here tonight as your deacon. I would not be here if I were still drinking. I'm proud of all of you, too. Thank you for being here and for being sober."

When I sat down, I was trembling, but I had a renewed sense of gratitude. I looked over at Kris, my rock, and Anna, my friend and supervisor, and Grace, my friend and faithful prayer warrior, and Katherine and all the people who had gathered around us and promised to support us in our ministry and I could only smile. Then I picked up a big piece of meat from my piled-high plate and was about to take a bite when Anna said, "Judith, what's that you're eating?"

"I don't know; what is it?"

"Beaver."

"Take my picture," I laughed playfully, "this is my first beaver."

(Top left) From left, Rev. Anna Frank, Bishop Mark MacDonald, and newly ordained Rev. Deacon Kris Lethin, Shageluk; (middle left) the author eating her first roast beaver at the ordination potlatch, Shageluk; (bottom) from left, Jimmy Dementi, Victor Rock, and newly ordained Judith Lethin playing gospel music during communion, Shageluk; (top right) Bishop Mark MacDonald blessing the bell and naming him St. Michael the Archangel, Shageluk.

WHEN I WAS A YOUNG GIRL
THOSE MISSIONARIES COME AND
START TO TALK ABOUT OUR LORD. I
WONDER WHO SHOULD I BELIEVE,
THOSE PEOPLE OR MY MAMA WHO
ALWAYS TELL ME ABOUT DINAXITÓ.

—Ellen Savage, Holy Cross

16.

THE DOLL MAKER

Not long after our ordination to the Deaconate, Katherine came to stay with us for a potlatch at St. Mary's in Anchorage. She had become my ministry partner when I traveled in Anvik, Shageluk, and Grayling, and we were becoming fast friends. I picked her up at the airport and took her home to rest while I baked my halibut for the potlatch.

When we walked into the church hall, Katherine said, "That is my relative, Ellen Savage, from Holy Cross," nodding towards a tiny elder seated by the window. "She makes dolls."

"Dolls!" I blurted, feeling like a 7-year-old. "I love dolls. Introduce me to her."

Katherine placed the cardboard box of fry bread she'd brought from Shageluk on the table and made sign over it. I added my halibut, made sign, and followed her as she began to weave her way through the crowded room towards Ellen. I couldn't help noticing the line of people waiting to say hello to the sweet elder wearing a blue flowered parka.

"This is Judith—she's the church lady who comes to Shageluk to help us," Katherine said. "She likes dolls."

"You must come and see my dolls," said Ellen. "I like people like you to have my dolls—you know, people from the church."

"When can I come?"

"Tomorrow," she said, "And bring your tape recorder. I will tell you stories."

The next afternoon Ellen was waiting for me in her tiny cabin in Mountain View, a subdivision on the north edge of Anchorage. She took my hand and led me into her home. A lavender scarf printed with peach roses held back wisps of gray hair; her deep-purple, hooded parka trimmed with lavender and white rick rack winked tiny seed beads. As I followed her inside, I felt as if I were stepping back in time. Heaps of purple and blue fabric spilled over on the sofa. Letters and papers crowded among the jam pots and salt and pepper shakers on an oblong wooden table. An oil pot burner hummed against the south wall, and the distinctive odor of stove oil lingered. A piece of king salmon was thawing beside a pile of china plates on the counter below a low bank of cupboards in an alcove that held the stove, refrigerator, and sink. Through an open door beyond the table, I could see a brown wooden desk, its surface covered with fur scraps, beads, thread and a doll. I ached to enter Ellen's sewing room and pick up the doll.

I sighed deeply and melted into a chair at the table, feeling like I belonged there, just one of the jam pots. Ellen patted my shoulder and moved unhurriedly between the counter and where I sat, first with a china mug, then a Lipton's tea bag, then a small bowl of sugar. Each time she returned to the table, she paused, touched my shoulder and seemed to explore my face with her gaze. I sensed an intimacy that was deeply comforting and familiar. I felt my heart opening as I allowed her languorous eyes to search me out, for who knows what. Did she know all about me though I had uttered but a few words: *I love dolls, when can I come?* These sound like coded messages to me now, as I slip back into the memory of that day. Time stood still, and I became still, as I allowed an old woman to make me tea and reach deep inside me to touch a longing I had not remembered was there.

"Good, you brought your tape recorder," Ellen said. "In the old days before the preachers come in, the old peoples tell us how to live good. They're our preachers. My mama used to tell us a little bit every day. She tell us to 'sit down and don't move.' If we move, she tell us, 'the words I'm telling you will fall off of you and you wouldn't remember nothing.'" I smiled as I realized this story was for me: "sit down and don't move or my words will fall off of you." I sat still, with my hands wrapped around my tea cup and the hum of the tape recorder marking time.

"Whatever come to her, she tell us about how to live," Ellen continued. "And that's how I live right now, just like my mama said: Talk to Dinaxitó every day and that way he'll take good care of you."

"Dinaxitó is the name the Deg Hit'an people call God, isn't it?" I asked.

She nodded, "Dinaxitó created the world and everything in it, the water and trees and birds and the animals. He created everything with a piece of his spirit in it. It was a time when all the animals could talk, and the people could all talk and understand one another and the animals. It was a story time."

A story time when all the animals and people could talk together—it was like the Beatrix Potter story, "The Tailor of Gloucester," that I had often read to my children. I smiled and nodded. But I could see this was more than a fairy tale. It was an archetypal story that transcended culture and language. I wondered if we would ever find our way back to that time. I wondered what the animals would tell us if we listened. I wondered what Dinaxitó would say today.

"What did Dinaxitó teach the people?" I asked.

"A long time ago there was a man walking down a road," said Ellen. "He come to a place where the road goes this way and that way. He wonders which way he should go. He look down. He see a string-like thing that goes down one road. It is all dark, like. He look down the other road. He see a string-like thing that goes down that road, too, but this string is all light. He decide to follow that light-string way. He walk and walk. It take him all day. He get tired. Still he walk. Then he come up a hill right into the clouds and there he see an old man. The old man is very surprised to see him. 'Sitthey,' he tell him. 'Grandchild, how did you find me?' The first man tell him he follow the light-string way. 'Oné—come,' say the old man, 'and I will show you something.' The old man, he pull back the clouds and show the man all the peoples down below. The old man pick up one of those people and hold him in the palm of his hand. 'See this man. He don't do good. He don't share or follow the rules, or anything. This is what I do to him.' And the old man drops the people and he go down, down, down, into a very bad place. 'See this man,' and the old man picks up another people. 'He do everything just good. He share all he gets and he take care of everything and follows the rules good. This is what I do to him.' And the old man sets the people down very gently, and he goes on and have a good life."

Ellen reached out and patted my arm. I managed a smile, then nodded my head and wondered if I could ever follow the rules or measure up to that kind of generosity.

"My daddy was a good hunter," Ellen continued. "He always gets lots of fur and fish." As the tape recorder whirred and Ellen's stories filled all the empty spaces, I became acutely aware that the cup of tea and the scene I was intimately a part of were warming and comforting me in a way I didn't entirely understand, but I kept looking through the doorway into Ellen's sewing room; every part of me wanted to hold the doll that stood on her desk, held upright by a wooden armature of some sort, who seemed to say, "I belong to you."

"Then there'd be old peoples, old lady who has hardly anybody around her. My mama would give her fish or ducks or meat or whatever. During the fishing time, my mama get fish wheel and fish trap and she would cut fish and we'd have lots, so my daddy would go to the fish wheel or fish trap and bring that whole fish to those peoples who need it. This is how they do it. And when we're kids we'd go to school and we'd come home, and my mama would say, you eat something and after you eat you go over to that grandma and grandpa and pack water for them, bring in wood for them, whatever they need because they cannot do much because they're old. So we used to do that. We get water for them, pack water. We never look for pay, because I didn't know, I didn't know money, that's what we do. If we're going for berries, my mama she said, you go to that grandma and get her basket so that you pick berries for her. So that way we fill up her basket. And we give it to her when we come back. This is our life, she tells us. This is your life you're working for because the old peoples will be happy and they'll know that you going to live a good life. That's how they pay you back. And those old peoples, when we do that, they're so happy. They just tell us that you'll have a nice life. They said, 'Look at that big mountain back there. It never move, it just sit there year and year. You'll be strong like that mountain,' they tell us. It's like a wish they give us. All those things I learn."

My God, I thought, a mountain blessing. To be strong like that mountain, fearless, rooted to the earth, graceful in the face of the wind's fury or winter's brutality. Thank you, Dinaxitó. That's what I wanted for myself—the humble capacity to trust myself, sit here year after year, a quality of endurance, not moving, but knowing my place, my purpose. The only way there, according to Ellen, was radical generosity: radical generosity and becoming once again a village, with the young chopping wood, carrying water, catching fish for the old, and the old blessing the young. See that mountain, you will be strong like that mountain.

More than anything I wanted to be like that mountain, but there was a hidden part of me that needed dolls. Dolls comforted the part of me that had been silenced as a child, the one who wanted to cry but hid under the lilac or the forsythia instead; the 7-year-old who was just becoming aware of her body; the one who fought to stay innocent and playful and trusting, and childlike.

Finally, Ellen took me by the hand and led me into her sewing room. She picked up the few threads and tiny bits of fur on her sewing desk and dropped them into an ashtray filled with ash. She saw me looking at the ashtray, and said matter-of-factly, "We always burn our threads and scraps, that way we don't disrespect nothing."

Ellen picked up the doll dressed in her beaver parka with the wolf ruff, and the calf skin boots, and the deer skin mittens, trimmed with red and white seed beads and placed it gently into my outstretched hands. I closed my eyes and brought the doll to my heart. I thought of the stories Ellen had shared with me, *sit still and listen, or my words will just fall off of you,* and the deep relationship she and Katherine had, and I knew I had found my safe place.

Doll made by Ellen Savage; now part of the author's collection.

I CARRY HOLY WATER WITH ME
EVERYWHERE I GO. I HEARD NOISES
SO I CAME OUT TO BLESS THIS PLACE
SO WE CAN ALL SLEEP JUST GOOD...
I GOT LOTS. I MAKE IT MYSELF.

—Ellen Savage, Holy Cross

17.

GRANDMA'S MEDICINE

The steady thrum-thrum, thrum of the drum lured me up the stairs in the Anvik Tribal Hall. Ellen was drumming and Katherine was marking time on her knee with her hand. They sat on folding chairs near the window, a large cardboard box and suitcase full of dance regalia nearby. Agnes was still up at the school with the children. I was limping badly from a no-see-em bite that I'd gotten when mowing our lawn in Seldovia the day before. The bite had begun swelling before I left home and was now very painful. But I had promised to come and was hell-bent on keeping my promise.

Ellen saw me limping and sat me in a chair. I grimaced when she pulled my sandal and sock off. My ankle had ballooned to the size of a cantaloupe on the 631-mile trip from Seldovia to Homer, Homer to Anchorage, Anchorage to Aniak, and Aniak to Anvik—a journey on four different airplanes that included an overnight in Anchorage. My toes looked like red grapes and I was surprised how quickly the infection had spread. As I fought back tears, I grumbled something about my body letting me down. I wondered how close I was to having sepsis.

"You need some Indian plant," said Ellen. "Don't move. I'll help you."

Ellen came back with a handful of deep green, heart shaped leaves that I recognized as Plantain from my garden in Seldovia. She disappeared into a storage room and came back with a large aluminum soup pot and a long wooden spoon which she placed on the floor in front of me. She ran fresh water through the coffee pot to heat it, then poured the steaming water over the garbled leaves until the whole thing resembled mashed spinach. When the water had cooled just enough, she lifted my foot, gently slid it into the water, and wrapped the warm leaves around my swollen flesh. The heat from the warm water and the juice from the mashed leaves was at once soothing. The pain and itching started to subside immediately.

"Sit still, and soon you'll feel just good," she said.

Katherine watched the whole affair grinning, "Ellen's going to fix you up. Pretty soon you'll be dancing just like the kids." Katherine and Ellen made more comforting noises as they went out the door to get some lunch.

I gazed out the window into the dark forest. It was so quiet in the Tribal Hall, with only the fox sparrows and robins singing outside the window. I closed my eyes and wondered how on earth a cowgirl from the Snake River ended up on the Yukon? Would I be okay? Should I try to see the health aide at the clinic? Should I get on the next plane and find a doctor in Anchorage? Inertia and the sound of the birds singing in the trees took hold of me, and I began to breathe and relax into the chair.

❖ ❖ ❖

Anvik's traditional name in the Deg Xinag language is Deloy Ges, the village that sits under the brow of the hill. The Yukon River, flowing 2,300 miles from its headwaters in British Columbia, Canada past Anvik on its way to the Bering Sea, has carved a steep bank where it glides past the low hills that separate the Anvik River from the Yukon. The Yukon is a superhighway in both summer and winter for people living in the region. Spring can be a treacherous time for travelers when the river ice begins to melt. Ice can jam at Holy Cross, where the river takes a sharp turn west, and cause the silt-ladened water to back up into all the lowlands.

I heard a story about one of the Chase boys who found the Rev. Dr. Chapman's communion box from the 1880's floating in those spring flood waters and hid it away for fifty years until it finally made its way to the Anvik Museum; an ironic gesture from a people who were beginning to reclaim their cultural and spiritual ways after a hundred years of suppression by the Christian churches and the Bureau of Indian Affairs schools. At Spirit Days, trusted elders were taking their rightful place as teachers and tradition bearers for the children. I was honored and humbled to be invited with Katherine and Ellen and Ellen's daughter, Agnes Jackson.

Soon I heard Agnes's voice, and the children clamoring up the stairs. They saw me sitting there alone with my foot wrapped in mashed green leaves.

"Judith, Judith, Judith, you've come!" the children shouted.

I held out my foot for everyone to see and I noticed that the swelling had already begun to subside, and the itching had almost completely disappeared. Good grief, this stuff really works.

"Eww, what's all over your foot?" asked Reenie, pushing her way to the front of the group.

"This is an Indian plant from Grandma Ellen," I said.

"Why can't you just use real medicine?" asked Dittie, wrinkling her nose.

"Apparently this is real medicine." I said, laughing. "This is Indian Medicine."

Agnes called the children over to the large box of regalia, and began fitting them in their vitthigits'igh xelan, their hooded parkas, for the dance practice. The girls had ruffled skirts on their parkas and the boys were jacket-styled. The excitement was palpable.

When Katherine and Ellen came into the hall, Katherine handed me a napkin wrapped around smoked king salmon strips and Pilot Bread. I thanked her, and then, like a kid, held up my foot again for show-and-tell.

"See, I said pretty soon you'll be dancing," Katherine teased.

Ellen opened a suitcase and began passing out white gloves and dance fans. "Taller kids in the back," shouted Agnes over the noise, but they could hardly keep their feet still or their hands to themselves. Two of the taller boys in the back row looked as if they had just been handed dueling swords. They leaped into the air and squared off with each other, ready to do battle. Agnes gave them a firm look and pointed forward. They straightened their bodies just as Ellen began to play her drum and sing. Katherine and I sat beside Ellen, smiling and keeping time with our bodies.

When the teaching and festivities were over for the day, I cornered Agnes and asked if she could make hooded parkas for the children who served as acolytes at Christ Church. She was tickled by the idea and said she would look for fabric when she got back to Anchorage.

We were ready for a good night's sleep, so we packed our gear into the Tribal Hall's two guest rooms, off the big room where we had been dancing with the children. Ellen and Agnes took one room and Katherine and I took the other. Late that night I heard sounds coming from the big room. I crawled from my sleeping bag to investigate and found Ellen throwing water all over the hall. I must have looked startled because she announced, "Holy water."

"Holy water," I repeated.

"I carry holy water with me everywhere I go. I heard noises so I came out to bless this place so we can all sleep just good."

"That's a lot of holy water."

"It's okay. I got lots. I make it myself."

"You make it?"

"Yeah, a long time ago, when I lived in Holy Cross, I used to ask the priest to make me holy water all the time, but one day he says to me, Ellen, your prayers are just as good as mine, you can make this stuff yourself. So, from then on, I just say those prayers myself and I have all the holy water I need. I never have to ask him for it again."

I climbed back in my sleeping bag, delighting in Ellen's audacity. "I got lots. I make it myself."

Grandma Ellen Savage, Holy Cross, and Grandma Alta Jerue, Anvik.

Ellen Savage, left, the author, and Katherine Hamilton at the Tribal Hall in Anvik during Spirit Days.

Author with some of the children who were acolytes wearing their new hooded parkas made by Agnus Savage Jackson, Anvik.

ISAAC FISHER WAS THE INTERPRETER FOR THE ANVIK MISSION. HE DIED IN THE 1927 EPIDEMIC. THAT WAS A TERRIBLE TIME. ALL THE ELDERS DIED. NO BABIES OR YOUNG CHILDREN DIED, BUT ALL THE ELDERS WHO KNEW THE SONGS AND STORIES AND TRADITIONS DIED. THEY STOPPED HAVING THE MASKED DANCE AND FEASTS BECAUSE NOBODY KNEW WHAT TO DO OR HOW TO DO IT.

—Alta Jerue, Anvik

18.

DAPPLED LIGHT

I returned to Anvik in the spring of 2000, and Angela Young invited me to stay with her and her mother, Grandma Mary, in her new log cabin near the school. When I came into the cabin, I found Grandma Mary sitting in an overstuffed royal blue chair near the window, humming and gently rocking. With dappled light falling across her face and her pale green hooded parky and the hand crocheted blanket at her back, she looked for all the world like a painting by Claude Monet. Her hands were pressed together, as though she'd been praying. She looked up when I sat down beside her. I smiled and nodded hello and began to move my own generous body in time with hers.

"I want the children to know that Jesus was Mary's son," she whispered. Her words seemed to float on a numinous wind that moved in chorus through the trees and through the tiny cabin and through my heart just then. "She wants us to love him." I smiled and nodded yes, as she looked deeper into my eyes and appeared to see me for the first time.

"She wants us to love him, and follow him," she said more urgently.

Again, I nodded, and Grandma Mary smiled and her face broke into a million wrinkles, and the soft skin around her eyes crinkled, and her brows floated up, and she leaned toward me and gently took my hand. Willingly, I followed her into that unfathomable place where she knew the love of Jesus and his mother.

Grandma Mary was born during the 1918 influenza epidemic

to a young woman known as Diva Xidoy, a name that means '*who's that at my door*' in Deg Xinag. She was later called Julia by the white people who lived in Anvik. Diva Xidoy could not take care of Mary so she gave her baby to Clara and George Reed. The Reeds raised Mary up the Yukon River in a place known as Bonzilla until it was time for her to go to school, then they moved to Anvik so Mary could attend the Mission at Christ Church.

I felt humbled by Mary's devotion to Mary and Jesus. I was aware that before first contact with Christianity, the Deg Hit'an people had their own cultural and spiritual beliefs about Dinaxitó that were taught to the children by the elders and the shaman. After contact, the diseases brought by the explorers, missionaries, and gold miners killed over half of the Native population in Alaska, leaving many children orphaned. It was a time of great suffering. I wondered if she'd been spared the terrible effects of boarding school because she had been adopted.

When Katherine, my ministry partner from Shageluk, and I came back to Anvik a few months later, Grandma Mary was lying in a hand-made spruce box at home. She had fallen and broken her hip and died a few days later. Her extended family and friends had come to the village to help cook the traditional meals that would feed the village for the four days before the potlatch. Men and young men set to work building the spirit house and digging the grave. Women and young girls sewed the skin boots, and hat and gloves that she would wear on her final journey into the light. A steady stream of workers and visitors came to the cabin to eat and visit and speak well of Mary.

On the morning of the potlatch, the men brought Mary's body to the community hall. Marsha, Susan, Julie, and Melody gathered to help Angela dress her in her new clothes. Katherine and I were invited to help. I had participated in a number of funerals on the Yukon, and had been allowed to watch the dressing of Grandma Alma in Grayling, but this was the first time I'd been invited to participate in this sacred burial ritual of the Deg Hit'an.

We all gathered in a circle around Grandma Mary. The two

oldest elders, Marsha and Katherine, stood with Angela near her head, ready to give instructions and to see that everything was done according to the old traditions. Julie and Susan, Marsha's daughters, were on one side of the box and Melody, the health aide, and I were on the other. Julie was the head teacher at the school. She often invited me to sing or play games with the children when I was in the village. Susan had a store in the front room of her cabin on main street and sold chips, sodas, candy, and canned goods. It was my go-to stop when I needed chocolate. Melody had invited me to help her dissect a fetal pig once for her medical certification and we'd laughed late into the night. Everyone here had children who came to Sunday school and took turns being acolytes during the worship services at Christ Church. I felt a warm kinship with these women who had invited me into this sacred circle.

Julie looked at me and nodded, "Judith, take her pants off."

I looked up in disbelief. Sweat broke out on my forehead. My mouth went dry. The only time I'd actually touched a body was after it was dressed in its traveling clothes, and then only to shake the gloved hand so the person's strength could come into me. I wanted to cuss. I wanted to run. I scanned the circle. Everyone calmly waited for me to begin.

"Okay."

As I leaned into the handmade spruce box, I became aware of two remarkable things: the unforgettable scent of death, and how still the room had become. The first caused me to hesitate, but the second caused me to look up. Grandma Mary's face held such a quality of serenity that I was immediately transported back to the morning the sunlight dappled her face and she'd told me we were to love Jesus and follow him. Follow him? Yes. Wherever he leads us? Yes.

"Thank you," I whispered.

I took a deep breath, grabbed onto her navy-blue pant legs and began to pull. The polyester didn't budge. I pulled again. This time the waistband moved about two inches. I leaned deeper into the box, held my breath, and slipped my hands around the sides of her waist and began to pull back and forth, back and forth until the cold, wet pants slowly began to slip free. I dropped them into the black garbage bag that Melody was holding, stepped back, and gasped.

I wanted to run outside and gulp in fresh air. I wanted to wash the wetness from my hands. I wanted to shake off my shame for hesitating. I also wanted to shout, "I did it! I did it!" But I couldn't move. I was mesmerized by the tenderness with which the women began to prepare Mary's body for her new clothes. She was their mother, their auntie, their elder. They loved her.

The gentle, yet confident, actions of the women dressing Grandma Mary and the soft murmur of voices as they discussed the right way to fold the handkerchief and tie on the belt began to flow over me like a gentle wind or a beam of sunlight. My breathing deepened, my shoulders began to relax, and in that moment, I realized we belong to the things we love the same way the trees belong to the wind and the fox kits playing in the forest belong to the sunlight. The things we love inform us and dwell in us and make us who we are.

Where do love and belonging come from? Where does gentleness come from? Where does the wind—as it curls over the hills—come from? We do not know, but we do know the sound the wind makes as it stirs the trees, and the feel of it as it brushes past our cheeks, and its undulating dance with the spruce boughs dappling the light that lifts the veil from an old woman's face when she smiles and talks about Jesus.

When Grandma Mary looked into my eyes and said she wanted the children to know Mary and Jesus, I somehow knew Jesus in a new way, too, and I was filled with joy and wonder. In that revelation, I could see that her desire to teach the children was not born of the fear, which so many Christians harbor, that the children would somehow be "lost" if they didn't know Jesus. No, there was a serenity of spirit that seemed to say, *even if we don't know Jesus, Jesus knows us, and Jesus loves us, and invites us to follow him into the way of love.* And we know, in that very moment, that we belong to love just as the trees belong to the wind, and we welcome it and we gulp it in, hoping to hold onto that mystery when times get tough.

Grandma Mary didn't choose me or choose any of the women who served her in that sacred way, but her faith and her cultural traditions assured her that she would be dressed with love and respect for the potlatch and her final journey into the light. Marsha and Susan and Julie and Angela and Katherine and Melody had welcomed me into their circle of love, and we belonged to each other from that moment on.

At last, I found soap and water and washed my hands, but by then a kind of peace had begun to replace the shame. I knew I was called to be at Christ Church as the Deacon who would officiate at the Christian burial rite the following morning. But it was also my privilege to be invited to participate in one of the oldest Deg Hit'an Athabascan rituals—preparing the dead for their potlatch—and, in that, I was changed. I felt humble and more alive. My work felt more hallowed. I was rooted to that place, a spruce tree undulating in the wind.

The following morning at the Anvik cemetery I noticed the patchwork of paper birch and black spruce standing watch on the hill facing the Yukon River, and the wildflowers that graced the family plots clustered here and there, and the spirit houses marking the individual grave sites; some standing straight and tall with a new coat of paint even as others melted into the landscape from age and neglect. Tall grasses and wild roses and purple Siberian iris pushed this way and that, greeting Grandma Mary and the Deg Hit'an people with an elegant sagacity that seemed to say, *thank you for still being here, on this river, on this land, with your language and your culture and your traditions, old and new, showing us the way to love.*

Grandma Mary Williams in the cabin she shared with her daughter, Angela Young, Anvik.

DINAXITÓ CREATED THE WORLD
AND EVERYTHING IN IT, THE WATER
AND TREES AND BIRDS AND THE
ANIMALS. HE CREATED EVERYTHING
WITH A PIECE OF HIS SPIRIT IN IT.
IT WAS A TIME WHEN ALL THE ANIMALS
COULD TALK, AND THE PEOPLE COULD
ALL TALK AND UNDERSTAND ONE
ANOTHER AND THE ANIMALS.
IT WAS A STORY TIME.

—Ellen Savage, Holy Cross

19.

ROBINS AND RAINBOWS

When I arrived in Shageluk on that May morning in 2001, a morning when the geese were flying and the days were already eighteen hours long and the villagers should have been celebrating winter's end, the airline agent picked me up at the airstrip and didn't smile or shake my hand or say a word. Traveling on the Yukon and Innoko Rivers was often challenging, but this trip felt devastating. I was completely outside my comfort zone, just showing up and praying that Jesus meant what he said, *don't worry what to say, what to do, I will always be with you*. I loaded my duffle bag and guitar into the back of the agent's beat-up pickup and slid into the front seat. Half the dials on the dashboard were missing. Mud encrusted everything from years of negotiating the dirt roads.

The airstrip was five miles from the village on the only high ground, but the melting snow washboarded the road and made the distance seem like ten. The drive past the old village, abandoned in 1966 when high water in the lake threatened to submerge it, was always too quick; every time I passed, I felt a longing to stop and explore, even indulging in a fantasy of fixing up one of the cabins and staying a while. There was beauty there in the way the scrub willow and birch trees embraced the weathered gray timbers. A mossy greenness and a hushed stillness hovered over the place like the last remnants of a song, *ya-ya… ya-ya… hi-ya…* maybe from an old woman making ice cream for potlatch when the people there practiced the old ways, and remembered to whom they belonged.

On that drive I'd heard a lot of stories from the agents who met the planes to pick up the mail and the groceries and the passengers—stories about who was traveling, who had been flown out on a medical evacuation, what was going on at the school. The men who met the planes had lived in Shageluk most of their lives and knew the place like black bears know all the denning spots just below tree line. Shageluk was the kind of place that made the young people want to stay put; there was an easiness about expectations. If you wanted a job, there were always odd ones, and if you wanted to drink there was always a party somewhere.

Early that morning Jeanette had called from Shageluk.

"Leroy and Clifford. Drowned. In the slough that drains the lake into the river. Near the bridge," Jeanette said.

Clifford was Marlene and Glen's oldest son, and Leroy was Jeannie's only son, and Katherine's grandson. I sat down on the bed and held my breath as the story spilled out in a torrent of clipped sentences. As I pulled together the fragments, I began to see the horrifying truth. The cousins, fifteen and twelve years old, had gone hunting after school on the lake ice and hadn't come home. The whole village had gone looking for them. The men had found their footprints in the crusty snow out on the lake. The trail led straight to the slough and ended abruptly at the bank. There had been no sign of struggle, no skid marks to indicate the boys had slid into the water, but the foot prints ended there, on the edge, and, after the men prodded the muddy waters, they found the boys, holding each other, arms linked together, dead.

"Can you come?" she asked.

I fought to stay focused; it was too much information. Leroy and Clifford had been in Sunday school class at St. Luke's and were so full of energy. They were both fun loving, ready to tease, quick with a smile. They loved hunting and being outdoors. Clifford was particularly keen on science. Jeanette was crying, and I was struggling to understand what I'd just heard.

"Yes, of course I can come," I said. "I'll get a seat on the first flight."

I was scared and I knew it. I began to cry. In the two years I'd served Shageluk and nearby villages, I'd already buried over a dozen people, but this news felt especially devastating. Two young men had gone out on the lake ice to look for spring ducks and geese and fell into the only open water for miles around. It just didn't make sense. I pulled my duffle bag out of the closet and filled it with jeans and tee shirts. As I reached for my Prayer Book, I saw St. George, the yellow teddy bear I used when I led grief and loss workshops, sitting on the dresser. The children loved St. George, and trusted him with their deepest secrets. I stuffed him in with the Prayer Book. I nudged George's head up so I could look into his somber face. "Thanks buddy, I need you."

When I finished packing, I reached for the telephone and called the Hagelund Airlines ticket agent at Anchorage International Airport.

"Yes, I can get you to Aniak," said the ticket agent, "But I can't guarantee a seat to the Yukon."

"I'll take my chances. You heard what happened in Shageluk?"

"Ya, I'll get you there this morning if I can."

"Thanks."

I didn't have to say much, and neither did he.

I picked up my guitar and duffle bag and walked out the door. In my car the full dread began to settle onto my shoulders. I felt powerless. I wondered if I'd get to Shageluk before the State Troopers. They're quick to respond when they need to be. They usually take bodies to Anchorage for autopsy, leaving the village empty and silent like some abandoned nest in fall time after the geese have headed south. Waiting and thinking while the bodies are gone can drive a person crazy.

✦ ✦ ✦

In Shageluk, the agent and I rode along in silence. I stared out the window looking for who knows what, answers maybe. The frozen lake, beyond the slumping cabins at the old village, looked hostile in the flat light. Navigating the narrowing isthmus, I was reminded that all things change in time; all things are eroded by the river current; all things slump and melt back into the earth.

As we crossed the steel bridge over the slough and entered the village, something was different. There were no children playing in the melting slush, no old people walking to the store or the post office, no four-wheelers. Even the usual gaggle of puppies was absent. I'd never seen the village this empty. The agent pulled up to the Kashim, but I could see from the road that no one was there, so I asked him to take me to the Mission House. The Troopers had obviously beaten me to the village and had taken the bodies to Anchorage for autopsy.

I dropped my duffle bag at the Mission House, stopped at the church for a prayer, then walked to the cabin where Clifford's mom and dad, Marlene and Glen, and his two sisters and brother lived. When I got to the clearing near their cabin, I saw an elder from Grayling talking with Marlene outside near the porch. "There's nothing I can say to make you feel better," he said. "I know. People tried to tell me things when my son was killed. Nothing helped. I have no words, no words."

I knew this elder's son had been killed in a shooting several years before, but, my God, if this elder had no words, what could I possibly say that would be helpful? I wanted to make sense of this loss that seemed so unfair, so sad. I wanted to be a comfort to Marlene and the family. I wanted to be helpful, but all I felt was inadequate and unsure of myself. I took a step back, hoping the trees would hide me and give me time to think, but Marlene saw me standing in the trees and came forward. We hugged.

She turned to go back inside her cabin, then looked back at me and pulled me in with a simple tug of her head. I followed, and we sat for a long time in silence. Marlene's sisters from Kaltag were in the kitchen boiling macaroni for salad and putting together sandwiches for the noon meal at the Kashim. I could hear the voices of the younger children playing in the bedroom. The phone kept ringing, and someone would answer it and write down who had called, and thank them, and say they would pass the message on. Marlene's husband, Glen, and some of the men had gone out hunting for a potlatch moose. At last, I whispered, "Can you tell me what happened?"

She talked and I listened. There was very little new information about how or why the boys died. Their footsteps led off the lake ice and onto the bank of the small stream that flowed into the Innoko River. There were no scuffle marks or skid marks in the snow around the stream; the trail just ended, like they had stepped out into space and then couldn't get back out because the bank was steep and frozen; there was no place to get a hand hold. There was speculation that one fell in, and the other jumped in to save him, but we would never know for sure. She cried. I cried. Somehow the morning passed.

At last Marlene said, "They died together, and they'll stay together now. Everything must be done together; one potlatch, one service, one grave site."

✦ ✦ ✦

On the long, slow walk up the hill to the cabin where Leroy's mother, Jeannie, lived with her daughters, I had time to think and pray. I knew Katherine would be there and that gave me some measure of comfort although I knew this death would be particularly difficult for her. Leroy was her grandson—her own deceased son was Leroy's father. Katherine's son and husband had both committed suicide in separate incidents years before, and Katherine often told me how bad she still felt from that time.

There were layers of grief on the Yukon and Innoko Rivers— layers and layers of loss that seemed to thicken like the muddy silt deposited on the delta where the Yukon meets the sea. Layers of dark sticky mud can nourish a place with time, but too many floods, too often, leave a landscape unstable, and inhospitable. Complicated grief is like that, too. Traditions and rituals and family and friends can help us recover from loss, but if those losses keep piling up, one on top of another—accidents, suicides, murders—we can never finish our grief work.

The younger children ran to me when I walked in. They began to sob. I looked past the girls and saw Jeannie huddled in a jumble of quilts and blankets on the daybed that was shoved up against the wall on the far end of the big room. "Why? Why?" She kept pleading, begging for answers over and over again. Her voice was shrill and thin, like she'd been up all night crying and trying to make sense of this terrible loss. I moved towards her knowing I could not give her what she wanted. When she saw me, she cried out again, "Why? Why?"

I shook my head and looked at Katherine, who sat near Jeannie on a small chair. Katherine looked at me then back at Jeannie, but didn't say anything. I sat down on the edge of the day bed and began to straighten the covers and tuck them in around Jeannie, who was now sobbing.

On the table in front of Jeannie I recognized a tiny vial of holy oil. I felt a release of tension in my shoulders. On my first trip to Shageluk two years earlier, I'd noticed Katherine's sadness. I'd prayed for her and anointed her with holy oil. She was so pleased with the prayer I gave the holy oil to her and said maybe she could pray for the children. Half the oil was gone; Katherine had been praying.

At last Katherine said, "Everything has to be done together; the potlatch, the service, and burial. They died together and they will stay together."

These were the same words Marlene had spoken. This must be a teaching from the culture. I didn't know exactly what it meant, but I knew they knew.

The following day was Mother's Day, and the irony staggered me. Katherine and I walked to the Kashim. All we could do was wait to hear from the coroner. Finally, Katherine said, "Let's go visit Grandma Elizabeth."

❖ ❖ ❖

"Ade,'" said Katherine as she pushed open the door into Grandma Elizabeth's cabin on the hill behind the Mission House.

"Gogidet," Elizabeth answered, and then she said, "Gee, everything is just sad."

Katherine said something else in their language and sat down on the folding chair by the stove. I took the space on the small loveseat by Elizabeth. She kissed my cheek and took my hands and held them in her lap. Her tenderness towards me reminded me of my grandmother Pence who always fussed over me when I came to visit.

"I tell my own grandchildren to be careful, don't drink," she continued. "I wish it was like long ago, nothing happened."

"What do you mean, like long ago, nothing happened?" I asked.

"We don't see accidents," said Katherine. "Only when people get old do we see death. We grow up down river so we don't see nothing until my daddy died when I was fourteen."

Katherine and Elizabeth continued telling stories and I felt myself sinking deeper and deeper into the old sofa, safe in the care of these two old women who loved each other, and who loved me. They had both suffered terrible loss, and somehow, they had come away from their experiences stronger and wiser. I was hoping, really hoping, that some of that serenity would rub off on me.

Finally, it was time to leave. Grandma Elizabeth kissed me goodbye. Katherine and I headed out the door and down the narrow path through the trees to the main road. Katherine hugged me then turned up the hill to her cabin. I turned left and retraced my steps to the Mission House where Jimmy had moose ribs cooking in the Dutch oven for supper.

On Monday morning Katherine and I sat again in the Kashim and drank coffee, and waited. Leroy's uncle called from Anchorage; the bodies had been released, but there weren't any charter flights available until the following day.

Katherine's face crumbled. "No!" I shouted into the phone. "That can't happen. You have to bring those children home today. We can't wait any longer. Let me call my husband and see if he can fly them home."

I called Kris's cell phone. "What are you doing right now?"

"I'm at Merrill Field and I've just taken the cowling off the church plane so I can do its annual inspection." Kris was still flying for the Diocese and supervising the maintenance of the airplane.

I filled him in. In minutes the flight was arranged. He would bring the boys home.

Several hours later the Cessna 206 appeared over the mountains from the east and began circling the village. The sight of the familiar red and white church airplane with the cross painted on its tail galvanized the village. We sprang to life. We raced to the airport in everything that moved: pickups, cars, four-wheelers. As I rushed with them, tears began to stream down my face in some kind of unconscious exhaustion-relief response. Whether my tears were from the relief that we were finally *doing* something, or the relief of having my husband almost there, or the sudden release of all the grief of the entire village that I'd been holding for three days, or the deep, penetrating grief of being a mother of four sons myself and unconsciously identifying with Marlene and Jeannie, I didn't know. But I could not stop the tears.

The plane touched down and rolled to a stop just as the last of the villagers pulled into a knot at the edge of the runway. When the cargo door opened and we saw the yellow body bags, the wail that erupted from the community was immediate and primal. All that grief let loose and spilled onto the runway like an ice jam exploding on the Yukon River.

The wailing gave way to soft weeping, and the women moved away from the cargo doors and the men reached forward and gently picked up the body bags and loaded the boys into the back of a pickup truck for the ride home. The return trip was slow, as though a great tenderness and heaviness had fallen over all of us. The driver negotiated the bumps with the greatest of care; we had precious cargo here. And we were in no hurry to reach our destination. As we drove into the village, a lone dog chained to a tree, tail drooping, watched silently. He knew, I think. Yes, even he knew.

We pulled up in front of the Kashim and the boys were carried in by uncles and cousins and fathers and placed in the corner, facing east. The door was gently closed. The women must not intrude. Opening the body bags and dressing the boys was men's work.

The next four days flew by, filled with preparations for the potlatch and funeral. The men were busy digging the grave and building the coffins and making the fence and roof of the spirit house to be placed over the grave. The women were busy sewing skin boots and hats and gloves and cooking three huge meals a day to feed the village and all who came from neighboring villages to pay their respects or help.

The evening of the potlatch finally arrived. I had spent the day coordinating funeral details with the families: favorite gospel songs, Bible lessons, readers. At the Mission House Jeanette made several batches of bumpy golden fry bread and Jimmy grilled a platter of king salmon steaks. "People are gathering," I announced. Jeanette, Jimmy, and I picked up the food offerings and headed to the Kashim. A large crowd had gathered outside the door, arms loaded with fish and salad and Indian ice cream, waiting for the family to arrive. Nobody complained about waiting. Everyone held a bowl or a platter or a cardboard box full of food.

Several trucks and four-wheelers pulled up from opposite ends of the village. The crowd opened up and the young men stepped forward and helped bring in the boxes and boxes of gifts and food from the immediate families. The families entered first and then everyone else followed.

Every chair and bench that could be found in the village had been arranged in a semicircle around the perimeter of the Kashim. By the time I entered with some of Jeanette's fry bread and made sign, the floor in the center of the Kashim was covered with boxes and bowls and enormous pans of moose and fish and fry bread and Indian ice cream. Once the offerings of food were blessed, family members got Clifford and Leroy's plates from the placemats and filled them with morsels of food from every bowl, box, and platter. The potlatch foods, like Indian ice cream, smoked salmon strips, moose liver, fry bread, Pilot Bread, cup cakes, cookies, and candies, were selected for the giveaway, and the pots of soup, stews, casseroles, and salads were placed on two long tables for the supper that would take place after the potlatch food and gifts were given out.

After that, the night was a blur of sitting still and letting the young men serve us. Even the children sat still, and accepted everything given to them. Somewhere in the belly of the potlatch is a haunting dream of feeding the relatives who have already died. Even the old woman up the hill, who has no children, knows her life has meaning if the children and young men and women remember how to dress her and feed her with this spiritual food when her time comes to journey into the light.

After every last glove and knife and skein of yarn was given away, after every box of Pilot Bread, every blanket and beaded key chain and dream catcher was passed out, everyone quietly got up to take their potlatch food and gifts home. Then we all came back for supper.

Early the next morning I headed to the Kashim to set up the altar for the service. The men were moving chairs out the door and into the back of a pickup truck.

"Too many people, so we're moving the funeral to the school," said Arnold when he saw me looking confused.

"Oh. Oh dear, there must be prayers for this sort of thing," I mumbled under my breath.

Uncertain about church protocols for moving bodies, I must have translated my concern to Arnold. He turned and growled, "Judith, we know what we're doing."

"Wait," I shouted as I ran after him, "You don't understand. I don't know what I'm doing."

He looked back then, with a half-smile, and grunted.

When the young men picked up the coffins, I ran back inside to grab my prayer book and then followed the procession up the hill to the school, praying, "In the midst of life we are in death, from whom can we seek help? From you alone, O Lord..." In the midst of death, God comes disguised as life: as candle holders and red beaded altar hangings made by the great grandmothers, and as men, gruff from drink, and as young children who've lost their brothers, and as grandmothers who show up again, and again, and again to cook and sew and pray. God comes in a *stranger's guise*, and even when I am estranged from myself, God comes. I stumbled along and said the words that I longed to hear myself, "Lord, you know the secrets of our hearts; shut not your ears to our prayers, but spare us, O Lord."

The school bleachers filled up, and all the chairs and benches on the gym floor filled up, and at last I began to sing the opening anthem, "I am Resurrection and I am Life, says the Lord. Whoever has faith in me shall have life, even though he die. And everyone who has life, and has committed himself to me in faith, shall not die forever."

The songs and the prayers and the lessons the families had chosen were a revelation of comfort and eternal things and wisdom beyond our understanding. I looked around the gymnasium and knew that every person there had lost someone through some kind of accident or premature death. They had buried sons who had committed suicide, and mothers who had died of alcohol poisoning, and an auntie who had jumped out of a boat on the Innoko River in front of them and drowned. One man had just come home from burying his father in Michigan. No one was spared. The elder from Grayling was right, words are not enough to take away this pain.

"There's not one person in this place who has not suffered loss," I began my homily. "I overheard an elder from Grayling telling Clifford's mother this week, 'There are no words, no words that can make you feel better or take this loss from you.'

"I've thought about this all week. I've watched and listened and finally, just now, realized that we may not have words but we have something more powerful here on the Yukon and Innoko Rivers, something more lasting than words that can be said and forgotten in a day or a week. I watched the men measuring and cutting and hammering the coffins and the spirit houses. I saw the young men coming in tired and dirty from digging the graves. That sawing and hammering and digging is a whole page of words.

"I watched the women cooking and feeding everyone who came to the Kashim. I sat with them while they sewed the boots and the hats and the gloves. That cooking and feeding and sewing is a whole chapter of words.

"And those of you who have come and brought fish and gifts and meat and sat and told your own stories, those gifts and those stories are a whole book of words.

"We may have no words, but our very actions are our words. No, there are no words. There are no words, but our deeds speak a whole library of words. Our deeds and our presence and our generosity and our kindness and our compassion and our willingness to tell our own stories to Leroy's and Clifford's families in their time of need somehow takes away some of our own suffering."

I looked over and saw Marlene and Jeannie and the younger children crying. Glen was staring straight ahead, and I wondered if he was trying to be strong for everyone else or was so devastated, he was numb. I remembered the night we had received the whole family into the church. Marlene had been raised Roman Catholic, and had had the children baptized in Kaltag. When I started coming to Shageluk, she decided to join the Episcopal Church so the whole family could take communion together.

"By your presence, Marlene and Glen and Jeannie and their children see what it's like to go on with life even in the depths of despair. By your presence, your own grief and suffering will, somehow, be relieved and made lighter. By your digging and hammering and sewing your own hearts will be comforted, your burdens lifted."

The river channel opened. One by one friends and neighbors got up and told a story about their own loss and the remarkable generosity of others. At last, we sang the final hymn. The oldest elder called everyone to crowd in, and at the count of three everyone made the traditional stomp to send the spirits of the boys on their journey into the light. The men got up to screw the tops on the coffins; then they carried the coffins to the pickup trucks, and the trek to the cemetery began.

It was early evening when we finished our work on the hill overlooking the Innoko River—every word, every prayer, every story finished. Silence filled the spaces between us as we filed down the narrow ridge to the Kashim. Gravity moved us forward even as exhaustion pulled us back.

"Judith, Judith," called the health aide, Betty, as she caught up with me on the steep slope. "Would you bless the clinic before you go? Everything sad happens there, and I can hardly go to work anymore."

Our eyes met, and I reached out and touched her arm. Nodding yes I said, "Later, okay?" I was exhausted, and besides, in the Episcopal tradition, deacons aren't allowed to do blessings. Blessings are the privilege of the priest or bishop. This created a real dilemma for me. If I blessed the clinic, I'd be breaking the rules. If I didn't bless the clinic, I'd be abandoning my pastoral responsibility. The people were really suffering, and there wouldn't be a priest or bishop showing up for months or maybe a year.

I had to think this through. Whatever I did, I would have to be able to defend my decision. I didn't want to be arrogant, but I did want to be sensitive to Betty and her grief. My feet slid on the loose stones as I looked away, too tired to say more. I was ready to be alone, ready to sit in the silence and let the images and words of the day, and this new dilemma, sort themselves out.

I stumbled into the Mission House, stopped for a cool glass of water from the fifty-five-gallon drum that Jimmy used when he gathered ice from the Innoko River, and slowly climbed the stairs. I fell into my sleeping bag, too worn out to eat. Voices and banging doors nearly woke me several times, but I was logy and didn't roust myself until after 11:00 p.m.

When I finally came downstairs, Jeanette was still up, playing a game on her laptop in the blue recliner in front of the wood stove. I told her where I was going, got a bowl from the cupboard and a jar of ice melt, and then I slipped out so I wouldn't wake Jimmy. I stopped on the trail between the Mission House and the church and searched for the perfect spruce bough to use for blessing. I spotted an eight-inch branch, smiled, thanked the tree for its offering, then gently broke it off at the trunk. The smell of fresh pitch revived my spirits. When I passed the clinic, I cached my bowl, water, spruce bough, and Prayer Book on a bench near the door, then headed up the road to tell the people at the Kashim who were playing bingo what Betty had asked me to do.

I had arrived early. The bingo game wouldn't break for supper until midnight. As I looked around the room at all the people, I marveled at their stamina. Bingo is the main way the villages raise money to support the families of the deceased, who must pay for all the plywood, paint, food, potlatch gifts, and travel for the families coming from Anchorage. I stepped outside, and the children playing on the slide and merry-go-round at the school saw me and waved. I headed to the schoolyard to wait.

Clifford's little sister, Glenna, flew down the slide and ran into my outstretched arms shouting, "Judith, Judith, quick, fall down on your knees and pray and listen for God's voice."

I pried her arms loose and stepped back enough so I could look into her eyes. She had recently been crying. Oh, God, out of the mouths of babes. I knew I must do what she asked. Very softly I said, "What do you hope I will hear God say?"

By this time all the children had crowded in close. "Find out if my brother and Leroy are okay," she said.

"Okay, everyone hold hands and help me listen."

I closed my eyes and cried out, "Dinaxitó, you know how sad we are, and how much we miss Leroy and Clifford. Please, please show us that they are okay—that they are with you and that they are safe and cared for and surrounded by all our relations, especially the grandmas and grandpas and aunties and uncles who have gone into the light before them."

I opened my eyes and let out a yelp. There, in the twilight of a near midnight sun, was the most enormous rainbow I had ever seen. It stretched from Shageluk Lake to the trail behind the village that led up to the cemetery. It was a full and complete rainbow—red, orange, yellow, green, blue, indigo, and violet. It wasn't there before I'd shut my eyes. The children saw it, too, and began to jump up and down. Just then a robin flew through the children's legs and up between Glenna and my encircled arms and over my right shoulder. All the children saw the robin and began to shout, "A robin, a rainbow, a robin, a rainbow!"

I stood motionless. Dinaxitó had delivered, big time. In this place where the people had been reading the signs of Dinaxitó through creation for thousands of years, Dinaxitó had answered our prayer with a robin and a rainbow. Earlier in the week two young black bear cubs had been seen playing on the lake ice and the elders had read that as a sign that the boys were safe in Dinaxitó's care. Now the children had their own sign—a robin and a rainbow.

As quickly as the children had gathered, they went back to the slide and the merry-go-round. I stood in the schoolyard a few more minutes and let the words and melody of a favorite old gospel hymn spill over me. "Precious memories, unseen angels, sent from somewhere to my soul. How they linger, ever near me, and the sacred past unfolds." Over and over, I whispered "Thank you, thank you, thank you, dear God, for your faithfulness."

I walked into the Kashim just as the last bingo game finished. No one moved or looked up. I sensed exhaustion in the slumped shoulders and the down-turned faces. People were there, but their minds and hearts seemed a million miles away.

"Betty asked me to bless the clinic," I blurted out. "She said everything sad happens there, and she's having a hard time going to work. Anyone who would like to help me is welcome."

I turned toward the door, not wanting to embarrass anyone who didn't want to come and expecting that they'd all rather not come. Betty was right, everything sad did happen there. As I reached for the door handle, I was body slammed by a thunderous rumble of chairs being shoved back; a clattering crash as they toppled over; a shuffling and stumbling of feet as the inert mass staggered towards the door.

The hair stood up on the back of my neck. Without looking back, I moved out the door and down the road towards the clinic with the roar still in my ears, and what felt like a mob on my heels.

At the clinic porch I finally turned and saw a crowd of 50 or 60 adults, pressed together, watching, waiting, their feet nervously scouring the stones on the muddy road. I still didn't know how I was going to solve the problem of not having permission or authority to bless the clinic. I didn't see Betty, but I saw two elders, my friend and companion Katherine and Raymond, Betty's dad, on the edge of the crowd, and I knew God had delivered them into my hands. I smiled and motioned them forward. "I need help."

Katherine nodded and moved towards me.

"I'll do it," said Raymond as he followed Katherine through the crowd.

I handed Katherine the stainless-steel bowl and Raymond the spruce bough. I lifted the Mason jar high and slowly began to pour the icy water into the bowl as I began to intone the blessing over the water from the Rite of Holy Baptism, which I did have the authority to do. The sound of the water splashing into the bowl brought us into stillness. Even the feet shuffling stopped. It was the sound of water just breaking loose from its winter place high in the mountains, like the laughter of water as it trickles past the red berries and the blueberries and the bog orchard, on its way to the sea, and we were drawn into the mystery of it, almost against our wills, almost as if the clarity of the sound awakened some deep memory in all of us. I looked up; a sea of earnest faces peered over and around one another's shoulders into the bowl. After what seemed like an interminable moment, we took, together, what felt like the first really deep breath of the day, or maybe even since this whole heartbreaking story had begun nearly a week earlier.

After blessing the water, I began to sing the ancient hymn, Trisagion, and motioned the gathering to follow me. "Holy God, Holy and Mighty, Holy Immortal One, Have Mercy Upon Us." Katherine held the bowl high and Raymond began to splash holy water with his spruce bough into every corner of the clinic with such fierceness and passion I felt a renewed surge of energy enter my feet and begin to move up my body. My voice became stronger and then I realized everyone else had begun to sing the Trisagion with me. "Holy God, Holy and Mighty, Holy Immortal One, Have Mercy Upon Us."

In front of the examination table, Katherine began to make an enormous gesture with her right hand. I had no idea what she was doing but whatever it was she was certainly doing it with all her old woman's power. My God, she was making the sign of the cross, and it was nearly as tall as she was and as wide as the chasm that engulfed this sorrow-filled place. Everyone began to sing louder. "Holy God, Holy and Mighty, Holy Immortal One, Have Mercy Upon Us."

Finally, when every corner and closet of the clinic was soaked with holy water and prayer and song, we spilled out onto the road and began circling the clinic. The children, still playing in the school yard, heard the commotion and shot down the hill on their bicycles to see what was going on. They joined the procession, first following, then circling, then leading. The five puppies from under the cabin next door heard the ruckus and staggered out of their warm nest and joined the procession, arfing and nipping pant legs as they dodged in and out. The once solemn gathering now felt like a rollicking Easter parade.

When we arrived back at the clinic's front porch, the singing subsided, but the children and puppies keep circling the gathering. I smiled. Everyone smiled. Suddenly Clifford's uncle pushed his way to the front and shouted, "Bless *me!*"

Raymond plunged the spruce bough into the bowl and shot a great dollop of holy water at the uncle and hit him right smack in the face. Both men yelped in delight. So did the crowd. I laughed out loud and shouted, "Alleluia!"

I looked into the uncle's enormous red-rimmed eyes and saw all the hurt and loss of a lifetime, especially of this week burying his nephew, begin to drain away. It was replaced by a deep, deep peace. A peace, it seemed to me, that comes from roots that plunge fearlessly into this damnable river clay—this silty, storm ravished, flooding-over place—then deeper still, until they hit bedrock, the bedrock of Athabascan culture, and language, and traditions. Traditions that have fed this place and these people for thousands of years, now mixed with Christian traditions that were beginning to understand and respect what had always been.

"Bless me," shouted a visitor from Holy Cross. "And me," shouted a child from Grayling. "And me, and me, and me…"

And then the water really began to fly, and laughter and joy and wonder filled the night and all the darkness that had followed me all week fled the hidden places of my heart and I breathed again, and came home to myself again, and to my place in this family and this village, once again. The blessing completed, little knots of laughing, smiling people wandered back to the Kashim for midnight supper, and I stood alone.

I had wrestled with Betty's request and my own dilemma as deacon and the rules about blessing, and I had chosen to act, not knowing what the outcome would be. God had delivered two elders to bless the clinic and the people. It felt like a moment of humility, both for me and for the church, and a triumph for the cultural ways of the people and the spiritual leadership of the elders. I knew I belonged here, as a teacher and a singer and a grandmother, but the elders were the wisdom keepers, and culture bearers, and spiritual leaders of the people. The elders and the people knew what they needed, and they had reached deep within themselves to meet those needs. I needed only to pray and sing, and then get out of the way and let it happen.

I whispered over and over, "Thank you, thank you, thank you, Dinaxitó for blessing us in this place." As I climbed the stairs to the Mission House, I hummed the chorus that had come to me in the school yard. "*In the stillness of the midnight, precious sacred scenes unfold…*" It was after midnight. A lone robin nesting in the woods sang out her glad reply.

Young people gathered at St. Luke's for Confirmation, Shageluk.

St. Luke's church with its new bell tower. Notice the author's guitar with her two traveling companions, St. George the Dragon Slayer, and Christmas Bear waiting patiently!

WHEN I WAS YOUNGER,
I REMEMBER GOING TO THE KASHIM,
WHERE EVERYBODY GATHERED
TO HAVE POTLATCHES. WHAT I
UNDERSTOOD WAS EVERYONE WAS
GIVING THANKS FOR WHAT WE GOT
HERE ON EARTH THAT DINAXITÓ
GAVE US. GIVING POTLATCHES, AND
ALL THAT GOOD STUFF THAT THEY
DID A LONG TIME AGO, WAS HOW
THEY ALWAYS GAVE THANKS FOR
EVERYTHING THEY WOULD GET.

—Martina John, Shageluk

20.
THE FBI

Early that fall I was back in Shageluk. "It's Judith!" I shouted as I pushed the door of the Mission House open with my shoulder and stepped into the cozy room. Jimmy Dementi was sitting in his favorite royal blue recliner facing the wood stove and the door and a huge picture window that looked down the trail to the church and the main road that wound through the village. He'd seen me coming and he was ready, holding his mug of coffee and looking solemn.

"The FBI is looking for you."

"FBI? You mean my husband?" I responded, and then we both began to laugh.

This had become our private joke. When Kris started looking for me, he was relentless. He'd call Henry Deacon in Grayling and Jimmy in Shageluk and soon the CB radios were crackling with, "Anybody seen Judith?" I was pretty darned hard to keep track of. The ironic double meaning of "FBI" wasn't lost on me either: Federal Bureau of Investigation and Full Blooded Indian.

The Old Mission House, built when the village moved to higher ground years before, had become my home away from home. The two-story log building had a great room that served as kitchen, dining room, and living room. There was a bedroom, water closet for the honey bucket, and pantry off to the right and a stairwell and small office on the left. The stairwell led to five bedrooms upstairs—enough room for a small army of vacation bible school teachers or visiting family or friends from neighboring villages who came to town for potlatch or spirit days or elders' meetings. I put my duffle bag, sleeping bag, and guitar at the foot of the stairs. I had stayed with Jimmy and Jeanette so often that I had my own designated bedroom upstairs.

Jeanette was still at the school, so I settled into her matching blue recliner with a cup of Jimmy's coffee. The coffee, the smell of something wonderful coming from the Dutch oven on the stove, and the soft old chair were comforting and familiar. I felt safe here. I knew I'd be cared for, cooked for, and looked for if I wandered too far off the trail. Jimmy and Kris shared another wonderful trait, they were men of few words. As Jimmy held tenderly the silence, I closed my eyes and rested.

Jeanette, whom Jimmy married after his first wife, Jean, died in 1988, came in the door from school. I finished my coffee and got up to help with dinner. Jeanette made a salad and I put the plates and silverware out. Jimmy took the lid off the Dutch oven and placed the heavy pot in the middle of the old Formica table on a pot holder. *Yes! Moose ribs, my favorite.* The ribs were so tender they fell off the bone. I declared they were the best darn ribs I had ever eaten. Jimmy rewarded me with a story.

"A couple of white guys fly out here every fall to hunt moose," he said. "I take them up the Innoko River. They take the steaks and roasts and back strap, and leave me the ribs and bones. One year when they showed up, I had a Dutch oven full of ribs on the stove. They sat down to eat with me. They never leave the ribs again," he said, and grinned.

The next evening was the funeral potlatch for a young man who had died, and the following morning was the funeral service. I was working for Southcentral Foundation in Anchorage and only had the weekend available to fly out, officiate the funeral, and then fly home so I said to Jimmy, "I need to catch the afternoon flight to Aniak."

"The burial is at the old gravesite across the river. I'll bring you back across at the airport so you can catch your airplane," he said.

"Thanks."

I followed the family down to the river bank. The men carried the coffin and loaded it in one of the waiting boats. The spirit house and fence were already loaded in another boat. I walked along with Jimmy and climbed into his boat with Jeanette, Katherine, and several others.

Jimmy started the motor and the boat glided out into the current from the bank for the short trip across the Innoko to the slough and the old cemetery. The birch trees were golden and the fireweed a burnt crimson topped with wisps of seed cotton. The grasses were shades of yellow, brassy gold, amber, and rust. The highbush cranberries were a deep red and pungent. The penetrating smell filled the forest with the expectation of death and endings and a kind of urgency to get the berries picked and the fish smoked and the meat hung in the shed for winter.

After the family and I said the final prayers and as family and friends began to throw handfuls of dirt onto the homemade casket, Jimmy motioned me *it's time to go*. We left the villagers eating smoked salmon strips and Pilot Bread and shoveling the dirt into the grave as we made our way down the sandy bank of the slough to the boat.

We didn't talk. We didn't need to. I was tired and ready to go home. When we landed the boat near the road that led to the airport, I put on my backpack and threw my duffle bag on the bank and then climbed out, balancing my guitar on the side of the boat. Jimmy got out with me.

"Oh, you don't have to walk with me."

He didn't say a word, just took the guitar out of my hand and picked up the duffle bag and started walking.

"I know the way. The airstrip is just down this road."

He nodded and kept walking. I protested several more times before I realized it was useless and shut up. We walked along in silence for a few minutes, then I saw something unusual in the soft mud on the side of the road. I looked closer and the hair stood up on the back of my neck. Grizzly bear tracks at least twelve inches long from toenail to pad were meandering in the same direction we were going. I looked at Jimmy. He looked at me. No smiles now. I looked over both shoulders, then inched closer to him. I tried to walk softly, maybe even on tippy-toes, but every step sounded like cattle stampeding down the mesa.

I kept peering ahead, fully expecting the bear to double back, ready for an easy lunch. I tried to remember what to do when you meet a grizzly bear in the forest, but for the life of me I couldn't. My mind went blank. I was barely breathing. As I gasped for air my mind began to work; I remembered a newspaper story about the woman eaten alive by black bears at Lake Louise. This was not helpful.

The airplane at the end of the airstrip came into view. The grizzly bear tracks meandered off into the forest and I began to breathe deeply again.

"Thank you," I mouthed silently when Jimmy looked at me again.

He nodded his head, and this time he grinned. Good thing the FBI is looking out for me.

The old two-story log Mission House at the end of a tree lined trail, in Shageluk, as viewed from the church.

Jeanette and Jim Dementi preparing supper in the mission house, Shageluk.

THERE'S NOTHING I CAN SAY
TO MAKE YOU FEEL BETTER. I KNOW.
PEOPLE TRIED TO TELL ME THINGS
WHEN MY SON WAS KILLED.
NOTHING HELPED. THERE ARE
NO WORDS, NO WORDS.

—Herman Deacon Sr., Grayling

21.

I ADOPT YOU

Katherine and I didn't speak. The smell of death was all around us. A late September rain had pummeled the crimson and yellow leaves of the high bush cranberry and birch trees, and the pungent odor filled all the spaces where words would have been on any other day. My oldest sister, Pat, had died five days earlier, on the Feast of St. Michael and All Angels, and Katherine had come to Anchorage to be with me, as is the custom of her people. She stood with me now in the parking lot of Meier Lake Conference Center, helping me load the last remaining dishes and icons from the funeral and reception.

Two days before her death, Pat said, "What do you think? Do we keep praying to our Lord? What good is it to pray? Is anything happening?" As she turned to face the wall at Providence Hospital, she whispered, "Oh, why does life have to be like this?"

Sitting beside her in the darkened room, I thought about her questions.

"I don't know why life has to be so hard. Life is hard. We pray because prayer opens us to God's love and peace. God doesn't want us to be sick or in pain. Prayer gives us the strength and grace to endure whatever life brings to us."

✦ ✦ ✦

Now, remembering Pat's words and my response, I was filled with a kind of drunken nostalgia and a jumble of feelings and conflicting stories told about my sister—that spunky girl, orphaned at six, who learned to be tough to survive; that disobedient ten year old who galloped old Whittle-de-dig across the Bruneau desert only to have him stumble in a gopher hole and go end over end with her flying over his head, and then jumping up, dusting herself off and climbing back on; that belligerent teenager who insisted on playing football in high school with the boys just to prove that Bruneau cowgirls were tougher than Homedale farm boys.

Stories of Pat's toughness collided with stories of her vulnerability in my thoughts as I tucked a Pendleton blanket around the china cups and saucers in the trunk of my VW Beetle. It's why our relationship was so complicated.

"Who will take care of me?" Pat had wailed the day she packed up the old Chevy for her last year of college at the University of Idaho in Moscow. The year was 1949.

"Do you want people to think you're weak?" our mother had answered.

I was five years old. Pat was twenty-one. I jumped up from my favorite place under the old cottonwood tree in our front yard and shouted, "I'll take care of you."

I'd been trying to take care of her for over fifty years.

Just a month before Pat died, I'd come over to make her a pot of soup and to wash her dishes. I was crying quietly as I stood in the darkened kitchen remembering how beautiful she was that day she stood in the front yard arguing with our mother. Her golden blonde hair waved into a long page boy. She was wearing trousers, all the rage since the war, and holding her suitcase in one hand and a box of Hershey Bars from the theater in the other. When I promised to take care of her that day, she smiled, then opened the box of Hershey Bars and gave me one with the assurance, "Hey kid, I'll write to you."

A strange noise interrupted my thoughts, and I rushed into the living room to find Pat slumped over in her wheelchair crying.

"What is it, sister?" I asked as I wrapped my arms around her.

"I never thought I wouldn't be able to take care of myself."

❖ ❖ ❖

A gust of wind sent the last few yellow birch leaves skittering across the parking lot in wild pursuit of place. I took the Wedgwood teapot from Katherine and placed it beside the china cups and saucers.

The rustle of the leaves and the pungent smells from the forest signaled for me the great looping circle of life, death, decay, then new life. Fall is the time in Alaska when women in hooded parkas bend over their favorite berry patch, gathering the blue and red berries that will go into their Indian ice cream served at potlatch. It's a time when a late run of salmon may still be hanging in the smoke house, traditional food served at every important occasion, evidence of the continuity of cultural traditions from long ago. Shouting and laughter can be heard over the buzzing of the chainsaw, as strong boys and men cut and prepare the logs that will be brought in by snowmachine and sled after the first good snowfall. Even the bears are in a frenzy of eating before they seek out a den for a long sleep. "It won't be long now," old-timers say, meaning the darkness and the snow and, of course, winter.

Everyone is a part of that circle, and if we're lucky or wise, we prepare for our own death with a certain grace and nimbleness of spirit. Sometimes we don't see that until very near the end.

The night before Pat died, she lapsed into a semiconscious state and began to mumble *ishouldabeenawegman… ishouldabeenawegman…* I leaned in close and slowed the words down so that I could understand what she was saying. Oh god, there it was—*I should have been a Wegman.*

"Do you mean you wish Dad had adopted you?" I asked.

"Yes," she whispered. "I should have been a Wegman."

Some of us bear our secrets for a lifetime, and when it's nearly too late, they slip out and reveal what was hidden there all along. Try as we might to live life on our own terms, we rarely get the chance. Life has a way of intruding, with all its messiness, causing us to project onto others strengths and weaknesses that are really our own.

Pat and I had been in a power struggle our whole lives. Pat was the eldest, and bossy. I was the playful one. I wanted to run off with my guitar and sing and pray and wear hats and shawls. She was quick to tell me I should stay home and take care of my husband and children. She thought *she* had to take care of *me*. I fought against that every chance I got, for I also had an overdeveloped sense of destiny and responsibility. I was the one who, at five years of age, decided that I was going to take care of my big sister. Now, sitting in the darkened hospital room, I could finally see the wound that she had carried for a lifetime, and all the old competitiveness evaporated. What remained was a deep sadness for us both.

Katherine handed me the icon of Mary and Jesus that I'd hung over Pat's hospital bed, and had brought to hang over the cremains at the funeral.

"Dogidinh," I said in Katherine's language. "Thank you."

I smiled. How beautifully Katherine's blue shirt matched the forget-me-not hue of the sky, and the wings of the *Celastrina argiolus* butterflies that circled my teapot. I took a deep breath and searched that wildflower sky for any signs of the red balloons our grandchildren had released at the end of the service. Pat loved forget-me-nots; Katherine loved blue. I loved blue and yellow winged butterflies and red balloons and children. Everything was going to be alright.

"Who's going to boss me around now that my sister's gone?" I teased.

Katherine looked at me and grinned. Her shoulders began to shake. Her bronze cheeks collided with the corner of her eyes, and those eyes—like half-moons lying on their bellies—skipped and sparked. Then she began to laugh out loud, and like a merry contagion, I crumpled forward into her arms and began to laugh with her. She put her hands on my shoulders and pushed me upright.

"I adopt you," she said.

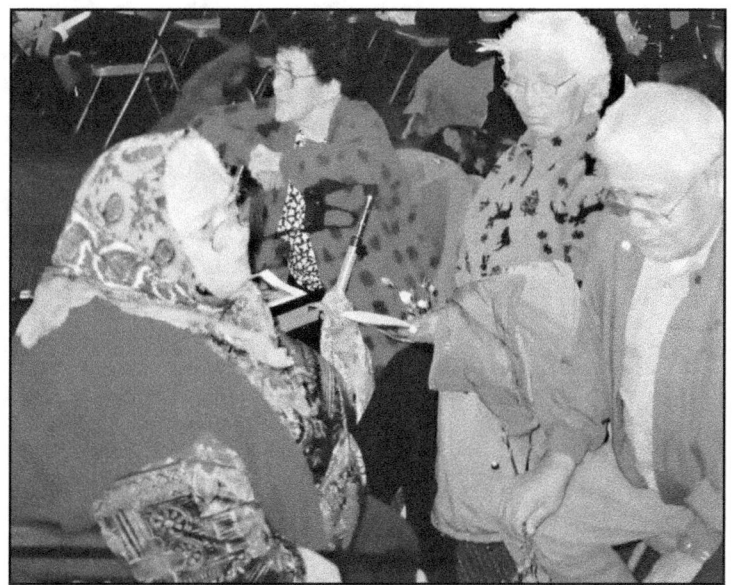

Dolly and Henry Deacon in the foreground, Rose Golilie, back left, all from Grayling, and author's ministry partner Katherine Hamilton, back right, Shageluk. All came to the author's sister Pat's funeral at Meier Lake Conference Center, Wasilla.

Pat Slack Symonds' University of Idaho class picture 1949.

WHEN WE SEE A BONE OR
A FEATHER ON THE TRAIL, WE PICK
IT UP AND PUT IT IN A SAFE PLACE.
WE DON'T STEP OVER NOTHING.
WE RESPECT ALL THE ANIMALS.
THEY ARE A GIFT FROM DINAXITÓ.

—Katherine Hamilton, Shageluk

22.

OLD FOX

When winter came, Katherine wanted to walk to the bridge that crossed the slough to visit a place so filled with sorrow that few words passed between us. It was mostly time to think. Mostly time to remember.

I'm remembering one of the dolls given to Native children to keep them still in the dark winter when the world lies locked in deep snow and ice. It's a rag doll sewn from turned cloth, a term my grandmother used when a woman had only one dress and she'd turn it so the faded parts could somehow be hidden inside, or the worn parts could be put where they could rest. A capable woman was one who could turn a dress several times, with no one the wiser. My great-grandmother was that kind of woman. I'm remembering this doll because it has a fur ruff made of rabbit fur and white fox fur.

I'm a cowgirl, really. I eat meat. I eat meat and I wear fur slippers, so what I'm about to tell you will seem strange.

As we approached the river, I saw a fox dressed in his turned coat of winter white. He didn't run. He lay in the snow and his deep black eyes watched me. I stopped. I quietly reached out to Katherine and pointed to this watcher-one who seemed unafraid, who didn't leap and run away as two old grandmothers passed by on the way to the bridge where Katherine's grandson drowned in springtime.

I stepped closer. The snow was matted, and then I saw the fur of this old fox was matted. I say old because his eyes spoke sorrow. I could just make out the cold steel of the trap in the matted snow.

I found a stick. I knew enough about trapped animals, and trapped men for that matter, to know I could be bitten. Keeping the stick between the old fox and me I slowly moved towards him. This was not child's play. This was life and death, and God knows, Katherine and I had seen enough death.

I watched him. Our eyes locked in some sort of cowboy, gunfighter standoff. A quick glance told me where the spring was, and I moved my stick unhurriedly there, then pressed the spring bit by bit until the jaws clicked open.

He lay there watching me still. I didn't understand until I saw his hind leg twisted and broken and a little bloodied. He got up, stiff and half frozen from his night of terror, and began to limp off towards the river, lippity-lippity, not very fast.

I wonder if Great Grandmother regretted leaving Missouri as she traversed the rugged terrain by Conestoga wagon into the Idaho Territory in 1866. I wonder if Katherine played with a doll like this on a winter's night in a tiny cabin somewhere near Swiftwater in western Alaska. I wonder if her daddy trapped the fox and made the ruff that kept her warm when the bitter winds blew over their frozen world.

The old fox stopped at the brow of the river and cast one last, long look at the old grandmother who'd set him free, and then he turned and disappeared out of sight.

This is an old style rag doll made from turned cloth. Part of the author's doll collection.

WHEN WE WERE YOUNG,
WE DIDN'T KNOW ABOUT LOVE.
THEN WE GREW UP AND WE BEGAN
TO DANCE. THEN WE FELL IN LOVE.

—Adolf Hamilton, Shageluk

23.

WOLVERINE MEDICINE

In May 2002, I got word that Margaret Hamilton had died and headed back to Shageluk. In the Kashim I found Margaret's husband, Adolf, sitting in front of her open casket. I slipped onto the bench beside him and waited for him to speak. Margaret's body was resting peacefully in front of us. Margaret and Adolf had been married 60 years and had sons and daughters, and grandchildren and great grandchildren—a river of children, I mused, going back generations, and hopefully forward many, many more—and most of them had come home to help the community prepare for her potlatch.

"When we were young, we didn't know about love," said Adolf at last. I nodded my head and made comforting noises.

"Then we grew up and we began to dance," he said. "Then we fell in love."

I sat up straight and looked at Adolf. "When you were young, you didn't know about love? Then you grew up and you began to dance?"

"Yes," whispered Adolf. "Then we fell in love." His face was radiant.

I felt like I was sitting in the middle of Psalm 30, "... *you have turned my wailing into dancing; you have put off my sack-cloth and clothed me with joy.*" I could imagine Adolf as a young man, meeting Margaret at a fiddle dance somewhere along the Yukon, eyeing her shyly, finally asking her to dance, and then falling in love.

Adolf's words stuck to me, and by the next morning they had woven themselves into my funeral sermon: "When we are young, we don't know about love. We see a lot of sad things, even bad things: accidents happen, people we love die, we may not have enough wood for winter, or fish for the smoke house. We may not know how the world works. We may blame others for our misfortune. We may even blame God. Then one day, something different happens. We cry out. God answers. We begin to grow up. We begin to dance with God. We dance with God through more good times, and bad times; when we're sick and when we're healthy; when we have money in our pockets, and when we're broke. Finally, we begin to trust that God will never leave us alone. God is there through the wonderful and terrible things that life brings to us, sheltering us, comforting us, ready to lift us up and help us start again. This dancing helps us fall in love with the God who has always loved us. This is the Gospel of Margaret and Adolf, making the invisible visible, dancing with each other, dancing with life, dancing with God, until they are so awash in love that all they can do is love."

I looked over at the grandchildren seated up front, who had volunteered to read the lessons and prayers, and again I smiled. I was proud of them, stepping up to help with the funeral service for their grandmother. I hoped they'd remember what I said about their grandfather and grandmother and about dancing with God until they know they are beloved.

After the burial, I returned to the Kashim to gather up the Prayer Books and put things away. As I shuffled the silver chalice and paten into the old communion box and folded the ancient linens, I became aware of three elder women standing near the door. Two of the women were from a neighboring village, and one was from Shageluk. They talked softly together and threw occasional glances my way—two of them seemed to include me in the conversation. One of the visiting elders held back and kept shaking her head. This was the same elder who, last year, had said to Katherine, "Why do you go around with that white woman all the time?"

"Why *do* you go around with me all the time?" I'd asked Katherine when she told me.

"Because," she said. "You make me laugh." At that we both laughed like old crones.

I quietly packed up the red beaded altar frontal that I had, once again, tacked to the old round poker table that had become my familiar makeshift funeral altar. I put the song books back into the cardboard box and turned to the table again just as the elder from Shageluk walked towards me. She seemed shy, yet determined. She was holding something in her hands. When she held out her hands, I saw a strip of wolverine fur about an inch wide and six inches long. I raised both hands together like I was about to receive Holy Communion. She placed the skin into my outstretched hands without a word. I nodded and whispered thank you. I'd heard murmurs about the power of wolverine medicine, but no one had said anything directly to me.

Years earlier, on one of my trips upriver with Scott Fisher, we were asked to bless the home of a man who was preparing the funeral potlatch for his father. We went from room to room with a tall candle and holy water reciting the familiar prayers meant to *banish every unclean spirit, and make it a secure habitation for those who dwell in it.* Almost on impulse our host threw open the closet for a blessing of objects that looked like funerary medicine—skins and feathers and other unfamiliar things—and prayers and holy water generously blessed the contents without question. We never spoke about it.

My great grandfather Arthur Pence, Sr. had an office full of sacred items from the Shoshone people, as well as artifacts and regalia. These sacred items were given to him because of his generosity and friendship with Shoshone people: he pulled their teeth when they ached, relieved their pains when their own medicine plants weren't enough, sat them down at his table for a meal when they were hungry, and even gave Bruneau John's sister, Polly, a place in the garden to pitch her tepee. After both Great Grandfather and Grandmother Pence died, their home sat empty for several years. Airmen from the Mt. Home Air Force Base reportedly broke in and stole everything.

These precious gifts were never recovered, a loss that is still felt in our family.

In Seldovia I have a long wicker basket where I keep things given to me by my First Nations friends: an abalone shell for burning sage and a rattle made from seed pods given by a Cree friend when we were in seminary together; sweet grass given by an Athabascan friend when we worked in the alcohol and drug treatment field together; a medicine pouch filled with corn pollen, tobacco, and white sage given by a mixed-blood friend after I prayed healing of memory prayers for her; a rattlesnake skin and rattles given by a Cherokee friend along with moccasins and a drum painted with four thunderbirds; a woven cedar bark hat, a necklace filled with eagle down and polished agates, a basket and two dolls from my adopted Haida sister; lapis, turquoise, and silver jewelry from my Tsimshian friend; a hand painted drum with the circle dot motif sheltering a polar bear, raven, two swans, and a snake from a Yup'ik friend; and now wolverine skin from a Deg Hit'an elder. I hold them gently, in a sacred trust, along with the many stories given to me that invite me to respect and understand a worldview that has sustained Indigenous people for thousands of years.

The next time in Shageluk I sought out Rudy, one of Margaret's sons. "I was gifted a piece of wolverine skin after your mother's funeral. Can you help me understand the significance of that?"

"Wolverine is fierce and full of courage. He's not afraid of anything, deep snow, or freezing temperatures. He can make trail through the roughest country. That's why Wolverine is the one who leads the way for a woman on her journey into the light."

✦ ✦ ✦

"You know," said Ellen Savage one day. "My daddy was a very holy man. He used to blow on the back of my neck before I go out the door to school to keep me safe."

"Shaman?" I ask.

"Might be."

"Who will take his place?"

"Who can say?"

She shakes her head back and forth and says no more.

✦ ✦ ✦

The afternoon I sat in the hall at St. Matthew's in Fairbanks waiting for Scott to drive me to the airport, my old friend and mentor David Salmon came in and sat down beside me. We nodded and greeted each other quietly, two old friends who had lost touch and were trying to fill in the intervening years with understanding.

"You left us."

"The bishop sent me down river. I've been working in Anvik, Shageluk, and Grayling."

After a long while David said, "Well, I guess those people needed you." Then he added, "You know my people call me shaman."

I smiled and nodded and said, "Yes, I'm sure they do."

✦ ✦ ✦

I held the wolverine skin in my hands as I drank my tea and thought about the men and women I know who were mystics, medicine people, and holy fools, and I wondered *who can say which people will carry the spiritual memories and gifts of a village or tribe or people*. Who can say why my great grandparents were spared when the Bannock warriors went on the uprising in 1878, or why my great-grandfather was given sacred gifts to care for. Who can say why I've been privileged to receive wolverine skin and a rattle and white sage. Is there anyone in this generation, like Ellen, who can *hold what her mama say, and what those preachers say, and not forget nothing* or like David, who will be recognized as both priest and shaman by the people?

✦ ✦ ✦

When I returned to Anchorage and the small apartment in

our oldest son's home, I realized how alone I felt. Kris had taken a position as CEO of Kikiktagruk Inupiat Corporation in Kotzebue. Our three older sons were married and starting families of their own, and our youngest son was in college. Rudy had said *wolverine is fierce and full of courage; he can make a trail through the roughest country…* It was time for me to make a plan and get moving with my life.

NOW, DON'T GET AHEAD
OF THE HOLY SPIRIT.
YOU DON'T HAVE TO DEFEND GOD.

—The Rev. Dr. Anna Frank

24.

FIRE BATH

Vancouver, British Columbia

"You'll need a cotton dress that you can roll around in the mud in," said Vivian Seegers, my campus buddy in the Native Ministries Program at Vancouver School of Theology. She'd just invited me to a sweat lodge in East Hastings. I'd returned to campus early from a family Christmas holiday in Sun River, Oregon, to study for the General Ordination Exams that would start the following day. I needed to detox from all the cookies and pies I'd baked for the children. This would be perfect.

"Let's go," I said.

Vivian led me into a small sparsely furnished room at the back of the old house used as a treatment center for First Nations women. She shut the door and said casually, "Take off all your clothes and jewelry, and put on your dress."

"Even my underwear?" I asked, incredulously.

"You need to be naked. Your skin needs to breathe."

As I stripped, I felt my cheeks flush and that old familiar body shame settle into my gut. My dress was a jumper that I'd usually worn with a turtleneck because the arm holes plunged to the waist. How in the heck could I keep my breasts from being exposed? I reluctantly worked the gold-nugget wedding band that I'd worn for thirty-nine years off my finger and put it in my sock. I'd started wearing the heart-shaped earrings that my mother gave me when I was ten years old after my sister, Pat, died. The earrings helped me feel close to both my sister and my mother. They went in the sock. Vivian shook her head, yes, when I pointed to the barrettes that were attempting to control my unruly hair; off they came, and my curls fell loose around my face. The barrettes and my glasses went into the sock. If this stripping away was meant to make me feel vulnerable, it was working. I now had nothing between me and the world except a very skimpy jumper.

When we went into the garden, a young man approached us and asked if I'd ever attended a sweat before. I said, "No." He looked doubtful and insisted I talk with Joe and ask him if it's okay for me to be there. This was the unceded traditional land of the Musqueam, Squamish, and Tsleil-Waututh Nations. I was painfully aware that as a white woman I was a guest, and a part of the colonial system, that had tried to wipe out First Nations people across Canada with racist policies, like boarding schools. I wanted to do the respectful thing; I would abide by whatever Joe said.

Vivian took my hand and led me over to meet Joe who was instructing the young men tending the fire. The igneous stones were already beginning to glow red hot.

"This is my friend, Judith."

"I'm a first timer," I whispered

He looked up. His eyes smiled, "You'll be okay."

Joe saw Vivian's drum, eagle-wing fan, pipe, and rattle: all the sacred objects she had received from the Sun Dance.

"Do you want to sing," he asked her.

"No," she said. "We do need to make prayer bundles though."

"Go ahead."

Vivian instructed me in choosing the right colors for my prayer bundles that would reflect my intentions. I knew I wasn't a scholar or theologian. I was a grandmother, a storyteller, and one of the oldest students in the M.Div. program. I told her I needed my mind to be clear for the General Ordination Exams, and my brain to be fully engaged. She said white was on the mental side of the medicine wheel, and I could choose white cloth to wrap the tobacco in. I said

I wanted to be free of fear and my heart to be at peace with whatever happened. She said I could tie my bundles with yellow cloth for emotional healing.

After we tied our bundles, we stepped outside and waited for the signal to re-enter. A steady rain soaked my hair, and cool water began to trickle down my forehead and neck. I stood barefoot, bare armed, bare necked, bare assed in the rain trembling, but I wasn't cold. I could barely see without my glasses. I squinted at the ground. I was standing in a puddle with mud squishing up between my toes. I knew I needed to enjoy the coolness now because soon, very soon, I would be on fire.

My eyes moved from the soft brown mud on my feet to the mound of earth at the mouth of the lodge that served as the altar. Several large deer horns, and all the sacred objects lay on it like an offering. The steady rain and the good earth imparted their own sacred blessings on them, and on us, as well. I'd never stood virtually naked in a January rain before. I closed my eyes and breathed deeply of the earthy smells and said thank you, over and over, to the rain, and the cedar trees, and Vivian and Joe and Jesus. It felt like a hinge day and I would somehow be different afterwards.

A reverent mood settled over the gathering. Casual conversation stopped. Overt movements gentled down. Vivian reached out and touched my arm. I opened my eyes. She motioned me to come close. It was time to go in. The elders and regulars entered first. Finally, Vivian moved to the altar and picked up her sacred things. She offered them to the four directions as she prayed. I lifted my prayer bundles to the four directions and whispered thank you.

Men circled to the left going in, and women to the right. As I watched the men and women settle into two rows around the fire pit, a memory of the day Kris and I worshiped at St. Seraphim's Russian Orthodox Church in Dillingham the year before came to me. There, the men stood on the right facing the altar and the women stood on the left. The priests, and deacons, who officiated worship, were the only ones who could pass the altar and enter the Holy of Holies.

I shivered. In the sweat, everyone passed the altar as we made our way into the center, the womb-cave, the place of fire, the Holy of Holies. In both traditions we each bring all that we have and offer it in prayer for the common good.

Joe welcomed us with kind words; then he welcomed the red-hot grandmother and grandfather stones as they were placed in the center of the circle. We also welcomed them and thanked them and offered prayers. I thanked Jesus for his presence and then I remembered Bruneau John and his sister, Polly. I asked them if they would like to join us as Shoshone ancestors and friends of my great grandfather. I said I hoped they would get along with the Cree. Joe seemed to be Cree. I stopped worrying, the Cree seemed to be respectful of many nations, including this old Irish-English-German-Swede.

I lost track of the number of stones, maybe four or five, maybe seven or eight. Anyway, the flap closed and Joe touched the bucket to the glowing stones and slowly poured the water over them. Wave after wave of scorching fire and water enveloped the gathered souls. The live steam felt at once terrifying and soothing. Joe raised his voice over the hissing of the water as he continued to welcome and thank the grandmothers and grandfathers for being present with us. Our voices echoed like a Greek chorus as we raised our thanksgivings and prayers. Someone began to beat out a deep steady rhythm with his drum. Vivian thrust her rattle into my hand and whispered, "Use this," then she picked up her drum and joined the first drummer. Quickly others joined with drums and rattles and singing. I, too, began to sing and rattle. I didn't know the Cree language, but I'd sung several healing songs with Mary Fontaine at our Native Ministries gatherings so I simply sang the words phonetically.

By the third round, I could feel my entire body beginning to melt into the earth. The cedar offering had an especially comforting effect, and I felt a deep calm. Vivian had told me when we tied our prayer bundles that if I got too hot, I could lay down behind her and lift the edge of the lodge an inch or so and suck in the cool air. I finally gave up and let my body slip down onto the earth. I inched my fingers under the wall and let the cool wind flow over my face. A poem by David Wagoner entitled "Lost," that I'd been using to prepare for Centering Prayer, began to circle in my mind. I must lay still, and recognize that the cedar tree is not lost. I am exactly where I need to be. I can treat this place as a powerful stranger. I can let myself be known even as I ask permission to know.

I don't know how long I lay like that. At last, I sat up, revived, and began to sing and rattle with new vigor.

When there was a lull in the singing, an old man in the back corner spoke, "I want the one sitting by the door with the rattle to sing."

Fire surged through my belly and chest. Was he talking to me? I was the one with the rattle sitting by the door. I had been given a song in a dream once, but it was a lullaby. Would that be appropriate? My mind raced; the old anxiety returned. I was paralyzed with indecision. I did nothing. At last, the man making the request began to sing and drum again.

When the ceremony ended, everyone quietly filed out of the darkness into the late afternoon twilight. The rain had stopped. Smoke from the sacred fire mingled with the scent of the wet cedars edging the garden and offered some comfort. I arched my shoulders and sucked in the tree medicine as I struggled to release the shame I felt for not singing. I must let the forest find me.

I held the rattle out to Vivian.

"Keep it," she said. "Use it when you pray for people."

"What will it do?" I whispered.

"If your energy is balled up, it will untangle it. If it's scattered, it will bring it home."

IN THE OLD DAYS, THE ELDERS
WOULD GATHER EVERY EVENING
IN THE CHURCH IN A CIRCLE AND
TALK ABOUT WHAT THE GOOD GOD
HAD DONE FOR THEM THAT DAY.

—The Rev. Helen Peters, Tanana

25.

NATIVITY

After graduating with my Masters of Divinity in May 2003, I visited family in Seattle, Portland, and Loma Linda, California and then flew to Seldovia to open Dancing Eagles Bed and Breakfast for the summer. In September I flew to Kotzebue to be with Kris as promised. I had barely six weeks to settle in before the sun dipped below the horizon for 175 days, cradling the landscape in twilight and darkness, except for the luminous canopy that glowed overhead with billions of galaxies stretching into deep space, haunting the landscape with vermillion and azure shadows. The quality of the light, the land that seemed to stretch into eternity, the generosity of the people gave me a newfound sense of peace and freedom. I had my rattle from Vivian, and I did use it when I prayed for myself. I secretly marveled at how untangled my spirit felt.

My days were lived as they came. I lunched with the folks at the treatment center five days a week and gave talks on spirituality and recovery. Kris introduced me to a young woman named Anahma Saito, who had started a suicide prevention program in the region. I threw myself into helping her and soon found myself traveling to Ambler and Kobuk to chaperone the teens who had written a suicide prevention play. The school in Norvik invited me to lead a values clarification retreat for 35 teens. Anahma asked me to lead a class for juvenile offenders at The Big Dipper coffee shop. She invited me to join a lady's sewing circle and taught me to sew hooded parkas. The bishop decided to ordain me even though I had failed four of the seven General Ordination Exams at Vancouver School of Theology—in spite of prayers bundles tied in white cloth—and plans were underway at St. Mary's in Anchorage for the big day. Yes, I was embarrassed by my failure, but I was free of fear and my heart was at peace with what happened. Yellow had done her job. I continued to serve the villages of Anvik, Shageluk, and Grayling.

When I flew into Grayling for Christmas services that December, it was minus 20 degrees below zero with less than five hours of daylight. Three feet of fresh snow had fallen just before the cold snap, softening the landscape and buildings and creating a whimsical winter scene right out of a Rie Munoz watercolor.

Marilyn, the agent for the airlines, was waiting on the airport apron with her snowmachine and heavy sled for mail and freight. She motioned me to put my gear in her sled and offered me a ride to Fred and Angela Howard's two-story log home. The main road was well plowed, but when we turned off on the trail, the moguls were deep and the track was narrow, making the going slow and laborious. The spruce trees and small shrubs, the abandoned pickups and sleds, the oil barrels and river boats lay hidden beneath the three feet of slumped meringue; only the partially dug out piles of birch logs and wood chips provided any relief from the white of winter.

Hummm... the smell of hot coffee, pancakes, and moose steak poured over me as I pulled the door open. Angie smiled and motioned me to sit. Fred poured me a cup of coffee. I managed to smother Mrs. Butterworth's on a generous plate of pancakes and moose steak before anyone spoke.

"There's no power back there," said Angie. "The snow's deep. I think the chimney fell off."

My heart sank, but I smiled weakly and nodded, "Okay, I'll check it out."

When I finished eating, I excused myself and walked through the snow to St. Paul's, dreading what I'd find: no power, no heat, and three feet of hardened snow. When I got within sight of the church, I started hollering. A perfectly straight path carved from the road to the church lay before me, and the porch, oh glory, was completely cleared, the door was open wide, and a pile of fresh cut firewood filled the narthex. A tall wooden ladder leaned against the north wall of the building, and smoke and sparks curled from the reattached chimney. Michael Hamilton stuck his head out the door and started waving when he saw it was me hollering. I threw my arms in the air and gave one last hoot and holler as I walked up the wide path to the church.

He grinned, then said almost apologetically, "You got no power for lights."

"Oh, not to worry, that part will be easy," I said. "You've already done the hard part. I'm sure we can find candle stubs for light."

When I entered the church, the floorboards snapped and popped from the cold, but the frost crystals were beginning to soften on the windows. The light was fading fast so I rummaged through the old dresser behind the altar screen until I'd found every last candle stub. I pulled two dozen jars and tin cans from a cardboard box sitting beside the dresser—many with crumpled tin foil in them already, so I knew they had been used as candle holders before. I began to place the longest candles on the window sills and along the back of the altar. I placed four candles on the lectern and then placed the box of stubs on the bench by the door.

"Oh come, all ye faithful," I sang under my breath, "Joyful and triumphant." I was buoyed by Michael's effort to get the church open and warm for the children. We really would have a beautiful Christmas service after all!

After I fussed and tidied up the benches and made sure everything was ready for the seven o'clock service, I stoked the barrel stove one last time, then walked back to Fred and Angela's for a bit of supper. When I opened the door, there was my favorite fiddle player, Victor Rock from Shageluk. He was grinning, obviously happy to be there. His fiddle and the small black pack he traveled with were sitting at the foot of the stairs.

"You'll play your fiddle tonight?" I asked.

"That's what I'm here for!" he declared.

"Angie, you'll lead the singing tonight, right?"

"Ya."

Supper was a blur of laughter and relief. What had seemed like an impossible task when I first arrived—minus 20-degree temperatures, deep snow blocking the way into the church, no chimney, no heat, no lights—had been solved by Michael's generosity; having fiddle music and Angie leading the singing was a huge bonus. I excused myself a little early and went back to the church to stoke the fire again, and pray.

I lit the tallest candles, standing almost straight in their jelly glasses and tin foil, and marveled at the richness of the golden light winking back from the old paned windows. I intoned the Christmas Collect that seemed, just then, so perfect and prophetic:

"Oh God, you have caused this holy night to shine with the brightness of the true Light: Grant that we, who have known the mystery of that Light on earth, may also enjoy him perfectly in heaven…"

Then I moved to the altar and surveyed the half-dozen jelly and pickle jars filled with their humble charges. My mind wandered to Henry Deacon, who had rescued the altar and all the beadwork from the old church in Holikachuk after the village moved to its present location on the Yukon. Holikachuk was on the Innoko River, and it flooded often in springtime when the water was high. In 1963 the village voted to move fifteen miles west to Grayling.

I had just lighted the altar candles when I heard the first snowmachine pull up to the church. I took fire from an altar candle and stood by the front door, ready to light each candle as the community gathered. Looking to the river, I could just see Little Rose Golilie coming around the side of her cabin with her grandchildren. They were helping her navigate her walker through the deep snow. Henry was on his snowmachine and had a chair in a sled for Dolly. Edna, and Big Rose, and Margie, and Mary came in with their families. Linda was there, and her daughters, who had been living with Angie and Fred, sat beside her. The elders and adults filled all the benches, and the children crowded on the floor in front of the altar. Looking around at the growing light, I said a quick prayer that no one would catch fire, then I nodded to Victor to begin the first hymn, *"O little town of Bethlehem, how still we see thee lie; above the deep and dreamless sleep the silent stars go by…*

After the readings from the Old and New Testaments, I stepped into the sea of children seated on the floor in front of the altar, held the Bible high, and proclaimed loudly, "The Gospel of our Lord Jesus Christ according to St. Luke."

Chanelle, Henry and Dolly's granddaughter, wailed, "I can't see."

Startled, I instinctively bent low and stretched my Bible towards the wailing child. She and all the children leaned forward and peered into the worn pages as though they could see into the very heart of the Nativity itself. *Only words*, I thought. The children were unfazed. The parents and elders instinctively moved their candles forward, encircling the children. The children continued to stare into the words, expectantly. I looked up—every parent and grandparent had followed the children's rapt gaze into the Holy Scriptures and each face was bathed in a rich golden light from their candles and what could only be imagined as *Shekinah*, a Hebrew term that means the presence of God in this place. Somehow, we had all tumbled headlong into this story that had mystified saints and scholars and scientists for over two thousand years: the mystery of a tiny child wrapped in rags in a stable coming as the savior of the world.

Time stood still, and as our humble candle stubs burned low, and the gathered children and parents and elders peered into the mystery of the word become flesh, we somehow *became* what all the Renaissance painters had tried to capture of that Holy night— Icons—Icons of the living God. Angels were singing somewhere.

"I can't see," the child had wailed, and we followed her into that holy place of seeing called faith, or belief, or mystery, and the words came alive for us all, and I knew I would never forget this night or hear this Nativity story the same way again.

The rest of the evening was a blur of images, and Holy

Communion, and Angela leading us in more Christmas hymns. At last Victor began the most holy of hymns, "Silent Night." This time the children each got their own candle stub. They sat perfectly still as the fire from the altar was passed to them.

> *Silent night, holy night,*
> *Son of God, love's pure light*
> *Radiant beams from thy holy face,*
> *With the dawn of redeeming grace,*
> *Jesus, Lord at thy birth.*
> *Jesus, Lord, at thy birth.*

After the closing prayer and blessing, plates and plates of home baked cookies came out from under benches, and in the midst of candlelight and laughter we had the biggest cookie party I'd ever seen. We ate and ate, and then the ladies skillfully began to shuffle the remaining cookies from plate to plate, so that everyone took home a sample from every family.

The following morning Fred loaded his sled with my guitar, duffle bag, sleeping bag, backpack, and Victor's fiddle and black bag for our journey to the airport. I slipped into the middle of the sled, in front of my gear, and Victor sat in the front of the sled with his gear behind him. We were packed in like sardines. Fred took off down the trail with his load and didn't look back. When the sled hit the first mogul I instinctively leaned back and then felt something let go in the sled. Too late, I realized it was my guitar. I managed to right myself just as Fred started up the second mogul. Again, I fell back, and this time I knew I was in trouble. Plop-kerplop, my duffle bag slid onto the trail. Another mogul, and my sleeping bag, backpack, and I all careened over the back of the sled onto the trail.

Victor, in the meantime, had been hanging onto the front of the sled and didn't realize what was happening behind him. When Fred started up another mountain of snow, Victor leaned backwards, lost his balance, and slid to the back of the now empty sled. I was lying in the snow on my backside, hollering and laughing; my gear scattered along the trail behind me, with Victor's black bag and fiddle dotting the trail in front of me. Seconds later, Victor was out of the sled face down in the snow, laughing with me. Fred finally looked back, and started to laugh. His cargo was strewn along the trail for ten yards.

"Hey," shouted Victor. "This is just like Ma and Pa Kettle. You're Ma and I'm Pa!" The madcap characters from the movies I'd watched as a child with my grandfather completely captured the moment. I'm sure I was trying to hold onto the holiness of the candlelight service the night before, but in less than a minute I was on my backside in the snow laughing like a holy fool. The moniker stuck. From then on, Victor greeted me as Ma and I called him Pa.

Judith and the Grayling Youth Group in the old mission house getting ready for a pizza party.

Judith, Rev. Wilfred Lane, and husband Kris, St. George's, Kotzebue.

Katherine Hamilton, St. Paul's, Grayling.

Young people gathered in front of the altar with the author at St. Paul's Episcopal church, Grayling.

REAL HEROES AREN'T THE RICH
AND FAMOUS. THEY ARE THEY ARE
THE ONES WHO SHOW GENEROSITY
AND KINDNESS TO STRANGERS.

—Arthur Pence, Jr., Bruneau, Idaho

26.

YER HUNGRY?

The cold front continued to press in on the lower Yukon, and it was minus 35 degrees when I was called to Anvik to bury the elder, James Hamilton, who had died of exposure on the Delaney Park Strip, a green belt that ran for eleven blocks between Ninth and Tenth Avenues in Anchorage. At the potlatch Sunday night, Brian John told me a story that I couldn't shake. When Brian was a small child, he would accompany his mother to visit James. "Yer Hungry?" James would shout. Then he would proceed to pull out a loaf of white bread and a package of baloney and put it on the table in his tiny apartment in Fairview. "Go ahead, eat," he would say.

My own family shared that rough and tumble sensibility with Jim. They didn't make a show of their faith, but they were kind and generous, ready to feed young children and old ladies, or anyone who showed up at their door. My father drove truck hauling cattle or sheep through Bruneau to their summer range in the hills in springtime. He would often stop and visit Aunt Mattie Trammel, who lived in a tiny house in Bruneau, with just a few chickens to keep her company after Uncle Frank died. My father would slip a brown paper bag containing a one pound can of Folgers coffee, a five-pound bag of sugar, a bone-in ham, a pound of butter, and a bottle of whiskey onto the round oak table next to the strawberry jam. Aunt Mattie would pull a pan of baking powder biscuits from the small black oven, the smell of golden goodness filling the dimly lit space, then grin and mischievously clinked two glasses on the table.

All night I chewed on that story until I finally realized that is what Jesus says to us in Matthew 25: 35, "For I was hungry and you gave me food, I was thirsty and you gave me something to drink, I was a stranger and you welcomed me." I couldn't stop thinking about all the times I had been fed and welcomed by the people; how many times the people had welcomed their prodigal sons and daughters' home to be buried with their ancestors, how many times they had prepared the potlatch, built the coffin and spirit house, dug the hole, sewed skin hat, gloves, and boots, then dressed their family member in their finest traditional traveling clothes. "Truly I tell you, just as you did it to one of the least of these who are members of my family, you did it to me."

I arrived at the church early the next morning and discovered that Carl Jerue, the village Chief, had built a fire after midnight and had also pumped 20 gallons of fuel into the tank for the Monitor stove. The oil stove was still running, and the temperature inside the church was a balmy 45 degrees. I restarted the wood stove, and by 11:00 it was 65 degrees. I was sweating. It was the first time I had been warm in winter in Anvik.

The service was a blessing of familiar hymns and prayers and Holy Communion, and at last the young men picked up the casket and we all processed out the narrow door to the waiting pickup truck. The wind was blowing a steady 20 miles an hour off the Yukon River, making the temperature feel more like minus 67 degrees with the wind chill. I was grateful for my red down parka and new felt-lined mukluks, and the fur hat Kris had been given when he was ordained deacon in Shageluk three years before.

At the cemetery the men discovered the coffin was just a few inches too long to fit into the hole. Women and children quickly disappeared into the nearest houses to get warm. Carl jumped into the hole with a pickaxe and shovel. One by one the younger men were overtaken by the cold and went to warm up, too. Carl and I were left alone. I turned my back to the wind and prayed for stamina for both Carl and myself as I watched him chip away at the frozen earth.

The men returned and quickly prepared the coffin and lowered it into its now perfect resting place. When I finished the Committal prayers, I paused before the final dismissal, and told the men. "Ellen Savage told me that her mother used to say, 'See that old womans over there, go carry water for her, go fill her berry basket, or go take her some fish. When we do that,' said Ellen, 'they would take us outside and say, *see that mountain over there? When you grow up you're going to be just like that mountain, you'll be strong and tall and a shelter for the birds and the animals, and nothing will move you.*' I think if Ellen were here with us, and she saw how you worked all night to build the coffin for James, and dig the hole in this bitter cold, and make fire in the church, she would say to you, *see that river, your life is going to be just like that river, long, and rich and powerful, and filled with good things to sustain you and to share with others*. It is an honor and a privilege to stand with you as we work together to celebrate the life of James Hamilton, a man of remarkable kindness and generosity. 'Yer hungry?' he would say to the children when they came to visit. May we all remember James, and what he did for others, and what has been done for him today, and be thankful. Alleluia, Christ is risen."

I WISH IT WAS LIKE THE OLD DAYS.
YOUNG PEOPLE DON'T HAVE
ACCIDENTS. EVERYBODY LIVES
JUST GOOD.

—Elisabeth Workman, Shageluk

27.

BLESSINGS

Spring came and the weather broke. I planned a trip to the Yukon for Easter. When I got to Shageluk, I headed straight for the Kashim. The tribe had held a wonderful Easter celebration for the children, with egg hunts, games, and prizes, and now we were gathered for a feast: baked King salmon, fried King salmon, King salmon strips, half-dried salmon with potatoes and onions, three bowls of fish ice cream with red berries and blueberries, several large pots of moose soup, baked ham, baked beans, macaroni salad, Jell-O with canned fruit, fry bread, Pilot Bread, cinnamon rolls, three different pies, two sheet cakes, and cupcakes with chocolate frosting.

Katherine and I were sitting with Jimmy and Jeannette. Jeanette waved at Allen John to join us. "Allen has started the fire in the church the last seven Sundays, so that Katherine and I could have Sunday school for the children and Evening Prayer."

"That's great," I said. "There's nothing more inviting than a warm fire!

Allen was shy about accepting the praise. Jimmy chimed in, "I used to be the Episcopal slave. My first wife used to say to me all the time *get wood, start fire.*" Everyone laughed. We all knew his first wife, Jean. She was strong. She had to be. She was the public health nurse and the priest in this region for many years. I heard her say once, "I birth them, baptize them, and then bury them when they start drinking as teenagers and have accidents."

I knew how heartbreaking that must have been. On my first trip to Shageluk four years earlier, the village counselor, Marlene, had asked me to intercede in a domestic violence incident and participate in a suicide intervention. My Senior Seminar at the University of Alaska had been in Suicide Prevention and Intervention, so on my second trip I decided to hold suicide prevention workshops in all three villages. I invited the elders from each village and the village counselors to participate. In Shageluk we had about 30 people gathered in the school gym—all the high school students, elders, and tribal council members. One man jumped up and left the room when we started talking about people we knew who had killed themselves. About thirty minutes later, he came back, crossed the circle, and sat in the empty chair beside me. It was Allen. His own son had committed suicide six months earlier and he'd never talked about it until then. After that we became comfortable friends. He would greet me warmly when we met, and often came to church.

When we walked to St. Luke's for the 7:00 Communion service the air was crisp and the snow still deep around the small plank building, but the warmth from Allen's fire was cheerful and welcomed us inside. The back table was covered with 20 crosses covered with tissue paper flowers that the children had made in Sunday school. Jeanette had picked an enormous bouquet of pussy willows and had them in a three-pound coffee can of water in front of the altar. During the service, the children would each get to hang their flowered cross on the pussy willows.

Katherine and I prepared the altar with the corporeal, chalice, paten, burse, and the beautiful white beaded vale that Flossie had made after my ordination. Just then the door burst open and three children, Kimberly, Alfred, and Johnny, rushed in.

"Can I ring the bell?" shouted Alfred. "No, me!" chimed in Kimberly. "I want to ring the bell," added Johnny.

"Whoa! Let's see if you can all ring the bell together."

Soon the church filled with elders and parents and more children. Jimmy was in the front row with his guitar. Young people eagerly vied to light the candles and read the lessons as Jeanette organized the service. Katherine and Allen took their places next to Jimmy. Favorite songs were requested, and we sang and sang as we prepared to reaffirm our Baptismal Vows and celebrate the Easter Eucharist.

"Christ is risen, the Lord is risen, indeed, Alleluia, alleluia!"

In my enthusiasm for Matthew's Easter Gospel, I read: "The angel said to the women, 'Do not be afraid; I know that you are looking for Jesus who was crucified. He is not here; for he has been raised, as he said….and indeed he is going ahead of you to *Shageluk*; there you will see him!"

"Shageluk," gasped Alfred, "How did he know about Shageluk?" The congregation erupted in laughter. Katherine and I looked at each other and giggled.

"He knows everything!" I declared. "And, furthermore, Jesus meant it when he said he would meet us here. He needs more helpers. Can't you see how old I'm getting?" I looked at each child and then asked, "Who will be the next priest to serve the people?" No one was laughing now. The old people were nodding, and the children were looking at their grandmas and grandpas for approval.

Looking around the sanctuary I remembered that great collect for Mission from Morning Prayer, "…pour out your spirit upon all flesh, and hasten the coming of your kingdom…"

At last, the spell was broken, and the service continued with the Eucharistic prayer and Jeanette and Jim serving communion while I anointed everyone with holy oil, from the small gold oil stock given to me by the Rev. Herb McMurtry for my graduation from the Native Ministries Program at Vancouver School of Theology. Herb had used it throughout his long ministry and had admonished, "*Remember me whenever you use this—I'll be there with you!*"

After Communion we all prayed together, "…*And now, Father, send us out to do the work you have given us to do, to love and serve you as faithful witnesses of Christ our Lord…*"

"Who will help Grandma Katherine and me take Holy Communion to Grandma Elisabeth?" I shouted above the din as children and families zipped up their coats and gathered their belongings.

Five hands shot into the air. "Me!" shouted Kimberly, Alfred, and Johnny all at once. Katherine smiled and nodded yes. "I'll go, too," whispered Allen softly. Looking around at their earnest faces, I couldn't leave anyone out. "Great! Let's all go!"

When I picked up the beautiful moose hide communion bag that Dolly Deacon and her daughter Becky Shelikof had made for my ordination and hung it over Alfred's shoulder, he smiled shyly. We all headed up the hill to the cabin where Elisabeth was waiting up for us. We could see the light on when we rounded the trail and came out of the trees near her dog lot.

We knocked loudly on the door, then all crowded into the cabin's tiny space. "Who is this with you?" asked Elisabeth—leaning forward to see better. I leaned towards her for my customary hug and kiss, then sat down on the sofa and motioned to the children to come… come… and introduce yourselves to Grandma. She doesn't get out much and doesn't know the names of all the village children.

Alfred, the young boy who had gasped at the idea of meeting Jesus in Shageluk, the one carrying the communion bag, stepped forward first and introduced himself to Grandma. She took his young face in her old gnarled hands and kissed him gently on both cheeks. He knelt down beside her, looking like he'd just been kissed by an angel.

Kimberly pushed little Johnny forward and introduced him, then herself to Grandma Elisabeth. She took their little faces in her dear sweet hands and kissed their cheeks, too. They knelt on the floor beside Alfred, enthralled.

Allen stepped forward and took her hand gently and greeted her. I shared how much Allen had done, building fire, so the children could have Sunday school. Allen squirmed and Elisabeth smiled.

I mentioned how the Easter Gospel invited the disciples to meet Jesus in Shageluk, and how we all giggled. I talked about how Jesus has a need for more disciples because people are lonely and there is so much sadness. People don't know how much they are loved.

Then I told the story of Jesus and his disciples and the night he was handed over to suffering and death. How he had taken a loaf of bread, blessed it, broke it, and said, "'Take, eat, this is my body, which is given for you. Do this for the remembrance of me.' And then he took the cup of wine, gave thanks for it, and said, 'Drink this, all of you: this is my blood of the new Covenant, which is shed for you and for many for the forgiveness of sins. Whenever you drink it, do this for the remembrance of me.'"

During Communion, Johnny stretched out by the stove to play with a toy he had found. We continued, and he listened as he played. "Grandma Katherine, will you lead us in the Lord's Prayer?" The children joined in, and knew every word.

I gave Allen the small birch bark basket made by Dorothy Savage Joseph from Holy Cross with the fry bread left from the altar, and Alfred the tiny silver chalice of wine, and asked them to serve Grandma Elisabeth. With great solemnity and some coaching on the words, Allen served the communion bread and my young helper, Alfred, served the chalice.

"Children," I said, "Remember how I prayed for all of you after communion at the church?" They all shook their heads yes. "How would you like to help me pray for Grandma Elisabeth tonight?" Their eyes got very big and they all nodded yes again, as they inched closer on their knees. I handed Katherine my holy oil stock and she made the sign of the cross with the healing oil on Elisabeth's forehead and then together we placed our hands over Elisabeth's hands, resting in her lap. One by one, Allen and the children placed their hands on top of ours.

Earlier, during communion, Johnny had become distracted by a toy, but when I declared, "Let us Pray," he dived over the top of my left shoulder and placed his little hands firmly on the very top of the pile!

"Amen!" he shouted.

Grandma Elizabeth Workman and grandchildren, Shageluk.

Lots of children at the candlelight service in Shageluk at Christmas with the author.

YOU DON'T HAVE TO GO TO COLLEGE,
OR KNOW EVERYTHING WRITTEN IN
BOOKS, YOU JUST HAVE TO LOVE JESUS.

—The Rev. Titus Peter, Birch Creek

28.

LIGHT INACCESSIBLE

"Judith, your ordination is scheduled for Superbowl Sunday," said Michael Burke, the rector of St. Mary's Episcopal Church in Anchorage. "Don't be disappointed if no one stays. In my experience, people come to church early and then rush home to watch the game."

"Not to worry," I assured him. "Whoever is meant to be here will be here."

The Saturday before the Ordination Bishop MacDonald hosted a clergy meeting in Anchorage, and priests and deacons came in from Point Hope, Nome, Tanana, Fairbanks, Juneau, Sitka, Petersburg, Eagle River, Seward, and Anchorage and stayed for the festivities. When all was said and done, 17 clergy were present the morning of my ordination, with four deacons and ten priests vesting for the procession into the sanctuary.

The two priests from St. Mary's, Michael Burke and Connie Jones, and the priest who had prepared me for confirmation 34 years earlier in Juneau, Mark Boesser, and his wife Mildred, were to present me to the bishop.

"If anyone comes from the Yukon," I said to Michael, "I want them to stand with me as well."

As the time drew near, people began to stream into the sanctuary: people I'd prayed with, led suicide prevention workshops with, married, people whose relatives I'd buried, people I'd played music with, and fiddle danced with–the people kept coming, and coming. Soon every chair was filled. Our four sons and daughters-in-law were in the front pew with five of our seven grandchildren. Four friends from the Roman Catholic church came. A nun who read about the ordination in the Saturday paper came. Chaplains from Providence Spiritual Care came. One friend from the Russian Orthodox church came. Nearly everyone from St. Mary's stayed for the celebration—they did not rush home to watch the Superbowl. And dozens and dozens of people from Anvik, Shageluk, and Grayling came.

I'd hired a trumpet player to join Wade Hampton-Miller and the Praise Singers, and the music was electric. Imagine Marty Haugen's well-known hymn *Gather Us In* with organ, piano, guitar, bass guitar, fiddle, mandolin, and trumpet. Young acolytes skipped in with butterfly and ribbon banners that fluttered and floated above the heads of the congregation. I read St. Patrick's Breastplate as an opening prayer and could feel my Irish roots plunge deeper into the soil of the place that had been my church home since I was nineteen years old. Bill Davis served as the bishop's chaplain and led the 17 clergy as they processed into the sanctuary to an Irish waltz.

When it was time, Michael invited a few of the Shageluk elders to come forward for the presentation, but when the other Native people saw them come forward, all the Native people came forward. I was enveloped in a sea of smiling faces.

"Where is she?" quipped the bishop.

"Here I am," I said waving from the back of the throng.

"Well, that's a first," he said. The congregation laughed out loud.

The wonderful diversity continued. My Inupiat friend from Kotzebue, Vivian Lane, read the Old Testament lesson, Isaiah 6:1-8; Connie Jones chanted *Psalm 138*; my black friend Charles Jackson read the epistle, 1 Corinthians 1:26-31; my Filipino friend and deacon Ben Messelium read the Gospel in Tagalog; my second grandchild, Ann, read the Gospel in English; Sarah Ruggles signed the gospel; and my oldest grandchild, Lynn, was the crucifer. Christina Talbot sang *I Sought The Lord*, and the Rev. Gayle Nauska chanted *Veni Sancte Spiritus*.

Bishop MacDonald told his favorite story about a man whose

car slid backwards down an icy hill through an accident scene in the middle of the night in a snowstorm in Minnesota. He not only missed hitting the two wrecked cars on either side of the road by a centimeter each—he leaped out of his car after it came to rest, and threw his hands in the air, taa-daa, grinning, as though he planned it that way all along. The analogy was to me, of course, and my journey to ordination. Point well taken. I had, after all, been named Ma Kettle by my friend, Victor. The Bishop also said the ordination felt like a Chinese wedding; all the toasting was a bit overwhelming for an introvert. Well, it was just what this extrovert needed, wanted, and loved.

During the Prayer of Consecration, all the clergy came forward and laid their hands on me, as the bishop laid his hands on my head and prayed …*Therefore, Father, through Jesus Christ your Son, give your Holy Spirit to Judith; fill her with grace and power, and make her a priest in your Church.* I felt like a torchlight that had been switched on at midnight. The weight of those hands pressing in, lifting up, channeling the Holy Spirit filled every part of my mind, heart, body, and spirit with grace and love.

St. Mary's Church gave the bishop a hefty Bible/prayer book combination to give me, and Dawn Allen-Herron placed the traditional red clergy stole that she had made over my shoulders. The stole was anything but traditional in a mottled red silk. A swirling rainbow of gold, orange, red, and purple silk cradled a white and cerulean blue cross that fairly exploded with gold threads and red jewels. The swirling rainbow gave birth to yellow, orange, gold and rose flames that danced up both sides to the shoulders. Everything was zig-zagged in gold and silver threads. A magenta raven on the wing anchored the bottom and harkened to an ancient Haida tale about Raven stealing fire from the sun; perhaps a portent or premonition of my adoption into the Raven Moiety by Merle Anderson from Old Massett, Haida Gwaii, Canada? All in all, it was a celebration of cultures to match the diversity of the diocese and the gathering that came to witness my ordination.

The Offertory hymn was Marty Haugen's "Canticle of the Sun." It certainly felt like all creation was shouting for joy. The trumpet player outdid himself. The energy in the room soared to match the brightness of the brass. Our son Dan and two of his children, Michael and Morgan, brought the bread and wine forward. Kris, as deacon, prepared the table, and the bishop stood on my left as I began The Great Thanksgiving and Eucharistic prayer D.

The Lord be with you, I began.

And also with you, responded the congregation

I looked out over the congregation as I proceeded to declare *God, living and true, dwelling in light inaccessible from before time and forever…* These were my people, faces beaming, nodding assent, acknowledging the rightness of our relationship…*you made all things and filled them with your blessing*…even as we blessed one another with our stories, our deepest secrets, our heartbreaks…*joining with angels, and giving voice to every creature under heaven, we acclaim you, and glorify your Name…And that we might live no longer for ourselves, but for him who died and rose for us, he sent the Holy Spirit…to bring to fulfillment the sanctification of all.* Everyone called. Everyone blessed, everyone sanctified to be a peacemaker, or teacher, or evangelist or parent, to comfort the broken-hearted, or speak truth to bullies. I was not alone. Oh yes, I was the one being ordained, but everyone there was a minister. The sanctuary was filled with God's people.

My long-time friend, Barbara Flaherty, brought holy water from St. Brigid's Well in Ireland for the final blessing, and Bill Davis carried the bowl as we walked among the congregation flinging it far and wide.

The potlatch was a celebration of feasting. We had muktuk from Kotzebue, caribou soup from Noatak, smoked King salmon strips from Grayling, half-dried salmon from Shageluk, baked salmon and halibut from Kachemak Bay, black forest ham, all kinds of salads, and two carrot cakes. Gifts were presented, stories told. At last, the bishop and clergy from out of town had to catch their airplanes, and friends and guests said their good-byes. Kris and I gathered up our family and headed home to rest.

Weeks later I finally got the courage to ask Kris, "Is my face shining? I feel radioactive, changed from the inside out, like light is pouring out of me." I could not stop smiling. He shook his head, no.

"Dang."

The author lost in a throng of Alaskans who are presenting her to the Bishop for Ordination at St. Mary's, Anchorage.

Bishop Mark MacDonald and clergy from around the Diocese at the ordination of the author at St. Mary's, Anchorage, February 1, 2004.

IF YOU SEE A GHOST ON THE TRAIL,
PREACH TO HIM. TELL HIM, JESUS
HAS PREPARED A PLACE FOR YOU
AND YOU ARE TO GO THERE NOW,
IN THE NAME OF JESUS.

—The Rev. Dr. Chief David Salmon, Chalkyitsik

29.

TWICE BLESSED

"The doctor says I will just get weaker and weaker," said Katherine as I settled onto the edge of the bed. "They give me morphine and say I can go home."

These were the words I dreaded hearing.

Katherine had been nauseous and exhausted all winter and hadn't felt up to traveling with me. She had come to Anchorage for a checkup in April. It was determined that her decayed teeth and swollen gums had caused lumps in her throat, and the lumps had become malignant. The cancer had spread down her esophagus into her stomach and liver.

I looked away. We'd shared so much; the news of her cancer was nearly unbearable. I looked back at Katherine and opened my arms for a hug. "Have you had a bath since you've been out of the hospital?" I asked.

"No. I never had one in there neither."

"Would you like to have a nice hot soak in the tub before you go back to Shageluk?"

"That'll be good."

I drew a warm bath. Katherine slipped out of her blue shirt and sweatpants. I steadied her arm as she stepped over the rim, and then I settled onto the toilet seat, hoping my presence helped her feel safe. Katherine was shy with her body. When she stayed with me in Anchorage, she liked to sleep in her clothes on the sofa with lots of pillows, sitting nearly upright. Thinking about her shyness led me to picture the door to her cabin in the village. It looked like it had been battered or chopped with an ax or a fist, and the doorknob was missing. The 2 x 4 jamb resembled a splintered leg with great patches of bone exposed. Katherine wrapped a heavy chain around the jamb and through a gaping hole in the adjoining plywood. She could pull the chain through the doorknob hole and lock it from the inside or outside when she was gone during the day or when she was home alone at night. I took the washcloth and gently scrubbed her back and neck.

After the bath, Katherine dressed and climbed back onto the bed. "I'll rest now," she said. "Dogidinh."

I stood in the doorway a long time. "I love you, sister."

"Gee," she said. "Just when we're getting to know each other real good, this happens."

❖ ❖ ❖

Katherine returned to Shageluk a few days later. Her daughter, Jeannie, and grandson, Patrick, went along to care for her. In the following weeks I found myself remembering things. I kept coming back to our visits to the bridge that crossed the slough, where her grandson had drowned with his cousin. How we pressed our hands against the girders and leaned in, like we could push back time. How we prayed and prayed and then she took the small vial of holy oil out of her pocket and made the sign of the cross on the cold steel. We didn't speak—we didn't have to. We had lost things, and found things, together.

Now, as I begin to reconstruct this story, a fragment of a poem by Naomi Shihab Nye comes to me: "Before you know kindness as the deepest thing inside, you must know sorrow as the other deepest thing. You must wake up with sorrow. You must speak to it till your voice catches the thread of all sorrows and you see the size of the cloth." I see that's what I'm doing, unwrapping the cloth from the bolt, measuring it, checking the color against all the other colors—yellow chrysanthemums and blue butterflies and a red fox in his winter coat of white. Who was Katherine, who am I, how did our lives twine and make meaning?

❖ ❖ ❖

Katherine was my guide on my first trip to Shageluk. She rode out with the agent and was standing beside his truck when the plane rolled to a stop. Her modest words welcomed me.

"You come?"

I nodded yes.

"How long you stay?"

"Three or four days," I answered.

"Oh, that's good."

After we dropped my duffle bag and guitar at the Mission House, we stopped at the church. Katherine slumped into one of the blue folding chairs and let out a sigh so deep I turned and gazed into her face. I knew nothing of her personal history then. I only knew her eyes were filled with such sorrow, and she looked so tiny sitting there, that I instinctively stepped forward and asked, "Can I pray for you?"

"Ya, that's what I need."

I took a small vial of holy oil from my pocket and anointed her forehead and then nudged her hands open and anointed her palms. The deep furrows in her hands looked like a map of the territory, and for a moment, I felt like I was looking into the very depths of the earth. Her shoulders trembled. I reached with my thumb and slid her collar back and made the sign of the cross on each boney protrusion. I held the small vial out to her. She took it and looked at me expectantly.

"Pray for the children," I said. This scene would come to characterize our relationship: few words, heavy sighs, holy oil, and prayer.

❖ ❖ ❖

Sometimes, when Katherine didn't know I was watching, she'd let her guard down. A haunting look—at first, I thought it was loneliness—would fill her eyes and push the corners of her mouth down, and her shoulders down. Sometimes a bitterness would creep into her voice when she talked about a *bad man who may be trying to hurt her daughter, sometimes*. That was as close as she'd come to talking about the violence caused by alcohol, but I knew even the elders were in danger of being raped when the bootleggers brought in a new supply.

In the beginning I was in as much denial as Katherine. I didn't want to talk about alcohol either, or openly notice the condition of her front door. I just wanted to listen to the birds sing and revel in the beauty of the tall summer grasses swaying in the breeze around her front steps.

Manageable compartments. As a child I could gallop into the mountains and watch the sunrise, then stay lost in that memory whenever I wanted. Maybe poverty and abuse do that to children—allow us to create manageable compartments.

Now, as I struggle to tell the truth, I recall, again and again, the images of that day walking with Katherine in the village of Shageluk, on the banks of the Innoko River, that winter's day when we returned, once more, to the bridge over the slough where her grandson Leroy drowned with his cousin Clifford; again we prayed at that place, that steel trap of a place, where the last living connection Katherine had with the son who had killed himself years before struggled in the bitter cold water, struggled in the panic-rising reality that he could not release himself, and he could not release his cousin, from that place. All they could do was cling to one another. And they did.

✦ ✦ ✦

I prayed for Katherine and her cancer all that summer. I was finishing my last unit of Clinical Pastoral Education at Providence Hospital and working the night shift there, so I was stuck in Anchorage. Our weekly phone calls became more infrequent.

Katherine was getting weaker and weaker, and even talking on the phone became an effort. I'd sit with my pot of tea and remember all the deaths that Katherine and I had attended together, all the potlatches, all the stories, all the funeral sermons I'd preached over the past five years. Death is a mystery; she comes in her own time, and on her own terms. Why was waiting for death so intolerable? Was it the dread? Was it the powerlessness, or the unknown, or even the denial that it's really happening? How many times can you say, "I love you?" How many times can you say "Good-bye?" Silence, in the final analysis, seemed the most fitting thing. Silence felt holy, it left room for sighing and tears and forgiveness.

✦ ✦ ✦

When I called Katherine in mid-July, she didn't want to speak to me. She was throwing up. I wondered if anyone was making tea for her, or if she could keep it down. Jeanette told me that Lucy, Katherine's sister-in-law, showed up every day to sit with her. Katherine and Lucy had married brothers. After Katherine adopted me, she started calling me "sister." Lucy picked right up on it and started calling me "sister," too. It made me happy then, but now, remembering, I feel a tremendous comfort.

Katherine taught me to show up. I didn't know the depths of my own buried grief then, but walking with her up and down the hills of Shageluk I would begin to give myself—in the silences we shared—to my own inner chaos. Someone said once, if we have no peace, it is because we have forgotten that we belong to one another. I didn't know where I belonged or to whom I belonged, but I felt safe with Katherine. She knew everyone. She knew their shame. She knew their sorrow. She knew their generosity, and she loved them. They were her people. They belonged to her and she belonged to them.

"Ngoxo chay nidhitlsenh. I made tea for you," Katherine would say when I'd come into her cabin. My own grandmother had made tea for me when I was a child. My cut-off feelings were finally busting through the door jamb, wiggling out of the gaping holes, where I'd kept them locked away.

❖ ❖ ❖

Caught in a trap, caught by the steel jaws of your own shadow, bones snap like dry twigs. You struggle, you scratch and bite then lay exhausted in the snow, waiting in morose silence for death to swallow you up. Old women's voices break the silence and ears prick, heart begins to race, dark eyes search the road for God knows who—friend or foe. In the moments between wondering and certainty, life floods in and all the important events of your life are relived, all the trails not taken are examined, all the dreams remembered. Panic rises in the throat and robs you of any remaining volition. Caught in a trap, all you can do is wait for two grandmothers to come over the rise and set you free.

❖ ❖ ❖

Feeling powerless so far away from Katherine in Shageluk, I began meditating on Psalm 46, "Be still, then, and know that I am God." I didn't know how to be still. I talked a good line about stillness, but I was always moving, humming, trembling, biting, sniffing, burping, blinking, bowing my head, lifting a shoulder, sucking in air, blowing it out loudly, tensing muscles, scolding them, releasing, swallowing, swallowing, swallowing, knotting up, letting go, letting go, letting go as if I could consciously release all the feelings I was holding, holding, holding on to—and release them and simply be still.

Maybe all this movement was simply aliveness. Perhaps stillness only truly comes at death. Yes, the quality of stillness at death is truly still. My sister Pat's body was still, at last, after she died. Yes, her still body had seemed filled with a quality of peace, poised, both complete and yet ready for the next transition.

I'm sorry I didn't sit with her body, her still body, her poised, waiting-for-its-new-beginning body. I would have learned a lot about stillness from her stillness. Her skin had an unearthly glow about it—probably a simple reason, like being hypo-oxygenated—but I didn't want a simple answer. I wanted a song, or a poem, or a god-answer. Her spirit was free and her shell of a body was also free and, in that freeness, there seemed to be a transparency that fairly glowed with the peace we call God.

I wondered if Jesus looked like that when they laid him in the tomb. Probably not. He suffered a terrible death. James of Arimathea and the rich man, Nicodemus, were in a hurry; it was the Sabbath; perhaps they didn't take the time to notice what Jesus' skin looked like. I was in a hurry, too. I didn't want to wait. I'd waited a lifetime. Now I see, I missed a chance to lean into the stillness with my sister. I could have taken her home. I could have sat with her stillness. Served tea with her stillness. Told stories about her in the stillness, and remembered her laughter, in the stillness.

But I didn't.

I simply didn't.

✦ ✦ ✦

Katherine and I, two grandmothers, returned together to that place, together to bear witness, together to cling to each other as the unholy sadness of that place visited us. We, too, experienced being caught in the steel jaws of that place. We too, could only hold on to each other for dear life in the god-awful shadow of that place, and afterward limp off—limp off with a backward glance as if to acknowledge that we were somehow grateful to be alive, I guess, somehow, limping as we were, broken, two old grandmothers.

✦ ✦ ✦

Jeannie and Patrick and now Jeannie's husband continued to care for Katherine. Four adults in that tiny three-room cabin—I imagined the smells must have been dreadful. Katherine's dying seemed dreadful, my ambivalence seemed dreadful—wanting to be there, not wanting to be there, not knowing what would happen next or how the disease would progress, not knowing how I'd respond. I found myself rehearsing—imagining what she'd look like, imagining what I'd do, what I'd say.

I wondered if perhaps rehearsing was my way of fending off the dread—making it more manageable. By rehearsing it, I could change the ending if I didn't get it right the first time, or the second time, or the third time. In fact, each subsequent ending could get better and better. Real life isn't like that—in real life when something happens, boom, you either get it right or are ashamed forever. More than likely when the time came, I'd be ordinary—somewhere in the middle between hero and villain. But I hated ordinary.

I wondered if there was evil in the whole rehearsal scenario—the drive to be spectacular was one of the great temptations of Jesus in the desert. Doesn't Jesus say in John's Gospel, *"Do not let your hearts be troubled…"*? Yes, that was it, *keep my heart on Jesus, and on Katherine's living, not on her dying, or my response.* That way death and life could live together in the stillness and in the noisiness, in the emptiness and in the fullness, in the ordinariness and in the spectacular.

✦ ✦ ✦

If being caught in what Carl Jung calls our shadow is like being caught in a trap, then we can expect that we may need help to get out. We can also expect to limp afterwards—limp because the leg bone has surely been broken—snapped like a fox bone in the jaws of a steel trap. We can expect to limp a long, long time, maybe seven generations, maybe only a lifetime if we're lucky.

✦ ✦ ✦

The first week of August my calendar cleared and I got on a plane for Shageluk. I dropped my gear at the church and asked the agent to drive me to Katherine's cabin. When I came in, Jeannie hugged me and asked if I would stay with her mom so she could go to the store.

Gladly. I turned off the TV and settled into the chair beside the sofa where Katherine lay.

"Ade' my sister," she whispered.

"Gogidet," I answered.

The small chair confined my generous body, and I shifted from hip to hip trying to relieve the pressure. Katherine lay still, her deep grey eyes fluttered, as she let the pain medicine take the edge off her suffering. I watched and waited, barely breathing as I felt the dread in me shift to sorrowing for my friend and adopted sister. The late afternoon sun pushed under the flowered curtain stitched from a piece of potlatch cloth that covered the window above the sofa.

"Katherine," I began at last, "What would you like me to do?"

"Just keep treating people the way you're treating them," she whispered.

I started, then pushed up straighter in the chair and leaned in so I could place my ear closer to her lips in an attempt to catch her whispered words. I didn't understand. I'd meant, what would you like me to do to ease your pain or your death, but the response I got was to *just keep treating people the way you're treating them*.

I was treating people the way Katherine treated people. Somehow in that treating, in that following, in that shadowing, I must have got it right, must be loving people like she loved people, unconditionally, even though she knew all about them.

✦ ✦ ✦

Two days later I returned to Anchorage for a few weeks, then was called back to Grayling to bury a young man. At the potlatch his father told me the younger sister used to say to her brother at the end of every phone conversation, "I love you, I love you, I love you." I started my funeral sermon the next day, "I love you, I love you, I love you—in the midst of deep grief what else can we say but, I love you, I love you, I love you. What else can we do, but love?"

I looked up and saw a tall handsome man named Gabe standing in the doorway of the church. There was standing room only, so he didn't try to come in. Throughout the service I kept glancing at the door. He was still there, and seemed to be watching and waiting for something. I thought this was strange—he'd never come to church before—but I went on with the service.

✦ ✦ ✦

Months before, at the Alaska Native Medical Center in Anchorage, an elder I was visiting had asked me to go down the hall and visit Gabe, who was there for some minor surgical procedure. But Gabe was the last person I wanted to visit; I only knew him as an angry voice that used to call the Mission House in the middle of the night when he'd been drinking. He'd always avoided me in the village, and I was a little afraid of him.

"I'll look in on him," I'd said. Afraid or not, I knew Katherine would expect me to visit him.

Gabe was sitting up in bed. I stood in the doorway and said a polite hello and how are you.

He said a few words like, "I'm fine, I'm fine." Then he fell silent.

I didn't know what else to say. I felt awkward and kept looking at the floor and the walls and the chair. He looked equally uncomfortable.

"Well," he blurted out at last. "Aren't you going to come in?"

"Thanks." I smiled weakly and moved to the side of his bed.

"Some other priest was in here yesterday, some old white guy. You know what he did?"

I shook my head.

"He come in here like he owned the place, told a few stories then said, let's pray. He didn't ask me if I wanted to pray, he just grabbed my hand and started praying. Made me mad."

I mumbled something like, "Yeah, that was Norman. He's pretty old, almost 90." *Remind me not to pray for this guy.*

He kept fidgeting with his blankets, and sighing. Finally, he blurted out, "You ever lost anything?"

I'd lost a turquoise necklace in Kotzebue the year before. I opened my mouth to say as much when he said, "My son fell through the ice. We never found his body. The church didn't come."

A thundering staccato, snapping twigs, slashing hooves echoed: *my son fell through the ice, we never found his body, the church didn't come.* I was knocked flat as by a charging bull moose.

Tears began streaming down my face. I wanted to hide my pettiness—fretting over a lost necklace and misunderstanding this father's anger—behind a tree, or a wood-plank door, or a brilliant sunrise, but the splintering hooves were relentless, *the church didn't come.*

I reached out and softly touched his arm. "I am so sorry for your loss," I whispered.

He began to cry.

I stood by his bedside a long time. The squirming stopped.

"Well," he said. "Aren't you going to pray?"

The gruffness was still there, but the anger was gone.

I don't remember what I prayed. Prayers are often hard to recall; they come from some place deep, intimate, and mysterious—it's as if God is praying in us and through us and to us all at once, inviting us into the stillness.

✦ ✦ ✦

When I turned from the altar after the Eucharistic Prayer, Gabe was still standing in the doorway. I held up a piece of fry bread from the potlatch that I had saved to use for Holy Communion.

"This bread is twice blessed," I said. "Last night one of the grandmothers brought it to the potlatch and made sign over it. It was served to me by one of the young men in the village. Today we have made prayers to our Lord and asked His blessing on this bread that it may be for us the Body of Christ. This bread was blessed last night by a tradition older than this church, and it's blessed again today by a tradition that came into this country seven generations ago. Just as this bread has been twice blessed, may we be twice blessed as we share it with one another. All are welcome at the Lord's Table."

Henry Deacon stepped forward to help serve the Chalice. I began to tear off small pieces of the bread and give them to the people.

"My first time in over thirty years that I'm taking it," said a familiar voice.

I looked up.

Gabe was standing in front of me, head bobbing and grinning, hands wide open.

"What?"

"Holy Communion," he said. "It's the first time in over thirty years that I'm taking Holy Communion."

I smiled, "The Body of Christ, the bread of heaven."

❖ ❖ ❖

After the burial in Grayling, Marlene and Glen took me to Shageluk in their boat. It was a cold, beautiful three-hour trip, with the thermometer dipping to 29 degrees that morning. The water in the Yukon was low, the sandy banks visible and full of sweepers left from last spring's flooding. The Innoko was low and still going down. We hit bottom four times. Here and there the birch leaves were beginning to turn a deep golden yellow. I had hoped to see that again. Katherine loved fall time best.

"Katherine is going to show us how to do it," said Jeanette when I walked into the Mission House. "She's going to show us how to die well." Then tears came into her eyes and she looked away. "She keeps singing in Indian and saying 'Ade' Papa'—hello daddy. Lucy thinks the elders are gathering."

Katherine believed our loved ones are around us all the time, and especially near the end of our earthly life. She had made sign over her food for them, prayed for them, acknowledged them, and now they were watching out for her, preparing to take her home with them into the light. Jesus says words to that effect too, in John 14: "I go to prepare a place for you—and I will come and take you to myself."

"Will you walk with me to see her?" I asked.

We could see that Katherine was very sick, but her breathing was steady. As I sank into the chair, I thought, *she has the heart of a wolverine*. The hole in her stomach, where the feeding tube was inserted, drained a greenish-yellow gunk that smelled terrible.

"She has a huge bedsore on her tailbone that won't heal," said Jeanette. "The hospital won't send more morphine or pain patches until we run out. We've had a terrible time keeping her pain free."

I didn't know why she wasn't howling in pain.

"Ade' Papa," she whispered.

Jeannie got a bowl of fresh water from the five-gallon bucket and began washing Katherine's stomach with sterile gauze. She did her best to keep her mother's wounds cleaned and dressed.

Jeanette and I watched Jeannie work. My mind wandered away to Columbus, New Mexico, where Kris and I planned to winter the following year to help start an interfaith retreat center, Our Lady of Las Palomas, with our friends Barbara Flaherty and Rita Holden. The day before, the September sun here had been gloriously warm and gentle. I wondered if New Mexico had a gentle winter sun; probably it did, in sheltered spots out of the wind. *El Sol es la cobija del pobre*, the sun is the blanket of the poor, I mused. Then I shook my head at my running-away thoughts and came back into the present moment.

The TV news was reporting on Hurricane Katrina and the terrible disaster in New Orleans, Louisiana, the coast of Mississippi, and the other Gulf States. The full impact wouldn't be known for days or weeks. Sitting beside Katherine's bed I felt a long way from New Mexico and the Gulf of Mexico. The outside world seemed to be catapulting into future shock. I didn't have the energy for the suffering of other people. I had my hands full right here.

After Jeannie finished washing her mother's wound, she went out for a walk with her husband and son. Jeanette went home to make supper for Jimmy. I turned the TV off and pulled the prayer shawl I'd been knitting for Katherine out of my backpack. I began to sing softly: *Holy God, Holy and Mighty, Holy Immortal One, Have*

Mercy Upon Us. Knitting and singing I could rest and breathe with Katherine and finally be present in the stillness.

✦ ✦ ✦

Fr. Thomas Keating says everything in the cosmos is born from the death of something else, so when a star explodes, something new is born. I'd like to think what was born for me when Katherine died was love—a deeper love for God, and the people, and consequently myself. Love makes it possible to go on, to forgive, to get up in the morning, to act courageously even when you are afraid, to surrender, to be kind to people and love them even when you know all about them, to be kind to yourself even when you remember the terrible things you have done.

Until I began traveling on the Yukon and Innoko Rivers, I did not know I belonged in the middle of suffering. I did not know I would learn from Katherine and the elders a way of seeing, a way of being that could knit suffering and kindness into a continuous cloth of belonging. I did not know there was no Katherine and me, only us; no God and us, only God. We are not separate or disconnected or alone, ever. God invites us to love God, and to serve God, and to become God, or as Meister Eckart so eloquently said, surrender completely, and let God be God in us.

The woody, spicy scent of frankincense filled the space between us, as I opened the tiny gold vial of holy oil and began to anoint Katherine's frail body, forever knitting us together in this sacrament of love. "Dogidinh', Katherine," I whispered. "I love you, I love you, I love you."

Katherine Hamilton and grandchild.

Katherine Hamilton and the author walking to Katherine's cabin, Shageluk.

The Innoko River.

Judith and Katherine Hamilton. We stopped at a pull-out on Turnagain Arm. Watching the Beluga whales before I took her to the airport for her final trip home.

KATHERINE'S POTLATCH

Food:

10 bowls of Indian ice cream: blueberry, salmon berry, cranberry
boxes and boxes of smoked king salmon strips
half-dried salmon baked with onions and potatoes
baked king salmon
fried king salmon
king salmon patties
moose soup with macaroni
moose chili beans
moose stew with potatoes and carrots
moose roast and gravy
moose liver, bacon and onions
moose tongue
fruit salads
pasta salads
soda pop
candy
cookies
cupcakes
apple pie
cherry pie
berry cobbler
chocolate cake with chocolate frosting
yellow cake with chocolate frosting
fry bread
Pilot Bread
cinnamon rolls

Gifts:

beaded earrings
beaded sun catchers
beaded key chains
blankets
gloves
socks
dish towels
washcloths edged with crochet and soap
yarn in every color
3 cases of Pilot Bread
2 cases of raspberry jam
28 jars of sugar free blueberry jam
Cases of jarred king salmon
yards and yards of fabric and sewing notions
20 yards of Christmas fabric and gold fringe
54 boxes of stick matches

ADMONITION

Katherine taught me to make sign, taught me to show up even in the dead of night when wind pushes snow into dark crevasses, when light is swallowed up in shadow, when rain falls incessantly, and fireweed and fern drench pant legs, and dimple the fragile pages of *The Book of Common Prayer*.

Show up when a meandering trail left by grizzly bear blurs into the mist at the edge of the forest, and people living and people dying blur, and children weeping and young women confessing press in, and running away seems easy.

Show up, no invitation necessary. Move slow. Follow the energy. When you don't know who will be there, when you're hungry or tired, confused, or sad, walk in, sit down, listen, cry, listen again, pray, share a story, laugh.

Show up on a river of light, legs splayed, galloping, hair flying, hang on. Walk. Trust your feet. Stay in your body. Feel the suffering. Don't run away. This too shall pass, the panic, the leap into raw imagination. Return here, now, stomach knotted, tears wiped clean, hands wet.

Trust your heart, not a bad thing to trust, the heart. Trust the God you imagine or imagine a new God.

Show up. Stay rooted in courage. This place, where you find yourself, is home. If you need comfort, hold gently a dolly, a puppy, a small child, icons speaking truth, innocence, vulnerability.

Show up, Mother.

Show up, Katherine.

Judith, Show Up.

Take flight with Raven. Don't fear the wind that bears you heavenward or the feathered ones who journey with you. Greet creation moment by moment and let these hollow-throated cries shake loose blessing.

THE LORD'S PRAYER
(IN DEG XINAG)

Dinaxito'
ngi ezre'
yan' ngizrenh.
Yitots'in' yoye
dhedo.
Yitots'in ngitl'ogh
xiye tr'ididltth'e.
Go dranh
nighandltth'in
dinadhon ghe'on.
Tr'ixet'ixdi xits'in'
dinatighelalin.
(Yitots'in) trixet'ixdi
xits'in dinak'odz
xudingilnek.

Deg Xinag Translation in 2000 by Jim Dementi, Katherine Hamilton,
Louise Winkelman, Lucy Hamilton, Raymond Dutchman, Agnes John,
Edna Deacon, Hannah Maillelle, and George Demientieff Holly

EPILOGUE

The Haida Way

In early February 2008, Kris and I drove from Our Lady of Las Palomas Interfaith Retreat Center in Columbus, New Mexico, into the Albuquerque International Sunport to pick up Merle and Knud Andersen. Merle and I had become friends while attending the Native Ministry Program at Vancouver School of Theology in British Columbia. I had invited Merle to teach a class in Haida cedar bark weaving for the Mexican women at the retreat center, and Wild West Weaving in Silver City. I had also arranged for her to teach at Western New Mexico University. Merle is a Haida weaver and regalia artist from the Haida Tribe, Raven, Yaahl Moiety, and Yaguu'janaas Clan, from Old Masset, Haida Gwaii. Her mother was Florence Davidson, a weaver, and her father, Robert Davidson, Sr. was a carver. Her grandmother Isabella Edenshaw, was a weaver, and her grandfather, Charles Edenshaw was a master carver.

When we got back to Compassion House, companions Barbara Flaherty and Rita Holden rushed out, waving madly. "There have been two white ravens playing in the yard all afternoon." Merle and I looked at each other in surprise. The hair stood up on the back of my neck.

"Of course, there were," I said. "White Raven is one of Merle's Crests in the Raven Moiety from Old Massett, Haida Gwaii. They were probably blessing Compassion House and the land in preparation for Merle's visit."

Eighteen months later, on August 22, 2009, during the Fortieth Anniversary Celebration of the first raising of a Haida Totem Pole in modern history at Old Massett by Merle's nephews, Robert and Reggie Davidson, Merle 'San'laa gudgaang' Andersen, adopted me as her sister. Merle's sister, Emily gave me the name Lablet Shedungs.

Then she added, "This means Flying Preacher, and that doesn't mean from here to there."

The following night at the Potlatch at the Kwiiyaans Community Hall, Robert and Reggie performed a powerful Raven Dance with drums and song. Raven sprang into the room wearing a grotesque black mask with bulging eyes and nose frightening the children. Old men laughed out loud. Old women grabbed the children and held them close, rocking to and fro, cooing. The singers and drummers shattered the consciousness of the onlookers with their echoing rhythms and the ya hee ya hee ya he he he ha that repeated itself over and over. We were carried along, unwilling participants, yet powerless to hold back. All eyes followed the black raven dancer as he dipped and lunged, dipped and leaped like some ancient messenger demanding to be heard.

In an instant, the black mask exploded, revealing a beautiful Light Man inside. Children screamed in delight then began shouting. Old men held their bellies and laughed louder. Old women gasped and then joined the children's loud shouts. Over and over the story repeated itself until everyone saw the Light Man.

"We are all like this—we are ugly, dead, frightening in the way we gossip about others, in the way we tell lies and try to deceive others, but, in fact, there is a beautiful Light Man hidden inside of each one of us if we will only stop pretending to be the dark, evil man," said Robert. "When I talk about someone, I imagine they are right here in front of me. I don't say anything I wouldn't say if they were right here. This stops negativity and gossip and judgment. This is the Haida Way."

Merle believed in the Light Man hidden inside of everyone, including me. She coaxed and cooed and gifted me with friendship, and sisterhood. She was tough when she needed to be, but always loving. When she taught me to weave a cedar bark basket, she looked at my crooked weaving and quietly asked, "Is this the way you want this to be?"

"No," I whispered, and patiently took out the spoiled parts and started again.

The night after my adoption, Merle and I were sitting quietly at her kitchen table. Our husbands and adopted sister, Anne Morawski, were on the porch drinking rhubarb wine.

Merle confided, "The first time I went to the Danish Lutheran Church in Vancouver one of the women said, '*What are you doing here?*'" Red rimmed eyes looked at me.

"I see your pain," I said. And then I wept, too. I wept for my Haida sister, and I wept for myself, at the shared powerlessness of a 49-year-old memory spilling out onto the lace tablecloth. The dim light of a late afternoon sun provided no relief from the glaring racism, the hurt still present. What are you doing here, and what am I doing here, and what is the breach between your presence and mine, between then and now? What are you doing here on Haida Gwaii that wasn't Canadian once—that, in fact, belonged to the Haida people from the beginning of time?

Laughter, as comic relief, forced itself from my throat as I recognized the irony of an immigrant Christian demanding an answer from White Raven.

My beloved Athabascan Elder, Ellen Savage, from the village of Holy Cross on the Yukon River, told me about a story time when all the animals could talk, and the people could all talk and understand one another and the animals. Dinaxitó created everything, the water, the trees, birds and animals, with a piece of his spirit in it. One day White Raven was watching Dinaxitó give colors to all the birds and animals. Dinaxitó called the little brown bird to himself and splashed red on her breast and robin was born. Robin began to sing. She sang and sang. She was very happy. Dinaxitó smiled.

Then Dinaxitó splashed blue on the next little bird and Steller's jay was born. Steller's jay strutted and chattered and scolded. Then he hopped off very happy. White Raven watched and watched as one by one Dinaxitó called the birds to himself and he gave them their colors—mottled brown and white for the little Song Sparrow, a soft grey and white for Arctic Tern, pure white edged with black for Snowy Owl. White Raven hopped on one foot and then the other, watching, watching. Finally, it was White Raven's turn.

"White Raven, you know I love you more than all the others. You have seen all the colors, what color would you like to be?"

One by one White Raven named the colors—yellow like Finch, no not yellow; green like Humming Bird, no not green; blue like Steller's jay—White Raven looked and looked at himself in the puddle, no not blue either. At last, in frustration, Dinaxitó mixed all the colors together and dumped them on White Raven, and that is how Raven got his colors!

Dinaxitó gave Snowy Owl and White Raven and all the birds their colors, and one by one placed them where he wanted them to be. This makes me understand that Dinaxitó also placed you and me where he wants us to be. May we come to know the beautiful Light Man hidden inside ourselves, so that we may also see the Light Man hidden inside one another. Thank you, Merle, for teaching me The Haida Way.

Judith and Merle Andersen, Old Masset, 2009.

My adoption at Christian's Longhouse in Old Masset, Haida Gwaii, British Columbia, 2009 Left to right: Emily Goertzen, Judith Lethin, Merle Andersen, Anne Morawski.

Knud Andersen speaking at Our Lady of Las Palomas Interfaith Retreat Center, Palomas, Mexico and Columbus, New Mexico.

Merle taught the Mexican women how to weave this small cedar bark basket and talisman necklace at Our Lady of Las Palomas Interfaith Retreat Center in Columbus, New Mexico.

Merle Andersen teaching Haida Culture at Western New Mexico University, Silver City, NM. wearing her White Raven vest and cedar bark hat.

WELLNESS IS THE WAY THAT
WE LIVE OUR LIVES.

—Jim Dementi, Shageluk

ACKNOWLEDGMENTS

I want to thank the team at Cirque Press for believing in this project and helping me stay focused on all the details to bring this book to fruition. Michael Burwell and Sandra Klevin, Publishers/Editors, Cynthia Lee Steele, Associate Editor *Cirque Journal*, and Kari Odden *Moontide Design*, your vision and creativity, and your capacity to build community and spark enthusiasm is contagious. I'm so grateful.

Images collide as I begin to thank the people whose lives inhabit these stories. The first image is a dream from 1986 when I was given bunches of daffodils to plant, and I choose a grassy mountain slope in Alaska. The second image is a memory from about that same time of church leaders from all over Alaska holding hands in one gigantic circle on the frozen ice at Meier Lake Conference Center singing *Holy Ground, we're standing on Holy Ground!* These two images fill me with a deep understanding: we are not separate from one another, from the earth, and all her creatures, from the trees, or the stars or the daffodils. We share an intimacy that binds us in a deep, inseparable kinship. More often than not, religious beliefs, cultural values, and language divide us—we each act like we are unique or superior. When I was young, I'm sure I acted that way too, but the Elders I've written about here picked me up when I failed to see a bigger God, and walked with me, made tea for me, shared soup with me until my own spiritual understandings grew to embrace my failings and our differences as gifts. Three Native couples—among the many who have blazed the way in the sobriety movement in Alaska—have been a particular blessing to me: Ernie and Rosanne Turner, Jim and Susan Labelle, and Doug and Amy Modig. I'm eternally grateful for all of you. You have taught me the power of vulnerability and truth speaking in building healthy communities. My life has so much meaning because of your teachings. Dogidinh', thank you.

Kris Lethin, my husband of 60 plus years, you have been my biggest cheerleader. Thank you, dear. You made me sit down in front of the first PC you bought 45 years ago and turn it on. I was sure the thing was going to blow up. It didn't, and I've been happily cutting and pasting ever since. I also want to thank our sons, their beautiful wives, our grandchildren and great grandchildren, for believing in me even when I missed holidays and birthdays or was just plain cranky and tired from wrestling with my own demons. I'm so proud of your generosity and kindness: William, Kazue, Lynn, Ann, Kyla; Dan, Cheri, Michael and Hailey, Morgan and Kent, and Jordan, Daniel and Justine; Kris, Nathaniel, Caleb; Tim, Savanna, Scarlett, Max.

When I realized I needed structure to help me write these stories down, I discovered a kindly man, a brilliant writer, and fearless mountaineer, David Stevenson, who directed the low-residency MFA program at the University of Alaska Anchorage. He'd assembled an equally wild cohort of teachers and mentors and, as they say in show business, the rest is history. Thank you, David. When I was paired with my first-year mentor, Sherry Simpson, I immediately confessed: "I'm so angry at the church. I'm afraid I'm going to throw up on everyone." She clamped onto my sagging shoulders and gave me a gentle shake, "I won't let you," she avowed. And she didn't. Thank you, Sherry, rest in peace. My second-year mentor, Eva Saulitis, urged me to tell a story that I'd never told anyone. After I pressed send, I had a massive stomachache as I waited for her response. Will she be shocked? Will she think less of me? What I got was totally unexpected, "Okay, that happened. Now we're going to make art out of it." Thank you, Eva, rest in peace. Nancy Lord, third year mentor, urged me to anchor my stories and characters in the landscape. Consequently, porcupine didn't simply die in the forest, his tiny paw stretched into a patch of dwarf dogwood at the base of an old spruce tree. By anchoring porcupine, I somehow recognized my own spiritual home, and was able to anchor myself there, as well. Thank you, Nancy.

Thank heavens for great editors like Jackie Pels, Patricia Heinicke, and Andromeda Romano-Lax. Jackie, you were the first editor I shared my work with. You gave me permission to celebrate the color yellow and the daffodils that now fill my garden. Patricia, you lit the lantern and gently urged me to go deeper into the forest. Your sweet spirit and profound respect for our First Nations friends urged me to reflect on my own trauma but not be diminished by it. Andromeda, you helped me find the place to begin. You gave me the courage to let go of most of my childhood angst. You encouraged me to keep moving forward. Each of you showed up when the student was ready. Thank you, all. I bow to you.

My Jungian Wisdom Circle, Diane Casper, Debbie Kohler, Jean Caton, Maria Mavroudi, Kat Yarborough, and Kay Cline have been worthy companions on the journey of individuation. Thank you, for journeying with me.

My Women Writing the West critique group, Eilene Lyon, Cyndie Zikmund, Alice Trego, Janice Kirk, Andrea Jones, and Tami Richards, you are all amazing writers, generous with your time, honest with your feedback, lavish with your encouragement. Thank you. Let's keep writing.

I'm grateful for Sharron Jones Hopkins, lifelong friend, with whom I've shared everything. I could fill another book with our adventures. I'm grateful for my Idaho and Nevada friends and family, especially cousin Linda Morrow Eastaugh who urged me to keep writing. Thank you, Barbara Flaherty and Rita Holden for starting the retreat center in New Mexico with me and for being early readers. I'm indebted to Sandee Elvsaas for sharing my love of children and daffodils. I've delighted in learning to forage for food in the forest and the beach from Lillian Elvsaas. I'm grateful for Judy Mullikin, and Nell Gustafson, for sharing my love of the Gospel and being early readers.

As I settle into finishing this manuscript, I have this great desire to plant more daffodils and give them all glorious names, your names dear readers, because I want you to know too that you are like these daffodils in their purest form—alive and pulsing, waiting for the right moment to emerge and bloom. Thank you.

Cessna N2185U serves as a fitting backdrop at the Shageluk airstrip: left to right: Katherine Hamilton Grace Hensler, pilot Kris Lethin, Bishop Mark MacDonald, Allan John, Clarence Painter.

Andy Fairfield and my husband Kris.

Left to Right: Kris Lethin, Larry Spannegal, unknown, Lowell Thomas, Jr.

Judith enjoying lunch on the step on their twin engine Cessna 337, 65 Sierra, enroute to British Columbia, Canada.

ABOUT THE AUTHOR

Judith Wegman Lethin is a writer, Episcopal priest, chaplain, and retreat master. A native of Idaho and Nevada, she has studied at the University of Nevada, Reno, Alaska Pacific University, Vancouver School of Theology, and the University of Alaska, Anchorage. She holds a Masters of Arts in Teaching, Masters of Divinity, and Masters of Fine Arts in creative nonfiction. Lethin has been a lifelong volunteer in organizations that serve women, children, and families. She served on the planning committee for the 1970 White House Conference on Children. She served on the National Advisory Board to the Bureau of Land Management (1974–1977) and chaired the meeting that wrote the first draft of the Organic Act. She received the Gold Pan Award for outstanding program director of 1990 from the Indian Health Service for writing and implementing *Ungwirwiiliik*, the first in-village alcohol treatment program for Native families. She served on the Alaska Mental Health Board (1994–1995), and the Governor's Advisory Board on Suicide Prevention (2003–2004). She received the David C. Charters award for outstanding service in Human Resources from the United States Postal Service (1996) and served on the Governor's Advisory Board on Alcohol and Drug Abuse (2003–2006). She designed and directed *Walking in Beauty—Roots & Wings*, a healing retreat for Alaska Native women recovering from the intergenerational effects of Boarding School (2017–2024). Lethin wrote and produced 100 daily prayers for a local Christian radio station. Lethin has published poems and stories in *Chaplaincy Today, Alaska Dispatch News, Cirque Journal,* and *Manifestations Journal*. She lives with her husband, Kris, and two golden retrievers, Ruby and Winter, in Seldovia, Alaska.

ABOUT CIRQUE PRESS

Cirque Press grew out of *Cirque*, a literary journal that publishes the works of writers and artists from the North Pacific Rim, a region that reaches north from Oregon to the Yukon Territory, south through Alaska to Hawaii, and west to the Russian Far East.

Cirque Press is a partnership of Sandra Kleven, publisher, and Michael Burwell, editor. Ten years ago, we recognized that works of talented writers in the region were going unpublished, and the Press was launched to bring those works to fruition. We publish fiction, nonfiction, and poetry, and we seek to produce art that provides a deeper understanding about the region and its cultures. The writing of our authors is significant, personal, and strong.

Sandra Kleven — Michael Burwell, publishers and editors

www.cirquejournal.com

BOOKS FROM CIRQUE PRESS

Apportioning the Light by Karen Tschannen (2018)

The Lure of Impermanence by Carey Taylor (2018)

Echolocation by Kristin Berger (2018)

Like Painted Kites & Collected Works by Clifton Bates (2019)

Athabaskan Fractal: Poems of the Far North by Karla Linn Merrifield (2019)

Holy Ghost Town by Tim Sherry (2019)

Drunk on Love: Twelve Stories to Savor Responsibly by Kerry Dean Feldman (2019)

Wide Open Eyes: Surfacing from Vietnam by Paul Kirk Haeder (2020)

Silty Water People by Vivian Faith Prescott (2020)

Life Revised by Leah Stenson (2020)

Oasis Earth: Planet in Peril by Rick Steiner (2020)

The Way to Gaamaak Cove by Doug Pope (2020)

Loggers Don't Make Love by Dave Rowan (2020)

The Dream That Is Childhood by Sandra Wassilie (2020)

Seward Soundboard by Sean Ulman (2020)

The Fox Boy by Gretchen Brinck (2021)

Lily Is Leaving: Poems by Leslie Ann Fried (2021)

One Headlight by Matt Caprioli (2021)

November Reconsidered by Marc Janssen (2021)

Callie Comes of Age by Dale Champlin (2021)

Someday I'll Miss This Place Too by Dan Branch (2021)

Out There In The Out There by Jerry McDonnell (2021)

Fish the Dead Water Hard by Eric Heyne (2021)

Salt & Roses by Buffy McKay (2022)

Growing Older In This Place: A Life in Alaska's Rainforest by Margo Wasserman Waring (2022)

Kettle Dance: A Big Sky Murder by Kerry Dean Feldman (2022)

Nothing Got Broke by Larry F. Slonaker (2022)

On the Beach: Poems 2016-2021 by Alan Weltzien (2022)

Sky Changes on the Kuskokwim by Clifton Bates (2022)

Transplanted By Birgit Lennertz Sarrimanolis (2022)

Between Promise and Sadness by Joanne Townsend (2022)

Yosemite Dawning by Shauna Potocky (2022)

The Woman Within by Tami Phelps and Kerry Dean Feldman (2023)

In the Winter of the Orange Snow by Diane S. Carpenter (2023)

Mail Order Nurse by Sue Lium (2023)

All in Due Time by Kate Troll (2023)

Infinite Meditations For Inspiration and Daily Practice by Scott Hanson (2023)

Getting Home from Here by Anne Ward-Masterson (2023)

Crossing the Burnside Bridge & Other Poems by Janice D. Rubin (2023)

A Variable Sense of Things by Ron McFarland (2023)

Tiny's Stories: An Athabascan Family on the Yukon River by Theresa "Tiny" Demientieff Devlin with Sam Demientieff (2024)

If Singing Went On by Gerald Cable (2024)

May the Owl Call Again: A Return to Poet John Meade Haines, 1924–2011 by Rachel Epstein (2024)

Out of the Dark: A Memoir by Marian Elliott (2024)

Kissing Kevin: An American Nurse in the Vietnam War by Sara Berg (2024)

Bury Me in Cherry Blossoms by Eric Braman (2024)

Last Call of the Dark by Mary Eliza Crane (2024)

Boardwalk Footsteps: Memoir of an Artist at a Remote Alaskan Cannery by Dot Bardarson (2024)

The Nancy Poems by John Morgan (2024)

A Wonderful-Terrible God by Judith Lethin (2024)

Dancing Away by Robert M. Fagen (2024)

Into the Khumbu by Alan Weltzien (2024)

CIRCLES
ILLUSTRATED BOOKS FROM CIRQUE PRESS

Baby Abe: A Lullaby for Lincoln by Ann Chandonnet (2021)

Miss Tami, Is Today Tomorrow? by Tami Phelps (2021)

Miss Bebe Goes to America by Lynda Humphrey (2022)

MORE PRAISE FOR
A WONDERFUL-TERRIBLE GOD

You can almost smell the wood smoke. In *A Wonderful- Terrible God*, Judith Lethin has written an intriguing memoir of her quest to find her true self in Alaska. She shares a path with us rarely discovered and never forgotten.

—The Rt. Rev. Steven Charleston, VI Bishop of Alaska, retired

A moving, uplifting, and beautifully written memoir that documents both a personal search for meaning as well as fascinating practices and lifeways of Alaska Natives in the villages, including cultural attitudes about death and grieving. Even readers unaffiliated with any specific faith will find consolation and catharsis in this tender and insightful memoir.

—Andromeda Romano-Lax, author of *Annie and the Wolves* and *The Deepest Lake*

A Wonderful-Terrible God is a personal story of healing. In the book, Judith Lethin shares with extraordinary vulnerability her personal journey to find her ultimate meaning and identity in the context and history of her life. Her stories echo what Blaise Pascale described in his 17th century work *Penses*: that the human quest for healing and release from the infinite abyss of craving for happiness and purpose as defined by the world and the cruel human ego—a definition of happiness that mostly requires the denial of everything that makes one human, can be filled only by a loving God that knows intimately what it means to be fully human—what it means to experience betrayal, suffering, trauma, and even death. Her story is a testament to the fact that no matter how heroic, rewarding, and meaningful it may seem to bear the crosses of others and to be their healer, true healing can only happen when you lay those crosses down and pick up your own.

—The Rt. Rev. Mark Lattime, VIII Bishop of Alaska

Judith's life-giving stories transport us into the Alaska she loves, ensuring that we fall in love with it, too. She illustrates beautifully what Indigenous people believe: We are all connected. We grieve when Beaver gives up his life, then rejoice in the holiness of his sacrifice to feed others. When Fire claims the lives of father and son, we cry tears of love and then sing songs of thanksgiving. Through these sacred stories generously shared, we discover joy born from sorrow, life victorious over death, and the beauty of holiness found throughout Creation. How wonderful!

—The Rev. Dr. Mary Crist (Blackfeet), Coordinator of Indigenous Theological Education for the Episcopal Church, U.S.A.

www.ingramcontent.com/pod-product-compliance
Lightning Source LLC
LaVergne TN
LVHW010308070526
838199LV00065B/5489